# Choreographies of Multilingualism

# OXFORD STUDIES IN SOCIOLINGUISTICS

General Editors:
Nikolas Coupland
Copenhagen University, University of Technology, Sydney, and Cardiff University
Adam Jaworski
University of Hong Kong

RECENTLY PUBLISHED IN THE SERIES:

# CHOREOGRAPHIES OF MULTILINGUALISM

*Writing and Language Ideology in Singapore*

Tong King Lee

*University of Hong Kong*

OXFORD
UNIVERSITY PRESS

# OXFORD
## UNIVERSITY PRESS

Oxford University Press is a department of the University of Oxford. It furthers
the University's objective of excellence in research, scholarship, and education
by publishing worldwide. Oxford is a registered trade mark of Oxford University
Press in the UK and certain other countries.

Published in the United States of America by Oxford University Press
198 Madison Avenue, New York, NY 10016, United States of America.

Library of Congress Control Number: 2022003550
ISBN 978-0-19-764465-2 (pbk.)
ISBN 978-0-19-764464-5 (hbk.)

DOI: 10.1093/oso/9780197644645.001.0001

9 8 7 6 5 4 3 2 1

Paperback printed by Integrated Books International, United States of America
Hardback printed by Bridgeport National Bindery, Inc., United States of America

# CONTENTS

# FIGURES

# ACKNOWLEDGMENTS

The idea for this book was incubated at a series of workshops themed "Writing (in) the City," conducted as part of an HKU-UCL strategic partnership project. I am indebted to Adam Jaworski for inducting me into this project, and for his patient advice and moral support during the entire course of my writing. Appreciation is due to the following colleagues who at different points shared with me their expertise, opinion, and resources that greatly facilitated this research: Li Wei, Chris Hutton, Mie Hiramoto, Philip Holden, Cindy Sturtz, Brook Bolander, Ritu Jain, Corey Huang, and Andre Joseph Theng. Equally deserving of mention are my two anonymous reviewers, who raised pertinent questions that enabled me to fill crucial gaps in earlier versions of this work.

I am also grateful to Sang Hong Chung of the National Library Board (Singapore), Lisa Lip of The Arts House (Singapore), and the proprietors of TheSuperBlessed.com, Statement.sg, and TemasekClothings.com for granting me permission to reproduce their copyrighted images. Every effort has been made to obtain copyright permission for the material used in this book, although this may not have been possible or practicable in all cases. Special thanks to Joshua Ip and Ng Yi-sheng for their personal communications with me on their work. Finally, this writing is supported by a research grant from the School of Chinese in the University of Hong Kong, for which I am grateful.

# ABBREVIATIONS

| | |
|---|---|
| ACS | Anglo Chinese School |
| ASEAN | Association of Southeast Asian Nations |
| CC | community club |
| CMIO | Chinese, Malay, Indian, Others |
| COM | cultural orientation model |
| CPF | Central Provident Fund |
| ECMT | English–Chinese–Malay–Tamil |
| L1/L2 | first language/second language (in schools) |
| MCTE | Malay–Chinese–Tamil–English |
| MRT | Mass Rapid Transit |
| MTCE | Malay–Tamil–Chinese–English |
| MTL | mother tongue language |
| NAC | National Arts Council |
| NDP | National Day Parade |
| NLB | National Library Board |
| NYT | New York Times |
| PA | People's Association |
| SG50 | celebration of Singapore's golden jubilee |
| SGEM | Speak Good English Movement |
| SGSM | Speak Good Singlish Movement |
| SLS | Sing Lit Station |
| SMC | Speak Mandarin Campaign |
| SOS | Save Our Singlish! |
| SPAS | Society for the Preservation of Authentic Singlish |
| SPOTM | SingPoOnTheMRT, Singapore Poetry on the MRT |
| SPWM | Singapore Poetry Writing Month, SingPoWriMo |

# CHAPTER 1
# Introduction

A conventional formula to begin any discussion on the sociolinguistics of
Singapore is to relate its basic demographics in terms of the ethnic distribution of its populace. It is of course fully justifiable to foreground the city's
unique ethnic constitution as a backdrop to discussing its language politics.
Yet to begin this way also risks enfolding the discussion immediately into a
top-down, macrostructural framework of cultural management, hence side-
lining the anecdotal, the quotidian, and the peripheral, which by definition
always lie outside the purview of such frameworks. At the risk of appearing
idiosyncratic, let us break with tradition by beginning with two episodes that
capture symptomatic moments pointing to the key issue addressed in this
book: the layered and intersecting ways in which multilingualism is imagined
and performed in Singapore.

## TWO EPISODES

Both of these symptomatic moments occurred in 2015, a watershed year for
Singapore in more ways than one. It was the year of the golden jubilee, ubiq-
uitously marketed as SG50. From the beginning of the year, the city-state,
which gained independence in August 1965, had been teeming with events
in the lead-up to the grand celebrations. The festive mood was interrupted in
March 2015 when the nation's founding father and first prime minister, Lee
Kuan Yew, died. Preparations for SG50 continued after a period of national
mourning, which added poignant weight to the National Day Parade (NDP)
of August 9.

While marking a symbolic threshold in the city's history, NDP 2015 also
broke new ground sociolinguistically. This is the first moment: for the first

*Choreographies of Multilingualism.* Tong King Lee, Oxford University Press. © Oxford University Press 2022.
DOI: 10.1093/oso/9780197644645.003.0001

time, the parade featured a segment where items from the Singlish lexicon, namely, *blur like sotong* (to be clueless), *chope* (to reserve), and the sentence-final particles *lah* and *leh,* were displayed on illuminated floats.[1] The parade's narrator called these and several other featured expressions from the local vernacular "something that is truly Singaporean . . . representing how the different aspects of our unique identity ties [*sic*] us together."[2]

This segment in NDP 2015 is significant because Singlish (also known as Colloquial Singapore English) had been (and still is) stigmatized in official discourses since at least the launch of the Speak Good English Movement (SGEM) in 2000. It is denounced as a vernacular variety, the inferior cousin of Standard English.[3] Hence, one commentator optimistically interpreted the NDP episode as a "significant evolution in the official discourse pertaining to Singapore's vernaculars" (Lim 2015: 267), a reading that gains pertinence in light of the etymology of the word "jubilee":

> The word *jubilee,* after all, finds its origins in Hebrew "ram's horn," blown in proclamation of the year of jubilee . . . which, in Judaism and Christianity, is a special year of remission of sin and universal pardon . . It can be seen as poetic justice that, in this jubilee year, at least some of Singapore's heritage languages, both old—the Chinese "dialects"—and new—Singlish—are forgiven the shortcomings once ascribed to them, and are recognised, and even celebrated. (Lim 2015: 267)

Leaving aside the question of whether this is an overly generous assessment, the NDP episode highlights two developments of interest. The first is the paradoxical tension inherent in the state's appropriation of the vernacular,[4] which, as will become clear, is systematically excluded from the state's multilingual

---

1. Along with these floats, Singlish songs and raps sounded in the background, their lyrics carrying still more Singlish expressions: *sour like kannah* (as sour as an olive, referring to one's unhappy countenance), *cannot tahan* (can't stand [sth. or sb.] anymore), *wah piang eh, walau eh* (both exclaiming astonishment, consternation, despair, or dismay; the Singlish equivalent of "oh my god"), *how like that* (what to do [about a negative situation]), *face so sour* (referring to someone's unhappy countenance), *wa steady ah* (exclaiming admiration for someone's capability or achievement), *pandai* (smart), *champion* (a parodic inversion of "champion" in English, used sarcastically to describe someone who acts in a way that brings about negative consequences), *confirm plus chop* (an assured confirmation), *at least got hope* (Singlish inflection of "at least there is hope"), *kiasu a bit* (be more competitive), and *don't play play* (don't fool around, get serious).
2. https://www.youtube.com/watch?v=bXlI01cNwrI.
3. For our purposes, there is no substantive difference between "Standard English" (used among linguists to differentiate from local varieties of English) and "English" (used in official discourses in Singapore). I use these terms interchangeably to contrast with Singlish in Singapore.
4. I use "vernacular" as a broad term to designate language varieties spoken in Singapore in general, including, inter alia, Singlish, various dialects of Chinese, and colloquial Malay, but excluding the official languages of Malay (Bahasa Melayu),

infrastructures and bilingual education system. It appears that the state is in this instance tapping into the potential of Singlish as an "extraordinarily powerful identity shibboleth" (Blommaert 2018: 29) to index a locale-specific ethos, aligning with a broader effect of national camaraderie that NDP seeks to engender.

The second is the phenomenon of written Singlish, which is relevant to the focus on written multilingualism in this book. The sociolinguistic literature on Singlish tends to locate it either in mundane, conversational settings or within language ideological debates. It is only more recently that scholars have turned their attention to Singlish as a written practice, for instance, in advertising contexts (Hiramoto 2019). This book participates in this latter line of inquiry, examining written Singlish alongside other languages across a range of genres and materialities.

Now let us skip forward to the second moment in November 2015, when the Singaporean writer, critic, and Singlish practitioner Gwee Li Sui delivered a TED talk mischievously titled "Singlish is a language for our future, lah!"[5] In this talk, now available on YouTube, Gwee makes a case for Singlish to be recognized in its own right, arguing that it harks back to Singapore's multicultural past ("Singlish is only as old as the concept of multicultural Singapore"). His implication is that the vernacular language is an integral part of the locale, not an aberration.

Importantly, Gwee maintains that Singlish, popularly seen as a variety of English entrenched in the vernacular, in fact indexes a cosmopolitan outlook. In a section of the talk with the telling title "Singlish globalises," Gwee speaks of Singlish as "a version of a global language" with a porosity enabling it to easily absorb resources from other languages into its repertoire. Gwee's strategy thus lies in rescaling Singlish toward the global, giving it an unexpected indexical potential that stands in contrast with the state's positioning (and appropriation, as in NDP 2015) of Singlish as an index of entrenched locality.

In a reflexive turn, Gwee remarks that Singlish enables its speakers to *potong jalan* (from Malay, cut-walk): "you *potong jalan* across distinct grammars and syntaxes; you create a way where previously there was no way to communicate." On the basis of this *potong jalan,* or transgressive capacity, of Singlish, Gwee establishes the trajectory of Singlish as analogous to the development of English, which has subsumed ingredients from several different languages over the course of its own evolution. The strength of Singlish, as expressed in the talk, thus lies in its propensity toward dynamic evolution that renders it a fluid site for translingual contact.

Mandarin, and Tamil. It should be noted that Singlish itself is an assemblage of elements from Chinese dialects, colloquial Malay, and English, among other sources.

5. https://www.youtube.com/watch?v=UT64iIwg9u8.

Therein lies the supposed globality of Singlish—a paradoxical idea that elevates a local tongue to the level of a global register. This underlines the radicality of Gwee's proposal, which is diametrically opposed to how Singlish is construed in official discourse.

With this, Gwee proceeds to debunk the prevailing myth that Singlish, owing to its demotic character, interferes with the proper acquisition and use of English—an argument long adopted by the state (Wee 2018: 84–88). The talk ends with a call to action for Singaporeans to take pride in Singlish, extolled as "a very unique, powerful, and unconscious national invention . . . [which] may well prove to be our 'Singaporean one' national resource, in a country that doesn't have any":

> Singlish may well be our great contribution to the world of inventions and to the world of languages. It is practical, it's good natured, it's funny, it's self-deprecating, it's succinct, it's futuristic, it's identity clarifying, it's communal and, most importantly, it's people powered. . . . With Singlish . . . if you therefore dare to keep your heart on it, while of course speaking good English, we can help make ourselves into the hub of how the future speaks.

Heralding Singlish as a language of the world and of the future, such laudatory rhetoric about this colloquial register had rarely been heard before, especially on such a visible platform as TED.

This book is not specifically about Singlish. Where Singlish is concerned, I am interested in the language as it is written rather than spoken. NDP 2015, as mentioned earlier, brings to the fore written displays of Singlish; although Gwee's TED talk is about speaking Singlish, he is also known for writing Singlish-inflected poetry and has published a book introducing Singlish *in* Singlish (see Chapter 4). In relation to this book's attention to multilingualism in writing, these two episodes can be read as moments that reveal long-standing tensions, but also new synergies, between different writing regimes in Singapore and their associated language ideologies.

More specifically, the two moments point to the problematic of Singlish against Singapore's complex and shifting sociolinguistic dynamic. The first of these, the Singlish displays at NDP 2015, represent an exceptional gesture on the part of the state in giving a nod to the local vernacular. The gesture is exceptional because it runs counter to the state's critical stance on the widespread use of Singlish as epitomized in the SGEM, a national campaign designed to enhance the standard of English among Singaporeans. It belies the state's ambivalence toward the vernacular, marked by dual impulses to rein in what it considers an aberrant variety of English and to appropriate that variety for strategic purposes, such as to foster solidarity with the grassroots populace and embrace an egalitarian outlook on high-profile occasions. Egalitarianism, or the struggle against elitism, is the thematic point of Gwee's TED talk. The talk is metonymic of a constellation of literary writings and metalinguistic commentaries that have matured into a bottom-up, ideologically resistant discourse, poised against the taylorist multilingual regime in which vernacular languages are perennially disavowed.

The tensions and slippages between these moments point to different modalities of engaging with linguistic plurality, namely, institutional multilingualism and grassroots multilingualism. These two modalities constitute the primary focus of this book. In particular, I investigate how these modalities, realized as concrete writing practices, articulate the idea of multilingual Singapore in ways that are contradictory but also complementary. Ultimately, this bipolarity between the institutional and the grassroots, though not without ontological grounding, can itself be called into question with new developments in the sociolinguistic landscape. In other words, these modalities govern the dynamic of writing on divergent scales (Blommaert 2010), creating a layeredness to the notion of multilingual Singapore while also intersecting each other.

Writing, as it is examined here, assumes many guises. These range from public signage with messages printed in patterned configurations of multiple languages to anthologies, exhibitions, and mobile applications presenting texts in various languages (entailing translation) to playful expositions on Singlish, as well as to more serious commentaries and manifestos defending Singlish against encroaching state policies, to heteroglossic literary writing that stylizes resources from the vernacular repertoire and finally to advertising billboards, commercial products, and text-based memorabilia commodifying the vernacular into a signifier of locality or an emblem of chicness.

As I elaborate later, these writing practices are *choreographies of multilingualism* in that they do not merely communicate information or emotion; they also perform subtle language ideological scripts that motivate their production. I am therefore invested not so much in the substantive content of written artifacts as in the affective structures that shape them, with regard to what Blommaert (2008: 4) describes as their material and ideational aspects, "in turn lodged in social, cultural, historical, economic and political contexts." Writing, then, becomes a window on how various actors think about identity in relation to language and, by extension, about multilingualism. In this way, the present study aligns with Blommaert's (2008: 4–5) view of writing as "an ethnographic object *par excellence*," one which, owing to its "sheer complexity and context-dependence," can only be "fully understood when an analytical tactic is used that focuses on the object in relation to its contexts." The next section addresses these contexts with respect to Singapore.

Taken together, the two episodes in the previous section give us a window on the language-ideological frames through which multilingualism is differentially imagined in Singapore. To appreciate their significance, we need to understand the broader institutional milieu in which they emerged.

This is the point where population statistics are inevitable. As of 2021, Singapore's resident population comprises 74.2% Chinese, 13.7% Malays, 8.9% Indians, and 3.2% Others (Department of Statistics 2021: 4). This composition is encapsulated in the multiethnic framework CMIO (Chinese, Malay, Indian, Others) and has been relatively stable over the past several decades. The CMIO division is a legacy of the British colonial administration (Tan 2021: 170). Since independence, it has been the state's key conceptual instrument for sustaining balance and harmony in the ethnically diverse polity, "in the hope that this would help mitigate any extremist tendencies that might otherwise try to impose a single language on the entire nation" (Wee 2018: 24).

As a conceptual grid, the CMIO is no doubt a simplification of actual demographics, where proliferative ethnicities far exceed the boundaries put in place by categorical labels, with the Chinese, Malay, and Tamil communities each containing diverse peoples from different origins. Yet as a superordinate principle of cultural organization, the CMIO has deep repercussions for other aspects of Singapore society. In particular, the management of multilingualism in Singapore aligns with this streamlined ethnic diversity. Following the CMIO model, Malay, Mandarin, Tamil, and English are instituted as the four official languages of Singapore, enshrined in Article 153A of the Singapore Constitution.

Malay, apart from being the common language within the Malay community, is also the de jure national language. This status is mostly symbolic, with the language used chiefly in formulaic contexts, such as the national anthem, military commands, and official state honors (Kuo and Chan 2016: 13, 64). The reason for this choice is geopolitical. Singapore is sandwiched between Malaysia to the north and Indonesia to the south, placing it within a predominantly Malay-speaking region within Southeast Asia. Malays are also considered the indigenous people in Singapore and the Malay Peninsula, preceding the arrival of the British in 1819 and the influx of Chinese and Indian immigrants thereafter. In 1963, under Lee Kuan Yew's leadership, Singapore joined the Federation of Malaya to form what is today called Malaysia, although this short-lived merger eventually led to Singapore's secession from the Federation to form its own country in 1965. Prior to independence, and long before English-language use became widespread, a colloquial, pidginized form of Malay, called Bazaar Malay or Baba Malay, circulated widely as a common language (Kuo and Chan 2016: 16). All these circumstances converge to afford Malay its privileged, if notional, status in the Constitution.

According to the CMIO logic, Mandarin and Tamil are, respectively, the common languages of the Chinese and Indian communities. This conception assumes that the language used in each community is monovarietal, which is of course a far cry from reality. Owing to their heterogeneous lineages,[6] but also because of recent trends in migration, Singapore's Chinese and Indian communities use a plethora of languages beyond Mandarin and Tamil: for the Chinese, these are primarily Hokkien, Teochew, Cantonese, Hakka, and Hainanese, mostly originating in the southeastern provinces of China. And for Indians, primarily Bengali, Gujarati, Hindi, Punjabi, and Urdu, with Hindi showing signs of outgrowing Tamil in recent years as the former enjoys higher economic currency in India than the latter (Jain and Wee 2019).

In official discourses, the three ethnic languages, also called the mother tongue languages (MTLs), serve as cultural ballasts for their respective communities, fulfilling the purpose of intraethnic communication. In contradistinction, English, the fourth official language, is positioned as "impartial and disinterested" (Kuo and Chan 2016: 11). Given this putative neutrality, it serves to transcend divisions among the MTLs, facilitating interethnic communication and racial harmony at the community level. Furthermore, it is the language of science and technology as well as of international trade, hence embodying, at the national level, the role of a cosmopolitan, technocratic medium that ties to imperatives of economic development. Finally, at the individual level, it serves as a meritocratic language for the enhancement of social mobility and global connectedness (Bokhorst-Heng 1999a: 8; Wee 2003a).

Importantly, the four official languages are conceived as enclosed, self-sufficient entities in *complementary distribution* with one another. Complementary distribution is a perspective on how languages relate to one another in multilingual settings. Its fundamental premise is that "[e]ach of the co-existing languages or language varieties in a given society serve[s] a specific function, and the specialized functions of different languages or

6. The ancestry of Chinese Singaporeans can be traced to various provinces in southern China, with mutually unintelligible tongues (Hokkien, Teochew, Cantonese, Hakka, Hainanese, and Foochow). There is the further division between Chinese immigrants who arrived in the late nineteenth to early twentieth century (and their descendants) and the local-born Straits Chinese (the Peranakans and their descendants) who had settled in Singapore before mass immigration at the turn of the twentieth century. The latter division has become largely irrelevant today due to intermarriages, with "Peranakan" becoming more of a heritage symbol. Singapore's Indians, too, are eclectic, initially originating primarily in South India and Ceylon and later joined by immigrants from other parts of India, especially in more recent years. As such, several Indian languages are spoken in Singapore, including Tamil, Malayalam, Telugu, Kannada, Hindi, Punjabi, and Gujarati. In this regard, Malays are in a slightly different position. They are technically the indigenous people of Singapore and historically consisted of the Javanese, Baweanese, and Bugis; the latter subdivisions are no longer considered active in Singapore, partly thanks to the cohesive strength of the Malay language (see Kuo and Chan 2016: 9–10).

language varieties [complement] each other, giving rise to cohesive and stable societal bilingualism and/or multilingualism" (Li 1994: 7). Although complementary distribution has been further developed in the literature (see Li 1994: 7–12), this basic idea of achieving stable societal multilingualism through functional distribution still encapsulates the design ethos behind Singapore's language policy.

## The bilingual education system

Singapore's official language policy, including its underlying logic of complementary distribution, is supported by the state's bilingual education system. First implemented in 1966 and achieving full maturity in the 1980s, the system requires all students in government schools to study English in addition to an MTL determined on the basis of patriarchal ethnicity (the ethnic group to which one's father belongs). Since the implementation of the New Education System in 1987, all government schools teach English as a first language (L1), using it as the medium of instruction for most academic subjects; the MTLs are taught as a second language (L2) by default, although there are exceptions. This results in what scholars have variously characterized as English-knowing bilingualism (Pakir 1991) or English-based bilingualism (Tan 2021: 162), where a student from an ethnic Chinese, Malay, or Indian family typically learns English as an L1 subject and, respectively, Chinese, Malay, or Tamil as an L2 subject.

This gives rise to an anomalous situation: what is called a "mother tongue" is in fact a second language for the vast majority of students, going against the grain of how that term is understood in language acquisition discourses (Kuo and Chan 2016: 16). Equally, there are circumstances in which one could claim to possess two "first languages": students who are academically stronger may take their MTLs at L1 level, viz. Higher Chinese Language, Higher Malay Language, and Higher Tamil Language, in addition to English as a compulsory L1 subject.[7] Therefore, MTL, together with the related terms L1 and L2, must be treated as a unique construct in the context of Singapore's bilingual education system, one that has an uncanny relation with the sociolinguistic concept of mother tongue, or what is sometimes called native language.[8]

7. Higher Chinese Language is offered in a small cluster of elite secondary schools called Special Assistance Programme schools, where Chinese as an L2 subject is not an available option.
8. The concept of MTL is further complicated in relation to the Eurasian community (which falls under the "O" [Other] category in CMIO) in Singapore. See Wee (2021a: 92–94).

Bilingual education in Singapore must therefore be understood within the dual rubric of the CMIO and the official language policy. The rationale of this educational system is to develop bilingual individuals in accord with the principle of functional differentiation between English and the MTLs, mentioned earlier. Thus, the institution of English as an L1 is motivated first and foremost by the instrumental reason of economic survival. "What is the responsibility of the government?" asked then-Minister Mentor Lee Kuan Yew in a parliamentary debate in 2004. He then offered the answer: "It is, first and foremost, to give everyone enough English language skills to make a living. Because if he cannot make a living, nothing else is important."[9]

Yet monolingualism in English is not seen as a desirable outcome; the language is seen to carry a virtual baggage of values, leading to a fear that "exposure to English can lead Singaporeans to become increasingly 'Westernized' or 'decadent'" (Wee and Bokhorst-Heng 2005: 164). Hence Lee Kuan Yew's conviction that "[b]ecoming monolingual in English would have been a setback. We would have lost our cultural identity, that quiet confidence about ourselves and our place in the world" (Lee 2000: 181). This line was echoed by other senior politicians, notably Prime Minister Lee Hsien Loong, who maintained that "[i]f we use only English, and allow our mother tongue to degenerate, we will, in time, lose our values and cultural heritage. The nature of our society will change for the worse. Ultimately, our self-confidence as a people will be undermined."[10]

This is where the MTLs enter to fill the gap, providing that which "gives him [a Singaporean] his identity and makes our society vigorous and distinctive," in Lee Kuan Yew's words.[11] It is important to note that this gap is a discursive invention produced through a deliberately simplistic indexical relation between the English language and Western (hence non-Asian, "decadent") cultural values. This in turn opens space for the MTLs to be mobilized along the same logic to index a core of Asian heritage and tradition underlying the three ethnic categories within the CMIO. In respect to Chinese, for instance, at the opening ceremony of the 1991 Speak Mandarin Campaign (SMC; more on this campaign later), then-Prime Minister Goh Chok Tong admonished that

9. Speech by Minister Mentor Lee Kuan Yew at the parliamentary debate on the report of the Chinese Language Curriculum and Pedagogy Review Committee, November 25, 2004, https://www.nas.gov.sg/archivesonline/data/pdfdoc/2004112501.htm.

10. Speech by Prime Minister Lee Hsien Loong, at launch of the 26th Speak Mandarin Campaign, November 15, 2005, at the National Library Events Plaza, https://www.nas.gov.sg/archivesonline/speeches/record-details/7dec15d8-115d-11e3-83d5-0050568939ad.

11. Speech by Minister Mentor Lee Kuan Yew at the parliamentary debate on the report of the Chinese Language Curriculum and Pedagogy Review Committee, November 25, 2004, https://www.nas.gov.sg/archivesonline/data/pdfdoc/2004112501.htm.

[a] Chinese Singaporean who does not know Chinese—either Mandarin or dialect—runs the risk of losing the collective wisdom of the Chinese civilization. . . . Mandarin not only allows Chinese to communicate easier with one another but also opens up many chests of treasures—Chinese literature, music, operas, paintings, calligraphy, ceramics and so on. When we can appreciate them, we will feel proud to be part of that rich history which is Chinese.[12]

While it is unclear (because it is not easily measurable) whether the bilingual education system has truly enabled Singaporeans to retain their cultural identity and assume a "quiet confidence" about themselves, the premium it places on English has no doubt enhanced the academic competitiveness of Singaporeans. This is particularly the case with Singaporean students' math and science achievements as well as reading literacy (Dixon 2005), which would no doubt give them an edge in terms of social mobility.

The bilingual education system has indeed resulted in a rise in bilingual literacy among Singaporeans (from 56% in 2000 to 70.5% in 2010 and 73.2% in 2015; Department of Statistics 2016: viii), but an important corollary of this trend is the increased usage and enhanced symbolic capital of English, to the extent that "its across-the-board usefulness may well pose a future threat to the maintenance of other languages in Singapore" (Simpson 2007: 385). The upshot of this is a generational shift in Singapore's sociolinguistic profile toward anglophone speakership. The number of households using English as a predominant home language witnessed a steady rise from 11.6% in 1980 to 20.8% in 1990 (Kuo and Chan 2016: 22), 23% in 2000, 28.1% in 2005, 32.3% in 2010, and 36.9% in 2015 (Department of Statistics 2016: viii). Notably, a 2019 statistic reveals that among local Chinese households with young children at Primary 1 level, 71% speak English as opposed to Mandarin or a Chinese dialect at home, as compared to 42% twenty years earlier.[13]

### The Speak Mandarin Campaign and the Speak Good English Movement

On a fractal level, the Chinese languages constitute their own site of asymmetric power relations. Historically, the predominant Chinese community

---

12. English version of speech given in Mandarin by Prime Minister Goh Chok Tong at the launching ceremony of the 1991 Speak Mandarin Campaign at the Singapore Conference Hall Auditorium on September 30, 1991, https://www.nas.gov.sg/archivesonline/data/pdfdoc/gct19910930.pdf.

13. Figures from Singapore's Ministry of Education, as cited by Prime Minister Lee Hsien Loong in his 2019 speech at the fortieth anniversary of the Speak Mandarin Campaign, https://www.straitstimes.com/singapore/speak-mandarin-campaign-marks-40-years-with-local-lexicon-pm-lee-hsien-loong-says.

in Singapore was (and, to a lesser extent, still is) characterized by mutually unintelligible topolects, predominantly Mandarin, Hokkien, Teochew, Cantonese, Hakka, and Hainanese. This lack of a common spoken medium within the ethnic Chinese community was perceived to be a social problem, as it could potentially result in and exacerbate tensions among the different dialect groups.[14]

To dovetail this diversity of Chinese vernaculars with official language policy, the government launched the SMC in 1979. The aim of the SMC was to promote Mandarin, based on the Beijing dialect, to the status of a prestige variety of Chinese vis-à-vis other Chinese dialects. This antidialect stance is evident in the slogans used in the campaign, especially in its first decade: "Speak More Mandarin and Less Dialects" (1979); "Mandarin's In. Dialect's Out" (1983); "Start with Mandarin, Not Dialect" (1986); "Better With More Mandarin, Less Dialect" (1988); "More Mandarin, Less Dialect. Make It a Way of Life" (1989) (Teo 2005: 129).[15]

To justify the campaign's rationale, four arguments have been forwarded since its inception (Bokhorst-Heng 1999b: 243; Kuo and Chan 2016: 47–54):

a. The educational argument: that dialects adversely affect students' learning of Mandarin and overall performance in examinations;[16]
b. The cultural argument: that Mandarin consolidates the roots of Chinese language and culture, serving to mitigate the perceived decadent effects associated with English language and culture;[17]

14. It may not be technically correct to say there was no bridge language among the Chinese before Mandarin became prevalent: one survey shows that in 1978, Hokkien was understood by nearly 80% of the Chinese population. Until then, it was one of three languages—alongside Malay and English, but not Mandarin—in which Lee Kuan Yew was reported to have delivered his National Day Rally messages (Kuo and Chan 2016: 17).

15. In response to generational shifts in language usage patterns, the SMC's aims have evolved over the past four decades, with more recent campaigns targeting youth by rebranding Mandarin as a "cool" or trendy language (Kuo and Chan 2016: 53–54; Teo 2005: 134–35).

16. For example, at the 1984 launch of the SMC, Prime Minister Lee Kuan Yew maintained that "[i]f we want our bilingual policy to succeed, we must lighten our children's learning load by using Mandarin as the mother tongue in place of dialect. Studies show that children from Mandarin-speaking families consistently do better in their examinations than those from dialect-speaking homes. . . . It must also be because they have no extra load of dialect words and phrases to carry" (cited in Kuo and Chan 2016: 48).

17. For example, at the 2005 launch of the SMC, Prime Minister Lee Hsien Loong said that "[k]nowledge of Mandarin gives us a sense of identity and roots. It enables us to appreciate and understand who we are and where we came from. It opens up a whole world of Chinese art, culture and traditions, which spans thousands of years of Chinese civilization. If we use only English, and allow our mother tongue to degenerate, we will, in time, lose our values and cultural heritage. The nature of our society will change for the worse. Ultimately, our self-confidence as a people will be undermined," https://

c. The practical argument: that Mandarin facilitates communication among Chinese peoples from various dialect groups;[18] and

d. The economic argument: that Mandarin has become more important with China's rise as an economic powerhouse, and therefore that Chinese Singaporeans must learn the language in order to maintain their competitiveness in the global economy.[19]

These multiple and shifting imperatives for the SMC demonstrate that languages, as Bokhorst-Heng (1999a) has suggested, are more than just languages in Singapore, in the sense that the motivations for promoting particular languages or language varieties are extrinsic rather than intrinsic to the languages themselves. Besides this instrumentalist orientation, the SMC also aligns with a prescriptivist approach to language planning (Dixon 2009: 122–23). The campaign triggered several measures to curtail the use of Chinese dialects in public communications, including gradually phasing out television and radio programs as well as commercials in dialects, and dubbing all Hokkien and Cantonese films imported from Hong Kong in Mandarin before making them available for public broadcast (Kuo and Chan 2016: 76).

With the systematic implementation of these measures, and in concert with the bilingual education policy, the SMC streamlined the linguistic landscape in Singapore with considerable success. Official statistics over three and a half decades show a steady decrease in the number of households using Chinese dialects as the most frequently spoken language at home, from 59.5% in 1980 to 38.2% in 1990 (Kuo and Chan 2016: 22), 23.8% in 2000, 18.2% in 2005, 14.3% in 2010, and then down to 12.2% in 2015 (Department of Statistics 2016: viii).

Yet Chinese dialects are still perfectly audible in Singapore as a grassroots register, sustaining the heteroglossic quality of local speech under the radar of official language policy. More pertinently, they participate in a subaltern

www.nas.gov.sg/archivesonline/speeches/record-details/7dec15d8-115d-11e3-83d5-0050568939ad.

18. For example, at the 1985 launch of the SMC, Second Deputy Prime Minister Ong Teng Cheong (later President) said: "The Chinese learn and speak Mandarin not only because it is the common spoken language of the Chinese community, representing our roots, but also because the economic value of Mandarin is increasing . . ." (cited in Wee 2006: 352), melding the practical argument with the cultural and economic arguments.

19. For example, at the fortieth anniversary celebration of the SMC in 2019, Prime Minister Lee Hsien Loong underlined the economic argument when he noted that people all over the world are learning Chinese, because "[t]hey all know that to work in China, to build relationships with the Chinese and to grab opportunities that come with China's development, they have to master Mandarin," https://www.straitstimes.com/singapore/speak-mandarin-campaign-marks-40-years-with-local-lexicon-pm-lee-hsien-loong-says.

politics, as seen, for instance, in the emergence of dialect classes conducted by Chinese clan associations beyond the ambit of the formal educational system, and in the commodified use of Chinese dialects (especially Hokkien) in local films and street musical performances to index a heartlander (noncosmopolitan) ethos (Lim 2009a: 62–65; Lim 2015: 264–65). Khiun and Chan (2013: 275) aptly describe these artistic expressions in local vernaculars as "vestigial pop," a term that highlights "the effects of repressive policies and political-economic change in delegitimizing and eroding their structures in both the sociolinguistic and educational realms."

The SMC finds a counterpart in the SGEM, launched on April 29, 2000. Just as the SMC set out to marginalize Chinese dialects, so the SGEM aims to streamline English usage with a mandate to eradicate Singlish. It was motivated by the government's perception that the standard of English among Singaporeans was in need of an overhaul. That perception was possibly triggered by the immense popularity of a sitcom figure named Phua Chu Kang. Phua Chu Kang is a characterological figure (Agha 2003) designed around the stereotypical image of a heavily Singlish-speaking heartlander Singaporean. His favorable reception among public audiences, however, landed him in trouble with the authorities, with the prime minister singling him out in a speech as a bad example for Singaporeans to follow as far as spoken English is concerned.

The Phua Chu Kang incident will be addressed in more detail in Chapter 4. Suffice it to say for now that it set off an alarm that Singlish would become so widespread as to adversely impact the standard of English-language use among Singaporeans. This led to the inauguration of the SGEM, whose initial mission was "to encourage Singaporeans to speak grammatically correct English that is universally understood" and "to help Singaporeans move away from the use of Singlish" (cited in Lim 2015: 264). This intention to rein in Singlish aligns with a statement by Prime Minister Goh Chok Tong made in 1999, one year before the SGEM began: "Singlish is not English. It is English corrupted by Singaporeans and has become a Singapore dialect . . . Singlish is broken, ungrammatical English sprinkled with words and phrases from local dialects and Malay which English speakers outside Singapore have difficulties in understanding."[20]

More recently, this anti-Singlish rhetoric seems to have been slightly attenuated; the SGEM's revised (and current) mission statement states that it "recognises the existence of Singlish as a cultural marker for many Singaporeans," which can be taken as a mild concession from its previous stance (Hiramoto 2019: 457). Notwithstanding this shift, the SGEM still projects a strongly

20. Speech by Prime Minister Goh Chok Tong at the Marine Parade National Day Dinner on August 29, 1999, at Sin Leong Restaurant, Marine Parade, https://www.nas.gov.sg/archivesonline/data/pdfdoc/1999082905.htm.

didactic character, stressing the importance of "understand[ing] the differences in Standard English, broken English and Singlish" and aims to help "those who habitually use fractured, ungrammatical English to use grammatical English" as well as "those who speak only Singlish, and those who think Singlish is English, to speak Standard English."[21] As an official platform, the SGEM unequivocally establishes Standard English as the benchmark of correct usage, thereby turning it into "a powerful diacritic" (Blommaert 2018: 48) and stigmatizing Singlish as a nonlegitimate medium.

## Linguistic elitism and its discontents

The SMC and the SGEM are united in their espousal of a purist language ideology. They demonstrate a decidedly modernist propensity toward stratification and elitism, fetishizing the official languages as well as pristine varieties within those languages by closing off potential interference from competing languages and varieties (see Wee 2021a, 2021b). This results in a normativization of language usage, in which Mandarin and Standard English are valorized at the expense of Chinese dialects and Singlish, respectively. Such regulated usage encompasses translation practices, which are found to "participate in maintaining a hierarchy of Mandarins and Englishes" in Singapore (St. André 2006a: 784) by way of shunning the vernacular in favor of the standard. Thus, in Parliament, where speeches can be delivered in all four official languages, the simultaneous English interpretations of speeches delivered in languages other than English are polished after parliamentary sessions to ensure the high quality of English records; and in court interpreting, defendants' utterances in Singlish or colloquial Singapore Mandarin (or other languages) tend to be straightened into a standard, legal English for the court's records (St. André 2006a: 775–77).

The structural divide between standard and vernacular extends beyond language into social class, as encapsulated by the heartlander/cosmopolitan divide. This distinction was first introduced by Prime Minister Goh Chok Tong in his 1999 National Day Rally speech to highlight two broad orientations among Singaporeans' language preferences (Singlish vs. English), career trajectories (local vs. global), and roles in society (cultural ballast vs. wealth generating). Tan (2003: 758) opines that, given the overwhelming majority of ethnic Chinese people in Singapore, the heartlander/cosmopolitan divide can be mapped onto the distinction between Chinese Singaporeans who are Chinese-educated and Chinese-speaking, and those who are English-educated and English-speaking. He further observes that the divide

21. https://www.languagecouncils.sg/goodenglish/about-us.

is not merely about language preferences and material differences; it is more starkly conceived in terms of value system and intrinsic loyalties. The heartlanders are characterized as providing the critical cultural and moral ballast needed by a disciplined society for its continued survival and prosperity. The cosmopolitans are economic dynamos enjoying "flexible citizenship," whose loyalties are fluid and motivated by transient connections of mobile employment and commercial opportunities. (Tan 2003: 758)

Although Goh proposed this divide as an objective rubric and did not overtly favor one orientation over the other, for Tan (2003: 759), the divide essentially "reifies the ideational–economic divide within the Chinese-Singaporean community in stark terms that shows no sign of being bridged." The divide is thus scalar (Blommaert 2010), in that it differentiates individual attributes, including language usage, along thresholds of socioeconomic prestige.

There is therefore a correlation between linguistic hierarchies enforced on the level of language policy and campaigns (standard/official vs. vernacular/nonofficial), on the one hand, and ideational–economic distinctions constructed through official discourse (cosmopolitan vs. heartlander), on the other. This connects directly to the structure of the present study. Institutional modalities of writing entrench the legitimacy of standard/official languages, promulgating a view of multilingualism that articulates a technocratic neatness and aspires to a global, future-oriented cosmopolitanism. These are countered by grassroots modalities of writing, which evoke a heteroglossic messiness associated with the heartlands as a source of nostalgic sentiments.

This latter mode of writing can be traced back to early experimentations, initiated by anglophone college students in the 1950s, with a Malayan literary language mixing English, Malay, and Chinese, also known by the portmanteau EngMalChin. EngMalChin literature did not quite become a phenomenon, but its experimental spirit found new incarnations from the 1980s onward in the work of theater practitioners, filmmakers, poets, and fiction writers, who explored a range of registers to inflect their language with a locale-specific tenor (see Chapter 5).

Yet the kind of grassroots writing that interests me goes beyond tapping into the demotic as part of literary experimentation: it self-consciously adopts a heartlander persona to articulate a sensibility that is ideologically predisposed against the elite establishment. Its stance is critical, and at times aggressive, but its style can be ludic and extremely entertaining. Within this scheme, the vernacular languages, as the remainder of official language policy, come to index egalitarian values; they figure as part of an aesthetic of a grassroots literacy (Blommaert 2008), a discursive instrument to resist top-down narratives of multilingualism. The heartlanders write back.

This study elucidates two broad paradigms in which multilingualism is conceived and performed in textual practices, which interpellate their audiences in different ways in relation to Singapore's multilingual orthodoxy, as defined by the state's language policy and multicultural discourse.

The first paradigm consists of the neat multilingualism of institutional discourses, such as official signage, public communications, and state-supported literary anthologies. Neat multilingualism denotes a structural formation in which the four official languages of Singapore are presented in streamlined and parallel juxtaposition with each other. It speaks to a multicultural praxis based around a visuality of quadrilingualism, and to a rationalization of languages along instituted boundaries that suppresses linguistic resources operating outside policy frameworks. Understanding such writing requires a multimodal approach (Kress and van Leeuwen 2021) to the visual, verbal, typographical, paratextual, and other signifying resources in these texts. This approach helps us uncover the emblematic force of linguistic signs (Blommaert 2010: 29–32) and the transversal of power relations in reiterative semiotic patterns.

The second paradigm comprises more dynamic and critical forms of creative expression, such as vernacular lexicography and social media-based poetry. In the hands of a younger generation of creative writers, features of vernacular speech are engineered into styling resources (Coupland 2007) to fashion literary and metadiscursive discourses that rehabilitate and exalt those vernaculars through rhetorical performance. We will look at examples of how the language of the streets becomes stylized into a playful register of English, shaping a multilingual vision from below, positioned in resistance to that imposed by bureaucracy from above. Here the enregisterment (Agha 2003, 2007; Johnstone et al. 2006; Johnstone 2009) of the vernacular is of particular import: it is precisely because of their marginalization by the language establishment that Singlish and Chinese dialects have come to be stylized into icons of cynical resistance against patriarchal structures.

The binary suggested here is meant as a heuristic, offering an analytical angle on the complex and evolving multilingual landscape of Singapore. As suggested above, it is a fluid binary, and there is a degree of overlap between the two paradigms: while institutionalized practices can strategically tap into dynamic repertoires that exceed the straitjacket of language policy, grassroots practices are showing signs of upscaling toward institutionalized structures. And, beyond this divide, the commodification of the vernacular into text-based artifacts for touristic consumption represents an emerging third frame, one governed by neither institutional nor grassroots ideologies but rather by the political economy of language-based identities within globalized linguistic marketing (Kelly-Holmes 2020). This last frame, addressed in

Chapter 6, diverts attention from the juxtaposition of the institutional and the grassroots, enabling us to project new routes toward—and beyond—multilingualism in the context of intensified economic globalization.

It is within this setup that I consider different writing practices in Singapore as competing choreographies. The term "choreography" generally denotes the stylized design and arrangement of kinetic sequences in dance and theater or, more generally, a premeditated exercise that entails the planning and composition of embodied movement leading to nonspontaneous aesthetic outcomes. The term also references the written notation of dancing, "the art of representing dancing by signs" (Oxford English Dictionary). Applying these senses to writing, I think of multilingual writing as a choreography in the sense that it is a semiotic representation involving the nonspontaneous configuration and display of languages in texts, pointing to their power relations against a specific sociolinguistic milieu. The actual techniques used to organize linguistic and semiotic resources in writing, whether separating or mixing them, may be described as the *technologies* of such choreography.

This use of choreography is informed by the sociolinguistic notion of performativity, where performance is understood as "a specially marked, artful way of speaking, one that sets up or represents a special interpretive frame within which the act of speaking is to be understood" (Bauman and Briggs 1990: 73). Applying this to writing rather than speaking, I construe multilingual artifacts as choreographic in that they put a nonrandom, nonarbitrary act of writing on display, "objectif[ying] it, lift[ing] it to a degree from its interactional setting and open[ing] it to scrutiny by an audience" (Bauman and Briggs 1990: 73). The will to linguistic performance generates the semiotic frames through which various social actors, be they institutional or grassroots, deploy communicative resources to enact different images of multilingual Singapore for public consumption. The lens of choreography therefore serves to foreground the nonarbitrary, ideologically constituted nature of writing practices.

By privileging written discourse, this study also responds to calls to fully recognize writing as a legitimate "object of the sociolinguistic gaze" (Lillis 2013: 2) alongside speaking. In postulating writing as a form of choreography with ideological consequences, it provides empirical support to show that writing is (based on Lillis 2013: 173)

a. an everyday, multimodal practice involving different "modes, materials and technologies" (from public communications to discursive publications to multimedia literature);
b. a social practice based around socioculturally and sociohistorically situated resources specific to the linguistic regime in Singapore (i.e., the quadrilingual template stemming from official language policy; the use of Singlish and Chinese dialects as resources for critical engagement); and

c. a "dynamic phenomenon" engineered by various actors (institutional and grassroots) for different ideological purposes (e.g., reinforcement vs. transgression of prevailing linguistic hierarchies).

This study's focus on the situatedness and materiality of writing in Singapore also converges with work located at the intersection of writing and cities. A case in point is a 2021 special issue in the journal *Social Semiotics* on "writing (in) the city," which aims to foreground "the powerful and particular role of writing as a resource for "making" the city—its design, image, and day-to-day practices" (Jaworski and Li 2021: 2). Exploring a wide range of genres and modalities—city logos, campaign posters, handwritten commercial signs, text-based T-shirts, as well as architectural multimedia performances—across diverse cities, the special issue signals a burgeoning line of inquiry into "the multimodality, materiality and multilinguality of writing as a mediational means of interpersonal and intergroup relationships, hierarchies, and imaginaries . . . and as a repository of the city's memory or biography" (Jaworski and Li 2021: 3). Such a perspective, according to Jaworski and Li (2021: 3), resonates with Michel de Certeau's understanding of writing as constitutive of everyday urban practices, as "a possibility of composing a space in conformity with one's will" (de Certeau 1984: 196).

## PLACE/STRATEGY VS. SPACE/TACTIC

This connection to Michel de Certeau's work brings me to a conceptual thread in the present study. My understanding of how different writing choreographies reify contrasting imaginaries of multilingual Singapore was initially inspired by de Certeau's theory of walking in *The Practice of Everyday Life*. de Certeau (1984) proposes a rhetorical view to the act of walking that conceptualizes it as a mode of enunciation (a speech act), introducing the crucial distinction between *place*/strategy and *space*/tactic. Although *place* and *space* are presented rather like polarities in de Certeau's theory, they are in fact dialectic and copresent, constituting dual perspectives on, and dimensions of, the spatial. I treat them here not as ontological entities but as analogical perspectives to help us elucidate competing narratives of multilingualism in Singapore.

For de Certeau, "place" refers to stable and static constellations of geographical points on the grid (a map, for instance); as an "instantaneous configuration of positions" (117), it represents a top-down spatializing of the city as governed by institutional ideologies and the exigencies of global capitalism.[22]

22. de Certeau's use of "place" and "space" is the reverse of how the same terms are typically used by cultural geographers and anthropologists. In Cresswell's (2015) words, de Certeau's idiosyncratic usage "stands the normal distinction on its head" (70). "Place" for de Certeau is the systemic grid imposed on everyday practices, which is

A *place* is constructed through strategy, "the calculus of force-relationships" (xix). Strategy represents

> the calculation (or manipulation) of power relationships that becomes possible as soon as a subject with will and power (a business, an army, a city, a scientific institution) can be isolated. It postulates a place that can be delimited as its own and serve as the base from which relations with an exteriority composed of targets or threats (customers or competitors, enemies, the country surrounding the city, objectives and objects of research, etc.) can be managed. (de Certeau 1984: 35–36)

An exemplar of this is the city museum, built within specific perimeters and carefully curated by authorities to convey a certain discourse—for example, to tell the story of the city's evolution through guided tours.

*Space*, by contrast, is "a practiced place," an effect "composed of intersections of mobile elements" and "actuated by the ensemble of movements" (117) of pedestrians in their everyday perambulations. It emerges through the deployment of tactic, a calculus that escapes the grid, so to speak, and "constantly manipulate[s] events in order to turn them into 'opportunities'" (xix). As opposed to the panoptic gaze and precise calculations of strategy, tactic involves

> accept[ing] the chance offerings of the moment, and seiz[ing] on the wing the possibilities that offer themselves at any given moment. It must vigilantly make use of the cracks that particular conjunctions open in the surveillance of the proprietary powers. It poaches in them. It creates surprises in them. It can be where it is least expected. It is a guileful ruse. (de Certeau 1984: 37)

Foregrounded here is the agency of the pedestrian, who can opportunistically hijack *place* (any area that has been institutionally designated by authorities for a particular purpose) by transgressing its parameters, thereby turning it into *space*. For example, by taking unplanned shortcuts, a pedestrian effectively invents a personalized route between two points. To use my city

the equivalent of "space" in cultural geography, whereas "space" for de Certeau encapsulates the dynamic flows that cut across prescribed structures, equivalent to "place" for cultural geographers. This is no doubt a result of translation (the terms "place" and "space" are respectively from *lieu* [location] and *espace* [space] in the original French). Consider, further, Marc Augé's (1995) term "non-places," referencing sites represented as impersonal, anonymous, and generally lacking a cultural specificity, as opposed to historically embedded locales. Since I am tapping into de Certeau's thinking, it may be confusing to reverse the polarities of his terms to fit with popular usage in cultural geography, as seen in Cresswell (2015) and Massey (2005). For that reason, I will be using the terms along de Certeau's definitions, but to differentiate from normative usage I will italicize them when they are meant in the de Certeauean sense.

museum example, a visitor might transform *place* into *space* by reversing the directionality in which the exhibition route is to be traversed, by permutating the order of viewing to come up with an alternative narrative of the city, or by punctuating the viewing experience with extended breaks, thereby resisting the linear continuity of the museum's discourse.

The strength of de Certeau's framework lies in the way it foregrounds the creative and critical potential of everyday practices, viewing these in terms of a power-and-resistance dynamic in relation to top-down bureaucratic structures. The framework is premised on a parallelism "between linguistic and pedestrian enunciation" (99), where "the clear text of the planned and readable city" (93), with all its "analytical, coherent proper meanings of urbanism" (102), is continually intercepted by networks of "moving, intersecting writings compos[ing] a manifold story that has neither author nor spectator" (93).

If we accept this linguistic conception of perambulation, can we not reverse the metaphorical equation to consider writing (the city) in terms of walking (the city)? Thus, in thinking through the cultural politics of writing in Singapore, I use the *place*/strategy and *space*/tactic dyads to provide rhetorical texture to my understanding of how institutional modes of inscription and publication aim at the top-down management of multilingualism, and how this is resisted from below by grassroots discourses espousing and performing a vernacular, nonelitist vision of multilingualism. Hence, while institutional modalities strategically produce a multilingual *place* evincing order, structure, and permanence, grassroots modalities accrue into a multilingual *space* that is mobile, ever evolving, and transient.[23] This de Certeauean inflection teases out the antagonisms and complementarities between different language ideological regimes, enabling us to understand how various choreographies of writing participate in the discursive struggle over what multilingual Singapore should look like.

Yet as noted above, it is not the case that institutional structures are static and oppressive and everyday practices dynamic and spontaneous. As demonstrated in the Chapter 6, there is seepage between the competing modalities of writing. Just as institutions can performatively engage in what is normally

23. There is the counterargument that, for de Certeau, all practices make *space*, and that since all writing, top-down or bottom-up, is practice as such, the *place*/*space* distinction is invalidated. This argument belies a slippage of terms: "practice" for de Certeau takes on the specific meaning of "everyday practice," excluding acts within bureaucratic apparatuses. For me, the term "practice" encompasses all modalities of writing, including the representation of writing: although *places* are supposed to be static grids compared to *spaces* accrued from everyday practices, does the former not also ensue from practices, though not the *everyday* practices that interest de Certeau (as well as cultural geographers)? The act of drawing up a map by an institution (or a metaphorical map, as in a policy document setting down rules and boundaries), for instance, is materially a kind of practice; even an empty grid must be constructed by someone, it cannot arise by itself.

seen as mundane practice, so too individuals may dovetail themselves into the institution, eliding any notion of pure resistance. Herein lies the logic of my intervention: to first establish and then eschew the dichotomy, thereby fleshing out the fundamental trajectories of multilingual writing in Singapore while maintaining a regard for the nuances between and alternatives beyond them.

## OUTLINE OF CHAPTERS

This book consists of six chapters. This chapter has provided a background to the language situation in Singapore with a review of its official language policy, bilingual education policy, and major language campaigns. It has also laid out the theoretical framework and conceptual methodology that inform the analyses that follow. The rest of the book devotes two chapters to each of the two modalities of writing under investigation (institutional and grassroots), before addressing the intersections between these modalities as well as developments beyond them in the closing chapter.

Chapter 2 is the first of two chapters examining institutional writing in Singapore, with a focus on the official dimension of the semiotic landscape. Based on a social semiotic analysis (Scollon and Scollon 2003; Kress and van Leeuwen 2021) of official multilingual discourses in the form of public signage or displays, it identifies a visual–spatial formula operating across a wide range of examples. The said formula is a quadrilingual schema distributing relatively equal visual–spatial resources to each of the official languages. Because of its ubiquity, this semiotic formula serves as a technology for choreographing semiotic landscapes. I argue, with recourse to Blommaert (2010, 2015), that the schema enacts the trope of neat multilingualism, as described earlier. Neat multilingualism evokes an affect of balance, which speaks to an order of indexicality ideologically informed by the macrostructures of official language policy and the bilingual education system. Official writing therefore operates on a scale that perpetuates public narratives on multiculturalism,[24] underpinned by the CMIO, in a top-down, panoptic manner. Adapting de Certeau's (1984) terms, the chapter argues that the resulting landscape is akin to a multilingual *place* produced by technocratic semiotic templates from above rather than a multilingual *space* emerging from spontaneous linguistic energies from below.

Chapter 3 shifts the setting from public spaces to discursive publications, taking the idea of choreography into the context of multilingual literature

24. Where public narratives are "[s]tories elaborated by and circulating among social and institutional formations larger than the individual, such as family, religious or educational institutions" (Baker 2019: 170, drawing on Somers 1992, 1997; and Somers and Gibson 1994). I use the term interchangeably with "statal narratives" (Wee and Bokhorst-Heng 2005) and "official narratives" to mean narratives circulated specifically by the state.

and literacy. Based on a corpus of government-funded literary anthologies published between 1985 and 2015, it identifies two variations within the top-down language ideology, forming two major translation models for Singapore's textual *place*. The first model is that of triple bilingualism, under which works written in the MTLs are accompanied by English translations but not vice versa or into other MTLs. The second model is that of multilateral translation, under which works written in each of the four official languages are translated into the other three, interweaving into a many-to-many matrix. The two models give rise to different language power formations. Triple bilingualism foregrounds the prerogative of English to function as a mediating nexus across all official languages, resulting in an asymmetrical mode of multilingual communication in which all languages are equal, but some (indeed just one: English) are more equal than others. The multilateral model features an immaculate symmetry, giving equal measure of symbolic capital to the MTLs and English, hence rekeying the English/MTL dichotomy into a balanced constellation. Despite their differences, both models thus reinforce the quadrilingual schema by instantiating the presence of official languages and the absence of vernaculars.

Chapter 4 is the first of two chapters that turn to grassroots writing, positioned antithetically in relation to institutional ideologies. It focuses on how Singaporean intellectuals articulate discursive resistance by enregistering the local vernacular. The case in point is the 2018 book *Spiaking Singlish*, lauded as the first book to be written in Singlish about Singlish. I argue that, by tactically appropriating Singlish as a performative register, the book develops the vernacular into a higher-order indexical (Silverstein 2003; Johnstone et al. 2006), tapping into its association with heartlander sensibilities. More specifically, I argue that the book develops a performative mode of Singlish, through which the vernacular becomes a fetish object. I then draw out several layers of controversy between Singlish practitioners and the language establishment. The chapter then discusses several key events that positioned state language policy and vernacular usage in direct opposition to each other. Finally, the chapter returns to *Spiaking Singlish*, critically discussing its contribution to the development of a citizen sociolinguistics (Rymes 2020) in Singapore, while also revealing elitist tendencies within the celebration of an egalitarian tongue.

Chapter 5 extends the argument of Chapter 4 by exploring grassroots writing within a community of practice developed around vernacular poetry. It also offers a counterpoint to the anthology data in Chapter 3 by focusing on noncanonical writing in which heteroglossia is a key stylistic feature. In contrast to institutional anthologies, which tend to compartmentalize writing into distinct quadrilingual categories that scale up to official policy discourse, heteroglossic writing instantiates a scaled-down (Rymes and Smail 2021) vision based on entropic rather than neat multilingualism. My case in point is

SingPoWriMo (Singapore Poetry Writing Month), a Facebook forum where amateur and professional writers participate in an interactive poetry event for thirty days in the month of April each year. In this event, writers respond to prompts set by forum moderators with their poems, hashtag their work, and comment on one another's writing. Through an analysis of examples from several runs of SingPoWriMo (2014–2020), with a special focus on its metadiscursive poetry in Singlish, I demonstrate how this brand of bottom-up writing makes use of unusual forms and mixed registers to choreograph quotidian creativities, project iconoclastic sensibilities, and debunk the state's multicultural fantasy (Chong 2010). The chapter argues that, just as speech acts are particular enunciations effected by speakers through their reappropriation of elements from a linguistic system (de Certeau 1984: xiii), so SingPoWriMo as a "light" literary community (Blommaert and Varis 2015) comprises "innumerable practices by means of which users reappropriate the space organized by techniques of sociocultural production" (de Certeau 1984: xiv), hence resisting the top-down discursive *place* structured by the quadrilingual schema.

Chapter 6 sets out to complicate the relation between the two contrasting scales of discourse (institutional vs. grassroots; systematic vs. spontaneous; strategic vs. tactical) that underpin the previous chapters. It presents evidence to suggest that different writing modalities are available to new and alternative choreographies, prompting us to adopt a more nuanced perspective on from-above and from-below trajectories of multilingualism. On the one hand, institutional writing, such as government communications with the general public, does not inflexibly espouse neat multilingualism; it may tap into heteroglossic, vernacular resources as part of a strategy to achieve contingent goals in communication. On the other hand, grassroots writing, such as independent literary initiatives, can be subsumed into more organized frameworks, thereby enfolding this writing into institutional structures and dovetailing into state funding mechanisms. Further complicating the picture is the increased commodification of local vernaculars in marketing environments in recent years, a development that offers a window on the socioeconomics of metrolingualism. Choreographies of multilingualism, then, exceed top-down versus bottom-up language ideological struggles, encompassing articulations of local identity against the pragmatic imperatives of globalization.

# CHAPTER 2

# Spectacles of multilingualism

## Reading the semiotic landscape

This chapter addresses multilingualism in Singapore's semiotic landscape, a concept that directs attention to "the interplay between language, visual discourse, and the spatial practices and dimensions of culture, especially the textual mediation or discursive construction of place and the use of space as a semiotic resource in its own right" (Jaworski and Thurlow 2010: 1).[1] It identifies a semiotic arc signaling a particular kind of discursive choreography, one that aims at a panoptic management of multilingualism in Singapore and that shapes the institutional dimension of the city-state's public communications. Focusing on the genre of public institutional signage,[2] I demonstrate how the

---

1. The idea of "semiotic landscape" extends that of linguistic landscape. It is the more appropriate term for present purposes, for although the data in this chapter pertain to displayed language, my interest lies not primarily with the verbal–linguistic but with the visual–spatial aspect.

2. For the purpose of this chapter, a sign is considered institutional insofar as it is emplaced by a public entity, regardless of whether that entity is strictly speaking a government body. Hereafter, I use "public" and "institutional"/"institutionalized" as interchangeable adjectives for this genre of signage. Other labels have been attached to this type of discourse in the literature: municipal (either "regulatory" or "infrastructural," as opposed to commercial; Scollon and Scollon 2003: 167); public (as opposed to private; Landry and Bourhis 1997: 26–27); professional (as opposed to amateur; Blommaert 2013: 62); top-down (as opposed to bottom-up; Ben-Rafael et al. 2006; Backhaus 2007: 80–83); from above (as opposed to from below; Coupland 2010); and in vitro (as opposed to in vivo; Calvet 1998). The binaries suggested by these terms have been subject to critique, perhaps rightly so (see Thurlow 2019). This does not mean, however, that we cannot identify broad trajectories along which signs are choreographed within various functional or ideological frames (Kallen 2010; Coupland and Garrett 2010; Coupland 2012; Moriarty 2014).

Choreographies of Multilingualism. Tong King Lee, Oxford University Press. © Oxford University Press 2022.
DOI: 10.1093/oso/9780197644645.003.0002

official languages of Singapore are formalized into a trope, a "relatively conventionalized (and therefore historical) [set] of metapragmatically attributive meaning" (Blommaert 2015: 107). This trope imposes a visual–verbal structure on public spaces, turning institutional signage in the urban landscape into an iterative figure of official multilingualism.

In concrete terms, we are looking at a compositional pattern that speaks directly to an officially sanctioned discourse on multilingualism in Singapore.[3] That pattern takes the form of a quadrilingual schema, affording English, Chinese, Malay, and Tamil (almost) equal recognition and symmetrical representation by way of an even distribution of visual–spatial resources. In so doing, the schema mirrors the taxonomy of languages and, by extension, of ethnic cultures as enshrined in official language policy and the CMIO (Chinese, Malay, Indian, Others) grid, as discussed in Chapter 1. Given that public signage as an institutionalized genre is driven by the state's taylorist discourse, the quadrilingual schema can be interpreted as "a technique of sociocultural production" (de Certeau 1984: xiv), motivated by spatial strategies and functioning as part of a larger bureaucratic apparatus.[4]

My starting point is that a semiotic landscape is an ideologically charged construction (Leeman and Modan 2009: 332), comprising signs that speak to a certain social, political, or economic framework (Shohamy 2015: 168). These signs materialize language ideologies by means of display conventions (Coupland 2012: 2), such as the choice, sequencing, and typography of languages. A display convention, according to Coupland (2012: 4),

> ASSERTS or PROPOSES a version of ethnolinguistic arrangements and the "shape" of a bilingual [or multilingual] culture. It may posit equal status and resources between languages, or imply an unproblematic, parallel co-existence between languages and social groups. It may posit hierarchical relations between languages and groups. It may challenge the legitimacy of a code and its idealized users, and so on. Bilingual displays are therefore moves in evolving discourses of cultural definition. (capitalization in the original)

Following Coupland, this chapter seeks to outline the "shape" of Singapore's multilingual culture as "asserted" or "proposed" by institutionalized display conventions. It offers a language ideological account for the "ethnolinguistic arrangements" manifested in the semiotic landscape, which, in the process of

3. Where "compositional pattern" refers to "the way in which the representational and interactive elements are made to relate to each other, the way they are integrated into a meaningful whole" (Kress and van Leeuwen 2021: 179).

4. Or, in the alternative terms of Lefebvre (1991: 38), the quadrilingual schema is integral to Singapore's "conceived space": the bureaucratic, scientific representation of space as imagined by scientists, planners, urbanists, technocratic subdividers, and social engineers.

embodying language policy (Shohamy 2006: 123, 2015: 168), becomes a strategic site of visual choreography.

The signs in question are therefore a multilingual spectacle.[5] Irrespective of their referential content, the institutionalized production of texts and images as complexes of translational frames is of emblematic import, where the official language constellation signifies by way of its visibility as an iterative schema. Featuring a fixed constellation of languages, emplaced in visible locations, and undergirded by an affect of balance, they are multimodal entities meant as much to be seen as to be read. As a fetishized genre whose visual patterning is central (Kelly-Holmes 2014), they perpetuate the myth of neat multilingualism, whereby different languages are construed as largely equitable partners on the basis of complementary distribution (Li 1994: 7–12, 2021: 214).

## THE QUADRILINGUAL SCHEMA

The quadrilingual schema does not simply capture a display convention. Rather, it points to a semiotic regime in which the spatial order of languages iconizes (Irvine and Gal 2000; Coupland 2012: 11) the state's conception of multilingualism in a single stroke. It thus represents a "normative organization of language," in particular "the tendency to standardize forms of language and language usage into highly politically sensitive templates" (Blommaert 2018: 35).

The schema is first and foremost marked by a symmetrical visual–spatial design. Let us start with two ubiquitous signs in Singapore, each with a different language sequence. Figure 2.1 shows a "danger" sign commonly seen at construction sites in Singapore, warning passersby to steer clear of engineering works in progress. Its message, "Danger—Keep Out!," is presented in the four official languages in the top-to-bottom sequence, English–Chinese–Malay–Tamil (ECMT). This sequence has gained a degree of stability across a significant range of public signs, although variations are not precluded.[6]

---

5. My use of the term "spectacle" is influenced by Guy Debord's (1995) idea of the "society of the spectacle," with its attendant emphasis on the complicity between the reign of the market economy and techniques of governmentality. Compare with Jaworski's (2018) notion of "writing spectacles," referring to large-scale texts characterized by their visual extravagance, immersiveness, performativity, iterative visual motifs, and diverse materiality. Also compare Sweetland's (2002: 515) "spectacular" uses of language, defined as the begging, borrowing, or stealing of a variety "by speakers who don't normally claim it."

6. The "danger" sign occasionally features the sequence English–Chinese–Tamil–Malay (the National Archives of Singapore has a photo, dated 1980, of the same sign with that order). Arguably, this is a minor shift that does not disturb the overall constellation, with English (the language of administration) and Chinese (the most widely spoken mother tongue language) remaining at the forefront.

**Figure 2.1.** Warning sign: "Danger–Keep Out!" with the ECMT order.

A number of visual and typographical details organize the space on the sign. The four language units are uniformly printed in red, the color almost universally associated with danger. And although we can't compare the typeface across all four segments because three different scripts are used, we can at least see that the English and Malay units, both in the roman script, share the same sans serif font. The exclamation marks at the end of each unit cohere into a vertical series. (The midline dash has almost the same effect, if not for its displacement by the comma in the Chinese segment as well as the lack of vertical alignment throughout.) Crucially, the four units occupy more or less the same amount of space on the board on which they are stenciled, leaving roughly equal margins on all four sides.

There is a minor difference in script size, but this difference is crafted to create an impression of sameness. The Tamil segment appears cramped as compared to the Malay segment, which in turn uses a slightly smaller font than the English. This is due to the different lengths of the warning phrase as it is expressed in each language and the typographical imperative to fit each language in a single line. This imperative is itself telling: why not stretch the Tamil segment over two lines, for instance? The answer lies not in the linguistics of the text but in the semiotics, particularly the need to create a visual–spatial effect of balance and equilibrium across the four languages.

Indeed, all of these features contribute to a holistic perception of symmetry. In the terms of Sebba's (2012: 106–8) framework for the analysis of multilingual written discourse, the *language-content relationship* is that of *equivalence*: each of the four language units carries the same appellative message and can thus be considered mutual translations in terms of their substantive verbal content.[7] The *language mixing type* is that of a *mixed type*: the four language units coexist and function as part of a larger heterogeneous unit (i.e., the multilingual sign). Note that what Sebba calls "mixed type" pertains to the presence of several languages on a single sign. Thus, in Figure 2.1, the four languages are "mixed" only because they cohabit space on the same physical sign; each language segment is unmixed, discrete, and in complementary distribution with the other segments, instantiating a quadruple monolingualism.[8]

The quadrilingual schema thus resonates with what Coupland (2012) calls "parallel-text bilingualism" in his study of Welsh–English display signs in Wales, except that we are dealing with four rather than two languages. As an "institutionally dominant frame," Coupland (2012: 12) argues that this model of bilingual display reinforces standard language ideologies under which linguistic syncretism has no place. Citing Monica Heller on her notion of double multilingualism, he maintains that, with parallel-text bilingualism, "while bilingualism is valued, it is only valued as long as it takes the shape of 'double monolingualism.' One is expected to speak each 'language' as though it were a homogeneous monolingual variety. . . . Mixed varieties, which of course are common in bilingual settings, are frowned upon (Heller 2002: 48; see also Heller 2003)" (Coupland 2012: 11). A comparable framework is attested in respect to institutional signage in Singapore where, instead of double monolingualism, we have quadruple monolingualism, whose shape is composed by four neatly delineated languages.

7. Other language-content combinations include *disjoint*, where each language unit offers different content, and *overlapping*, where only part of the content is available across different languages (Sebba 2012: 107). Other scholars, notably Reh (2004: 8–15) and Backhaus (2007: 90–103), have proposed different labels to describe similar patterns, creating a confusing matrix of overlapping terminology. Thus, Sebba's *equivalence* corresponds to Reh's *duplicating* (the same text appears in two or more languages) and to Backhaus's *homophonic* (mutual translation or transliteration among languages fully available). Sebba's *overlapping* is coextensive with Reh's use of the same term (parts of the text are shared between two or more languages, while other parts appear in one or the other of the languages), while Backhaus's *mixed* encompasses Sebba's and Reh's *overlapping* as well as Reh's *fragmentary* (the text appears in full in one language, with parts of it translated into the other language[s]). Sebba's *disjoint* corresponds to Reh's *complementary* (distinct parts of the text appear in different languages with no overlap in content), which is Backhaus's *polyphonic* (mutual translation or transliteration among languages not available), but this is not to be confused with Sebba's *complementary* texts (see note 9 in this chapter). Backhaus further proposes *monophonic*, where a piece of information is available in a stand-alone language.

8. Compare with the "language-neutral type," where a language segment is ambivalent as to which of two or three languages it is encoded in, invoking them "at once, and at the same time, none of them" (Sebba 2012: 108). This type is irrelevant to cases where the languages at issue bear different orthographies.

Following Sebba (2012: 109), the sign in Figure 2.1 would therefore be called a "parallel text," characterized by "matched units, symmetrically arranged and containing identical content in each language, without any language mixing."[9] Close inspection of a similar sign, however, reveals a critical factor missing from Sebba's framework. Figure 2.2 shows the sign of a community club (CC) in Singapore. At first blush, the sign strikes one as similar to the one in Figure 2.1, with the name of the building "Bishan North Community Club" appearing in the same four languages, vertically arranged, and evincing the same visual balance and typographical neatness. While the two signs would both be classified as parallel texts in Sebba's analytical rubric, this rubric neglects the significance of the order in which the languages appear.

The sequence of the languages on display in Figure 2.2 is Malay–Chinese–Tamil–English (MCTE). As compared to Figure 2.1, the most conspicuous shift here is the displacement of English by Malay as the first language to appear on the vertical reading axis; significantly, English comes last, with Chinese and Tamil sandwiched in between. Taking, for the sake of argument, the ECMT sequence as the point of reference, such permutation is likely to be motivated. To understand this motivation, we must appreciate the differential symbolic capital of the various languages as well as the material circumstances of the sign's emplacement.

The first key to understanding the MCTE sequence is that it is the order in which the four official languages are mentioned in the constitution.[10] The lead language, Malay, is also the national language of Singapore. As mentioned in the previous chapter, this status is largely symbolic, because Malay is far from (and has never been) the most widely used language in Singapore; it is spoken by barely 14% of the population today (Department of Statistics 2021: 4). The question now arises as to how Malay's symbolic status relates to its positioning on top of the other official languages, as in Figure 2.2. This takes us to the spatial semiotics of language sequencing and its meaning effects.

According to Kress and van Leeuwen (2021: 190–98; see also Scollon and Scollon 2003: 91–95), within a top-to-bottom viewing frame, the placement

9. Compare with "complementary texts," where language-spatial relationships are asymmetrical (some languages are more salient than others) and language-content relationships are disjoint (each language segment offers different content) (Sebba 2012: 109).

10. Clause 153A (Part XIII), Constitution of the Republic of Singapore: "Malay, Mandarin, Tamil and English shall be the 4 official languages in Singapore" (https://sso.agc.gov.sg/Act/CONS1963?ProvIds=P1XIII-). Note that in the early years of independence, Malay was also officially described, though not legally instituted, as a "common" language; this informal status has long been acceded to English. See a pertinent statement from the prime minister's office issued on October 1, 1965, https://www.nas.gov.sg/archivesonline/data/pdfdoc/lky19651001.pdf.

**Figure 2.2.** Name sign of a community club with the MCTE order.

of an element on a vertical axis provides a certain "information value." Specifically, an element that appears at or near the top of a unit of communication (e.g., an advertisement or the text-image layout of a newspaper article) represents the Ideal, that is, the realm of aspirations and desires "divested of contradictions, exceptions and nuances." Top placement, in other words, signifies "an idealized or generalized essence."

By contrast, an element appearing at or near the bottom of a frame represents the Real, evoking the specific, the practical, and the down to earth. This bottom placement implies an ideological backgrounding, extending a "subservient" role to an element in a visually "lower," hence ideologically less prominent, position, as compared to the "lead" role assumed by a top-placed element. In advertising contexts, material appearing at the top tends to be assertions of a general nature, spelling out a more symbolic, idealized, and emotive vision, "the edifice of promise." On the other hand, material appearing at the bottom of an advertising interface tends to provide specific product information, pointing to "what is" rather than "what might be" (Kress and van Leeuwen 2021: 190).

Applying this to our example in Figure 2.2 yields a social semiotic interpretation of its visual structure. The top placement of Malay brings the viewer's attention to its idealized status as the national language—idealized precisely because that status is more symbolic than substantive. Being on the top also means Malay is ostensibly the most ideologically salient language (see Kress and van Leeuwen 2021: 191). By the same token, English, now relegated to the bottom end of the axis, is rendered least prominent in semiotic terms. As a result of this arrangement, the three mother tongue languages (MTLs) now appear before English.

This is not inconsequential. We have seen in Chapter 1 the official language policy and the bilingual education system combine to give English a premium over the MTLs. Hence, the bottom placement of English on the sign gives rise to a social semiotic value in tension with its prestige status in contemporary society. By the same token, the top placement of Malay suggests a semiotic preeminence in tension with its actual usage in everyday life. To the extent that Malay is far from a lingua franca in Singapore today—it had much more currency in earlier decades in the form of Bazaar Malay—this MCTE order is arguably marked, though by no means singular.[11]

An alternative argument is that, since the MCTE order is attested in, indeed derives from, the Constitution, it can equally be said to be unmarked; in this case we may very well postulate in the reverse that the ECMT order is marked. Be that as it may, the important point is that each of these language patterns represents "a special interpretive frame within which the act of speaking is to be understood" (Bauman and Briggs 1990: 73; substituting writing for speaking in the case at hand). In other words, both sequences are entextualizations of a certain stance on linguistic hierarchy. Despite the nuances between them, both are nonrandom and nonarbitrary; they instantiate a choreography from an institutional vantage point by reinforcing the visuality of the quadrilingual schema.

To understand the interpretative frame invoked by the sign in Figure 2.2, we need a second key, namely, the function of CCs in Singapore. These clubs are district-level entities run by the People's Association (PA), a statutory board tasked with the mission "to promote racial harmony and social cohesion in Singapore" and "to build and bridge communities in achieving one people, one Singapore."[12] According to the PA website, CCs are "common spaces for people of all races to come together, build friendships and promote social bonding. CCs also connect residents and the Government by providing relevant information and gathering feedback on national concerns and policies."[13] CCs are therefore grassroots-oriented organizations connoting strong *heartlander* as opposed to *cosmopolitan* leanings (Tan 2003: 759), each serving a relatively small neighborhood.

11. For example, name signs at the entrance of government schools (excluding certain aided schools affiliated with the church or Chinese clans) use the MCTE order; see Tan (2014: 447).
12. https://www.pa.gov.sg/our-network/about-us.
13. https://www.pa.gov.sg/our-network/community-clubs.

The PA's mission statement and its introductory passage on CCs share a common emphasis on fostering racial togetherness as part of building a cohesive social community. Herein lies the crux for understanding the MCTE pattern in Figure 2.2. Because the CCs in particular and the PA in general place a premium on racial harmony, the bottom placement of English can be read as manifesting a desire to highlight the MTLs, and by extension, their connections with a heartlander sensibility. English, as explained in Chapter 1, is constructed in the official discourse on multilingualism as an ethnically "neutral" language delinked from any particular category under the CMIO rubric. As the language of social mobility and global connectedness, it is also associated with a cosmopolitan, future-looking orientation. This indexical value renders English a less viable resource in the context of CCs, whose mandate puts them on a strictly local (i.e., town or neighborhood level) scale of things.

By contrast, the MTLs, with their direct mapping onto the ethnic categories of C(hinese), M(alay), and I(ndian),[14] call up a localized, nostalgic consciousness that dovetails with the racial-harmony and community-bonding objectives of CCs and the PA. It is this indexicality that justifies their premium space on the vertical axis of languages in relation to English. The relative identity values of English and the MTLs in the context of a CC sign, however, do not hold when those same languages are organized on signs like the one in Figure 2.1. This latter sign, emplaced at construction sites, is not directly associated with the articulation of racial-ethnic relations; its relative instrumentality arguably pivots it toward the ECMT sequence, which is pervasive in the semiotic landscape.[15]

The ECMT and MCTE sequences evoke different time-space imaginations based around their (global or local) affinities, which is to say they embody different chronotopes (Blommaert 2015). The ECMT represents a forward-looking trajectory of Singapore as an advanced economy with international aspirations, situated at the macronexus of global trade and postindustrial capitalism. The placement of English first, the language of economic mobility, signifies this vision. The MCTE, in contrast, highlights the MTLs, and the placement of Malay first speaks to a strategic scaling to the micro and the local, with all their vernacular connotations of solidarity and communality. Inasmuch as the MCTE sequences hail from the Constitution, it harks back to yesteryear and to a different sociolinguistic space, recalling a lost milieu when

14. O(thers), being an eclectic category, is not tied to a specific language.
15. Such pervasiveness is evidenced, for example, in the government's official website on COVID-19 (https://www.gov.sg/article/covid-19-resources#posters), which offers free downloads of a litany of parallel posters in English, Chinese, Malay, and Tamil, listed consistently in that order. Although the site of emplacement here is official, the subject matter in question is a global health issue of overriding instrumental importance, which would justify the ECMT sequencing.

the MTLs (Malay in particular) were still relatively vibrant and when the dominance of English was yet to be.

A detail in Figure 2.2 is worth attending to. At the top of the figure, we see the words "Bishan North Community Club" cast in large, block letters in the form of a language sculpture stretching across the roof of a glass structure. The three-dimensional corporeality of this free-standing sculptural place name (reinforced by the all-caps typography of the letters) bestows on it, and on the embodying language, material salience over the multilingual entrance sign with its embossed letters (Jaworski and Lee 2019). It appears only in English, and this repetition of the English name on two proximate signs is itself performative.

From where I stood to take the picture, near the entrance of the CC, the English sculpture overarched the multilingual sign (and me). This was a low-angle shot that tilted my gaze upward. As a consequence, the name sculpture was in an elevated position vis-à-vis myself, giving it symbolic power over me (Kress and van Leeuwen 2021: 138–40; Scollon and Scollon 2003: 95–98). By extension, and notwithstanding the anthropomorphism, we might say that the English-only sculptural sign exerts symbolic power over the multilingual sign at the entrance.

In the vertical space between the two signs, a silent power struggle is staged where the official languages engage one another in semiotic tension. What I said earlier about mitigating the preeminence of English in favor of the MTLs in the CC setting will now have to be qualified, though not necessarily invalidated. It is as though the English-only sculpture on the roof imposes itself, literally from above, onto the MCTE sign at the entrance, symbolically reining in the foregrounded MTLs on the latter. Such a reading unveils language ideological tensions embedded in the semiotic landscape, where languages function not only as codes but also as resources for strategic identity work. It also points to a complex dynamic within the panoptic management of multilingualism, where imperatives toward global, future-oriented cosmopolitanism interact with and are moderated by imperatives toward the local, nostalgic heartlands.

Yet despite their variant sequences, the two signs in Figures 2.1 and 2.2 converge on a broader scale of things. They are specific examples of a social practice (Scollon 2001: 4; Scollon and Scollon 2004: 12–13): the institutional production of public signage, where the four official languages consolidate into an iterative, translational signifier—the quadrilingual schema. This schema, indexically evocative of statal narratives on multiculturalism, streamlines the four official languages into bounded, self-sufficient categories while locking out languages falling on the "wrong" side of the language policy paradigm, including Chinese dialects, Singlish, and non-Tamil Indian languages. Whether ECMT or MCTE, the schema issues from a legal-institutional discourse that imposes a representational frame on Singapore's multilingual imaginary.

Discourse, as Stuart Hall (1997; following Foucault) tells us, "governs the way a topic can be meaningfully talked about and reasoned about": "Just as a discourse 'rules in' certain ways of talking about a topic, defining an acceptable and intelligible way to talk, write, or conduct oneself, so also, by definition, it 'rules out', limits and restricts other ways of talking, of conducting ourselves in relation to the topic or constructing knowledge about it" (44). In the case at hand, the quadrilingual schema "rules in" English, Chinese, Malay, and Tamil (regardless of sequence) at the same time as it "rules out" other languages and language varieties. In so doing, it frames an "acceptable and intelligible way"—from the perspective of the establishment, that is—to think multilingualism in Singapore.

The examples in Figures 2.1 and 2.2 instantiate this schema, and hence the language ideological discourse motivating it, in different contexts of emplacement. They represent different tokens, "sites of engagement" speaking to a broader type of writing, or a "nexus of practice" (Scollon and Scollon 2004: 12).[16] More precisely, they are "emblematic figures of identity," in Agha's (2007: 237) terms, sitting at the intersection of the state's discursive construal of language relations for the public performance of multilingualism and the recursive performance of such relations in institutional signage—that is, "in the give and take of social interaction" (239).

## VISUAL EQUILIBRIUM: TOWARD A NEAT MULTILINGUALISM

The rest of this chapter presents further evidence from the semiotic landscape to elucidate the general principles governing institutional signage. This signage partakes of a "rationalized, expansionist . . . centralized, clamorous, and spectacular production" (de Certeau 1984: xii) of public written discourse. They belie a visual–spatial choreography in that their design schemes are underpinned by the quadrilingual schema, under which the four official languages are presented as parallel, bounded units with no crossover between them. This is neat multilingualism, a Cartesian, rationalized multilingual setup whose coordinates are immaculately measured.

In what follows, I discuss various examples according to three kinds of material frames: single frames (in which four languages appear in one poster or notice), twin frames (in which two posters or notices, each carrying two languages, make up one information unit), and quadrilingual frames (in which

16. "Site of engagement" refers to the specific historical moment and material space in which an action unfolds. A site of engagement is "a single token of the type"; when repeated over time, it accrues into a nexus of practice, which refers to "a type of action, not a specific token" (Scollon and Scollon 2004: 12).

four monolingual posters or notices, each in one of the official languages, make up one information unit).

## Single frames

Where single frames are concerned, the texts in each language unit are symmetrically distributed within the space of a sign and evenly weighted in relation to their font, size, color, and other typographical features (Scollon and Scollon 2003: 129). The four languages may be configured along a vertical axis, in which case, as noted previously, a top-placed language is accorded the information value of the Ideal and a bottom-placed one that of the Real. We already see this at work in Figures 2.1 and 2.2. Figure 2.3 shows another example with more complex wording, where the quadrilingual schema is set out vertically following the frequently sighted ECMT order.[17]

The ECMT order effects a code preference (Scollon and Scollon 2003: 116–28) within an otherwise perfectly balanced frame, underscoring the priority position of English. (The CMT arrangement may be influenced by the order in which the three languages appear in CMIO.) Two variant sequences, English–Chinese–Tamil–Malay and English–Malay–Chinese–Tamil, are occasionally encountered. In the latter two sequences, the permutations are notably among the MTLs. Arguably, these shifts do not radically destabilize the normative code preference: English generally comes on top, save in emplacement sites where there is a motivation to foreground the symbolic status of Malay (as in Figure 2.2). Chinese and Tamil never appear as the leading language within the schema.

Where the four languages are configured in a Cartesian grid, as in Figure 2.4, we are faced with a left-right syntagm compounding a top-down paradigm. To understand the left-to-right reading path (Kress and van Leeuwen 2021: 211–15) or vector (Scollon and Scollon 2003: 143), we have recourse again to Kress and van Leeuwen's (2021) visual semiotics, which tells us that left placement implies a piece of information is Given, that is, an "agreed-upon point of departure" (187), while right placement implies it is New, that is, something unknown or "perhaps not yet agreed upon by the viewer" (187).[18]

17. In some cases, public signs may apparently feature three languages: English (Malay), Chinese, and Tamil, as in the name signs of train stations. There is an orthographic explanation for this: spelling a proper name, for instance, "Chinatown", takes exactly the same form in Malay as in English. These signs should therefore not be read as trilingual, as they appear to be, but still quadrilingual, with the "absent" Malay (English) unit being conflated with the English (Malay) unit.

18. This corresponds to the Theme–Rheme relation in Hallidayan linguistics and applies specifically to left-to-right literacy cultures. The converse would apply to

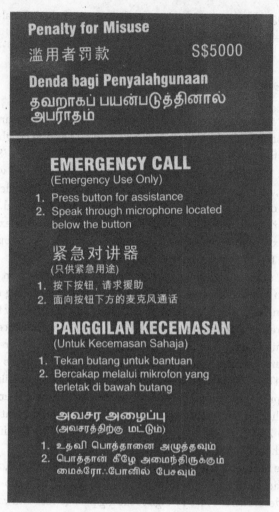

**Figure 2.3.** A sign in a train car about the emergency call facility.

As with a top-to-bottom orientation, the relative position of a piece of information within a left-to-right frame has ideological implications: the Given, we are told, is "commonsensical" and "self-evident," whereas the New is associated with such qualities as "problematic" and "contestable" (Kress and van Leeuwen 2021: 187)—the information at issue, so to speak. This Given–New divide is ideological in that "the information is presented *as though* it had that status or value for the reader and that readers have to read it within that structure, even if that valuation may then be rejected

right-to-left literacy cultures, such as Middle Eastern cultures based on Arabic (Kress and van Leeuwen 2021: 188–89).

**Figure 2.4.** A sign on a train station platform about the emergency communication button.

by particular readers" (Kress and van Leeuwen 2021: 187 [emphasis in the original]).

Thus, in Figure 2.4, the code preference is for English to appear on the top left. What this means in visual semiotic terms is that apart from being the Ideal, English is also the symbolic Given, the taken-for-granted linguistic point of departure. In this particular sign, Chinese is allocated to the top right, Malay to the bottom left, and Tamil to the bottom right, creating multiple tiers resonant with language ideological meaning. Chinese (on the right) is less of a Given compared to English (on the left), but as the most widely spoken MTL, it can be said to be more visible (on the upper tier) than Malay and Tamil (on the lower tier).[19] On the bottom tier, Malay is placed to the left of Tamil, so it is the Given ("commonsensical," "self-evident") between the two, relegating Tamil, demographically weakest among the official languages, to the semiotically most disadvantaged position in the grid.

19. That said, it should be noted that the positions of Malay and Chinese are at times interchangeable (see Hoa 2020: 164).

The same dynamic comes into play in Figures 2.5a–b, which show two signs on the windowpane of a train car in a twin-frame format. Two language units appear on each frame: one with English and Chinese and the other with Malay and Tamil. The two signs mirror each other semantically, duplicating the same communicative message ("Mind the Gap. Do Not Lean Against the Doors"), as well as visually, using the same design template and color scheme.

The spatial affordance of the twin frames prompts us to consider how each sign is laterally emplaced in relation to the other, moving us from "placement within a frame" to "placement in the world" (Scollon and Scollon 2003: 124). In the train car, the two bilingual signs in the figure appear alongside each other on a horizontal axis, with the English/Chinese sign appearing on the left of the Malay/Tamil sign. Within each sign, the same linear pattern is fractally scaled (Irvine and Gal 2000), with English appearing to the left of Chinese, and Malay to the left of Tamil, respectively. Following Kress and van Leeuwen (2021), a visual semiotic interpretation of the twin signs in Figures 2.5a–b,

**Figure 2.5a.** "Mind the Gap" sign in a train car (English/Chinese).

**Figure 2.5b.** "Mind the Gap" sign in a train car (Malay/Tamil).

lined up in an ECMT sequence from left to right, is once again this: English is the Given, with implications for its taken-for-grantedness; whereas the MTLs represent the New: relatively unknown, "not yet agreed upon," with Chinese, Malay, and Tamil ranked in descending order of givenness.

The dual-frame configuration in Figures 2.5a–b is widely used, conceivably preferred when there is too much information for all four language units to be fitted into a single frame. It produces and enhances an overall effect of visual equivalence, within which the quadrilingual schema comes through intact. A further example is shown in Figures 2.6a–b, where English/Chinese and Malay/Tamil couple together on separate frames, with Figures 2.7a–b featuring the alternative pairing English/Malay and Chinese/Tamil. Unlike in Figure 2.4, the syntagm in these cases is not always clear. The twin signs may or may not be juxtaposed in their site of emplacement, although when they are jigsawed together, there is usually a code preference for English, such that viewers would typically encounter the frame carrying the English message first (see Scollon and Scollon 2003: 124).[20] At any rate, the vertical code preference on each bilingual frame indicates a strong consistency, with English appearing above Chinese, and Malay appearing above Tamil (in Figure 2.7: English above Malay, Chinese above Tamil). Generally, the power relation implied by this visual semiotic is most favorable to English and least favorable to Tamil, over which Chinese and Malay gain relative weight in terms of information value.

Notwithstanding the semiotic differential created by left-right and/or top-down placement, what is striking about the dual-frame setup on the whole is the sense of a visual rhetoric. The twin signs are not only exact mutual translations in terms of their referential content; they are also reduplications of each other, with identical design compositions, graphic icons, typographical choices, and color schemes. Within each set of twin posters is a clear design intention to produce structural homogeneity, encouraging viewers to see them, and by extension the languages they embody, as a continuous slate calibrated by mirror images.

20. A reflexive note is in order. In Figures 2.6 and 2.7, I have arranged the a and b subfigures in a manner suggesting a linearity that favors English. In fact, how these twin signs relate to each other syntagmatically varies with the spatial contingencies of the emplacement site in question. Some twin signs, for example, appear at a certain distance from each other on a horizontal plane (i.e., they are not juxtaposed), such that one cannot determine the linear order of the four languages as they are perceived by empirical viewers. With these things, a degree of idiosyncrasy should be expected, such that it is not impossible for a Malay/Tamil frame to appear on the left of an English/Chinese frame, though my observation tells me that in cases of juxtaposition, the frame with English usually prevails. So, in arranging my figures in line with the conventional code preference system, am I not complicit in reproducing the symbolic power relation among the four languages, as predicted by an interpretation along the lines of Kress and van Leeuwen? The same point applies to my subsequent examples featuring four monolingual frames.

**Figure 2.6a.** A notice in a train station on changes in operating hours (English/Chinese).

**Figure 2.6b.** A notice in a train station on changes in operating hours (Malay/Tamil).

**Figure 2.7a.** An LED sign outside a public elevator on using personal mobility devices in the neighborhood (English/Malay).

**Figure 2.7b.** An LED sign outside a public elevator on using personal mobility devices in the neighborhood (Chinese/Tamil).

## Quadruple frames

What comes to the fore in the dual-frame design is the overt use of parallelism and repetition to bind multiple physical signs into one cohesive entity, thus tracing a neat linearity across the quadrilingual schema. This visual structure is most exuberantly performed in cases where, instead of two bilingual frames, we have four monolingual frames for every unit of information. Figures 2.8a–d show an example of this setup.

## ASYMMETRICAL FORMATIONS

Asymmetrical nuances can subsist in apparently symmetrical frames, invariably in favor of English. Within a quadrilingual layout that is prima facie well balanced, minute details may reveal unequal power relations. My earlier examples have already demonstrated the existence of a code preference, as indicated by the relative placement of the languages on top-down and left-right axes; this section turns to other types of evidence suggestive of asymmetries within the quadrilingual schema.

Typographical asymmetries can be detected in otherwise well-balanced frames, invariably leaning toward English as a salient code and implicitly construing the MTLs as translations. In Figure 2.9, the headnote "Notice," appearing in English only, has more salience through a combination of center justification, capitalization, increased font size, and background contrast. In Figure 2.10, the English "Caution!" is much more pronounced than the corresponding words in Chinese, Malay, and Tamil, with its larger font size, bold font weight, and top-center placement (compare the MTL segments aligned on the middle right).

Such asymmetrical treatment can inflect the design of dual-frame signage as well. Thus, on the bilingual screens in Figures 2.11a–b, the English and Chinese headings are respectively larger than their Malay and Tamil counterparts. This reproduces the fractal power relations (mentioned earlier in relation to Figure 2.5), between English and the MTLs on the one hand and between the MTLs on the other. The "fare review exercise" poster in Figure 2.12 is a more complex example. It features a large, capitalized, and color-coded English title with the three MTL titles running below it in lower case (for the Malay segment) and in a smaller font. The content on the poster is divided into several blocks of information, each conforming to the ECMT order, with English achieving visual coherence and salience with a larger font size, color coding (blue, against the black-coded MTLs), and upper-case capitalization (specifically, for "what are the changes to our fares" and "public transport vouchers").

Some cases of asymmetry are less subtle and result in substantial imbalances in content distribution within the quadrilingual schema. Figure 2.13

**Figure 2.8a.** A sign in a train station on safe boarding practices (English).

**Figure 2.8b.** A sign in a train station on safe boarding practices (Chinese).

Figure 2.8c. A sign in a train station on safe boarding practices (Malay).

Figure 2.8d. A sign in a train station on safe boarding practices (Tamil).

**NOTICE**

Please pay the correct fares.
Tap out your fare card only
when you exit the bus.
(This also applies to <u>feeder services</u> & <u>all concession cards</u>.)

通告
请付正确的车资
在下车时才触卡
(包括<u>支线</u>及<u>所有优惠卡</u>)

**NOTIS**

Sila bayar tambang yang betul. Sentuh keluar
kad anda hanya bila anda turun dari bas.
(Ini juga dikenakan kepada <u>perkhidmatan feeder</u> dan
<u>semua kad konsesi</u>.)

பயணிகள் கவனிக்க
அன்புகூர்ந்து எப்போதும் சரியான கட்டணம் செலுத்துங்கள்
பேருந்திலிருந்து இறங்கும்போதுதான்,
பயண அட்டையை 'வாசிப்பான்'-இல் தட்டவேண்டும்.
(இந்நடைமுறை இணைப்புப் பேருந்துகளுக்கும்
சலுகைப் பயணஅட்டைகளுக்கும் பொருந்தும்.)

*SBS Transit*

Figure 2.9. A sign inside a public bus on paying fares.

shows a multilingual banner emplaced in a local neighborhood to warn residents about an outbreak of dengue fever. Overall, English is more heavily weighted in terms of position (it appears on top of the MTLs), space (two lines for the English and one line for each MTL), and size/typography (the English letters are in a bigger font size with full upper-case capitalization, and the word "dengue" is color coded with enlarged and bold letters). The three MTLs combined take up an approximately equal amount of space on the sign as the English tagline. This asymmetrical language-spatial relationship (Sebba 2012: 106) is complemented by a fragmentary language-content relationship, where more information is provided in English than in the MTLs, thus giving the impression that the overlapping bits of information

**Figure 2.10.** A "caution" sign in a park.

are translations from English into the MTLs (see Reh 2004: 10). Appearing in English only are the words "Yellow Dengue Alert" (cast in a large font on the righthand side of the banner), the instructions to obtain further information on social media below the main taglines ("Get updates on dengue clusters" and "Download my ENVapp"), and the slogan "Our Lives. Our Fight. Do the 5-Step Mozzie Wipeout Today" in the yellow bar at the bottom, alongside the English-only name of the sign producer (National Environment Agency).

### English as scaffolding

Asymmetry finds expression in a unique semiotic configuration in which English functions as a scaffold for the MTLs. My example comes from a 2019 exhibition organized by the National Heritage Board, a statutory board of the Singapore government. The exhibition revolves around the design of the Founders' Memorial, a large-scale public facility "commemorating Singapore's

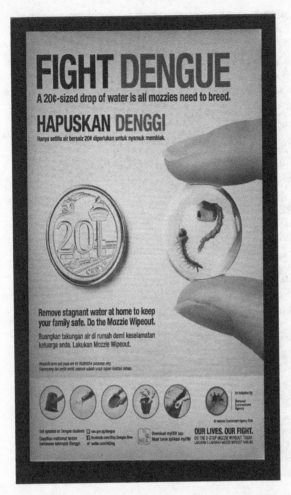

**Figure 2.11a.** An LED sign outside a public elevator on preventing dengue fever (English/ Malay).

founding values and ideals."[21] The event showcases submissions from an international architectural design competition held in connection with the memorial's construction.[22] Figures 2.14–2.15 show two types of multilingual panels providing viewers with information relating to the concept, design, and construction of the Memorial.

21. https://www.foundersmemorial.sg.

22. In the spirit of public engagement, viewers are invited to choose their preferred design and log their preference into a digital system for the judging panel's reference, "to be part of the making of the Memorial": https://www.nhb.gov.sg/nationalmus eum/our-exhibitions/exhibition-list/founders-memorial?sc_lang=en.

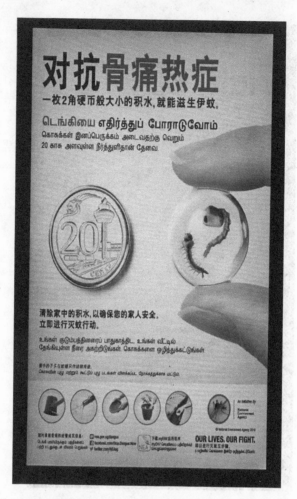

**Figure 2.11b.** An LED sign outside a public elevator on preventing dengue fever (Chinese/Tamil).

Figure 2.14 exemplifies a neat quadrilingual setup in line with the symmetrical frames we have already examined. The text here is a quote from the prime minister on the significance of the prospective memorial, available in four language versions in mutual translation. The spatial configuration is, on the whole, balanced. That said, the English panel is afforded more visual salience compared to the MTL panels: its color is of a brighter (red) tone; its encompassing box is slightly larger, with the English text printed in a larger font (compare the Malay panel at the top right) and in white (hence marked as compared to the MTL texts, all printed in black); and it is placed in the center left of the display board.

Contrast this with the panels in Figures 2.15a–c, which adopt a different format I call triple bilingualism (see also Chapter 3). This is a variant of the

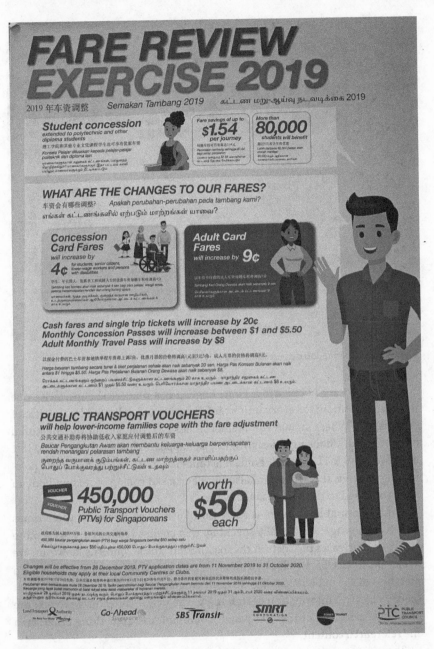

**Figure 2.12.** "Fare review exercise" poster.

quadrilingual schema where English is paired up with each of the three MTLs, giving rise to three consecutive sets of parallel texts (English/Chinese, English/Malay, and English/Tamil). The texts are equivalent in content across the four languages, inviting us to see them as being in a relationship of translation.

**Figure 2.13.** A banner on dengue fever in a neighborhood.

Two points are noteworthy. First, English has numerical superiority due to sheer repetition; for every unit of information (as indicated by the title of each panel: "Where should the Memorial be?"; "What should the Memorial be like?"; and "Choosing a design"), English appears thrice as opposed to just once for every MTL. Second, English is rendered more salient by its left positioning vis-à-vis the MTLs, and also by the marked coding of its text body in red as opposed to the MTL texts in black.

On a technical level, there is no reason for English to appear three times for every message. Logistically speaking, this creates redundancy, uses more space, and increases the costs of the installation. These concerns, however, are irrelevant in face of the ideological import of the triple-bilingual formula. To members of the public speaking different languages, what is showcased is not merely objective information pertaining to the new architectural project; the discursive structure of the text panels communicates something other than the referential content.

These signs perform a visuality consonant with Singapore's bilingual education policy (see Chapter 1): in pairing English with each MTL across three panels, the triple-bilingual setup becomes a homologue of the English-plus-MTL schema underlying the language education policy, while still sustaining the general visibility of all four official languages. To the extent that its symbolic value exists alongside, and even supersedes, its instrumental–semantic

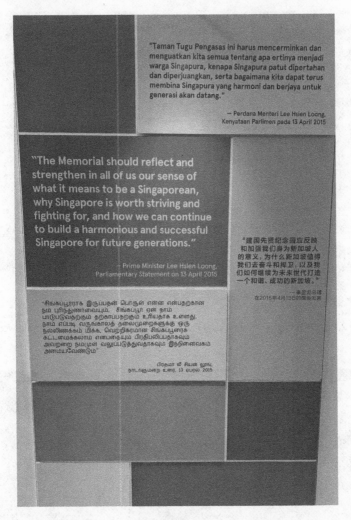

"Taman Tugu Pengasas ini harus mencerminkan dan menguatkan kita semua tentang apa ertinya menjadi warga Singapura, kenapa Singapura patut dipertahan dan diperjuangkan, serta bagaimana kita dapat terus membina Singapura yang harmoni dan berjaya untuk generasi akan datang."

– Perdana Menteri Lee Hsien Loong,
Kenyataan Parlimen pada 13 April 2015

"The Memorial should reflect and strengthen in all of us our sense of what it means to be a Singaporean, why Singapore is worth striving and fighting for, and how we can continue to build a harmonious and successful Singapore for future generations."

– Prime Minister Lee Hsien Loong,
Parliamentary Statement on 13 April 2015

"建国先贤纪念园应反映
和加强我们身为新加坡人
的意义，为什么新加坡值得
我们去奋斗和捍卫，以及我
们如何继续为未来世代打造
一个和谐、成功的新加坡。"

— 李显龙总理
在2015年4月13日的国会发言

"சிங்கப்பூராக இருப்பதன் பொருள் என்ன என்பதற்கான
நம் புரிந்துணர்வையும், சிங்கப்பூர் ஏன் நாம்
பாடுபடுவதற்கும் தற்காப்பதற்கும் உரியதாக உள்ளது,
நாம் எப்படி வருங்காலத் தலைமுறைகளுக்கு ஒரு
நல்லிணக்கம் மிக்க, வெற்றிகரமான சிங்கப்பூரைக்
கட்டமைக்கலாம் என்பதையும் பிரதிபலிப்பதாகவும்
அவற்றை நம்முள் வலுப்படுத்துவதாகவும் இந்நினைவகம்
அமைய வேண்டும்"

பிரதமர் லீ சியன் லூங்,
நாடாளுமன்ற உரை, 13 ஏப்ரல் 2015

**Figure 2.14.** A quadrilingual panel at the Founders' Memorial design showcase.

value, the configuration embodies a linguistic fetish (Kelly-Holmes 2014) pivoting on the nexus of English.

As an offshoot of the quadrilingual schema, the triple-bilingual matrix underscores the importance of English by iterating it across multiple panels. The bilingual panels therefore have the effect of sharpening the English-MTL divide. This has the meaning effect of raising the status of English to that of an encompassing language, the primary point of reference, or the Original; it simultaneously scaffolds and circumscribes the MTLs, relegating them to the implied role of nonautonomous languages (see Coupland 2012: 7–9), translational derivatives, or the Other within the constellation.

**Figure 2.15a.** Two English/Chinese panels at the Founders' Memorial design showcase.

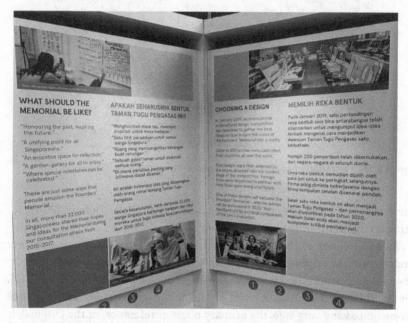

**Figure 2.15b.** Two English/Malay panels at the Founders' Memorial design showcase.

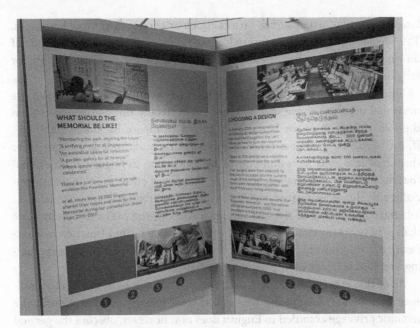

**Figure 2.15c.** Two English/Tamil panels at the Founders' Memorial design showcase.

## Asymmetries within symmetries

The asymmetrical configurations above confirm Backhaus's (2006) observation that language power relations are perpetuated within the visual hierarchy of languages as represented on multilingual signs. In Tokyo, for instance, official signs tend to feature Japanese more prominently than minority languages, such as Korean and Chinese. Heinrich (2021) observes the same power structures in relation to multilingual signage for the Tokyo Olympics: what language administrators call *tagengo taiō* (multilingual support), aimed at *kotoba no baria furī* (removal of linguistic barriers), is premised on a simplistic Japanese/English binary. Under this binary, all non-Japanese languages are swept under an anglophone rubric and marginalized out of the semiotic landscape. This is hardly a surprising practice, aligning as it does with Japan's monolingual regime, where non-Japanese languages tend to appear subservient to Japanese "as supplementary translations, and care is taken that this relationship is unmistakably expressed" (Backhaus 2006: 63).

To a certain extent, the visual–spatial advantage English possesses over the MTLs in quadrilingual signage can be explained in terms of Backhaus's power hypothesis: English, as the hegemonic language of administration, serves as an umbrella language encompassing the MTLs, accounting for their differential values based on placement and inscription. As in society, so in semiotics. Yet the Tokyo situation is not entirely applicable to Singapore, whose language regime sustains itself on a cautious balance of the official languages. This ideology of balance is captured in the national pledge, where citizens of Singapore are said to be "one united people/regardless of race, *language*, or religion."[23]

Thus, unlike official multilingual signs in Tokyo, where Japanese enjoys unrivaled primacy, those in Singapore are generally not as unequivocal on the role of English as the language of power (compare Backhaus 2006: 64). If, in Tokyo, "the mere existence of official signs containing languages other than Japanese constitutes a noteworthy concession to linguistic minorities" (Backhaus 2006: 64), then in Singapore, languages other than English—crucially, only those designated as official—have more than a "mere existence." As integral components of the quadrilingual schema, the MTLs represent more than a "noteworthy concession" on the part of English. They function as a necessary counterpoint to English, and are substantively important in perpetuating a replicable image of linguistic egalitarianism.

All of this is notwithstanding that English may still be afforded more salience than the MTLs in specific frames, as I have demonstrated previously. The semiotic privilege accorded to English does not, however, obscure the general stability and visibility of the quadrilingual schema. The sheer presence of the four official languages (and not others) in tandem strongly shapes the visuality of public communications toward a visual–spatial equilibrium, and any perceived asymmetries should be seen as playing out subtle power dynamics within this overall structure of balance—or what I describe in this chapter as an affect of balance.

## EMBLEMATICS AND EXCLUSIONS

The preceding examples demonstrate that the quadrilingual schema has a powerful emblematic quality that exceeds its linguistic quality (Blommaert 2010: 29–32). Let us briefly return to the "danger" sign (Figure 2.1). The meaning of the text on this sign may appear substantively important for its perlocutionary force. But, in fact, it is not primarily the language per se (the locution) that signifies; it is the material sign perceived as a gestalt. The "danger" sign is part of an instantly recognizable genre thanks to its ubiquity. One does not actually have to read the word string "Danger–Keep Out" from left to right in full, and certainly not in all four languages, to get the warning message. Seeing alone suffices: the sign communicates by way of a replicative visual–spatial pattern configured around a recurring language pattern. Also part of the signification are a familiar materiality (red scripts against a

23. https://www.nhb.gov.sg/what-we-do/our-work/community-engagement/educat ion/resources/national-symbols/national-pledge (emphasis added).

white background on a rectangular frame) and a situated semiotic (Scollon and Scollon 2003: 146) deriving from the sign's emplacement in the "right" place.[24]

The same can be said of the sign in Figure 2.2, which exists not merely as a locational threshold but also, even principally, as an institutional identity marker. It is all very well that the name of the building has a signposting function, but the multilingual image of the entrance sign has a second, and quite different, layer of meaning, namely, an emblematic meaning based on the entrenched visuality of a stable constellation of official languages. As is so often the case, the whole is greater than—or at least different from—the sum of its parts. Each language tier on the sign communicates its semantics in a different form, but together they operate as a holistic formula to recall a sense of structure and construct an affective regime of balance.[25]

This point comes into sharper focus when we consider signage featuring nonlocal languages. Like the "danger" sign in Figure 2.1, the sign in Figure 2.16 is placed outside a construction site, except that it is directed to foreign workers (mainly South Asian and Southeast Asian) rather than the Singaporean public. In terms of composition, there are six rather than four languages: English, Chinese, Malay, Tamil, Thai, and Bengali. Here we see both the instrumental and performative dimensions of multilingualism at play within one frame.

The English-only headnote makes it clear that the message is addressed to foreign workers, requiring them "to produce their original work permits without demand." Presumably, the message targets specific communities of laborers speaking Thai and Bengali, which explains the appearance of these two languages. There is thus a substantivity to the use of foreign languages here. But the question then arises as to why Thai and Bengali, the languages of the intended audience, should appear at the bottom of the sign, indicating their status as the Real. To put it conversely, given that local residents are evidently not the target audience, it is ideologically significant that the message should even be made available in the four official languages, and furthermore that this ECMT sequence should precede Thai and Bengali on the vertical reading axis as the Ideal.

To appreciate the semiotics of this sign, we must consider the functional division of labor among the languages involved. On the one hand, Thai and

24. The "right" place here would be construction sites or other locations with potential danger. By the same token, placing the same sign in the middle of a museum gallery would create "transgressive semiotics" (Scollon and Scollon 2003: 146), turning the sign into something entirely different, namely, an aesthetic artifact.

25. The linguistic and the emblematic are not zero-sum concepts as far as multilingual representation is concerned. To say that a multilingual sign is emblematic does not cancel out its semantics; the two can ride on each other's backs. Thus the text may carry linguistic value, though its multilingual constellation may be wholly emblematic.

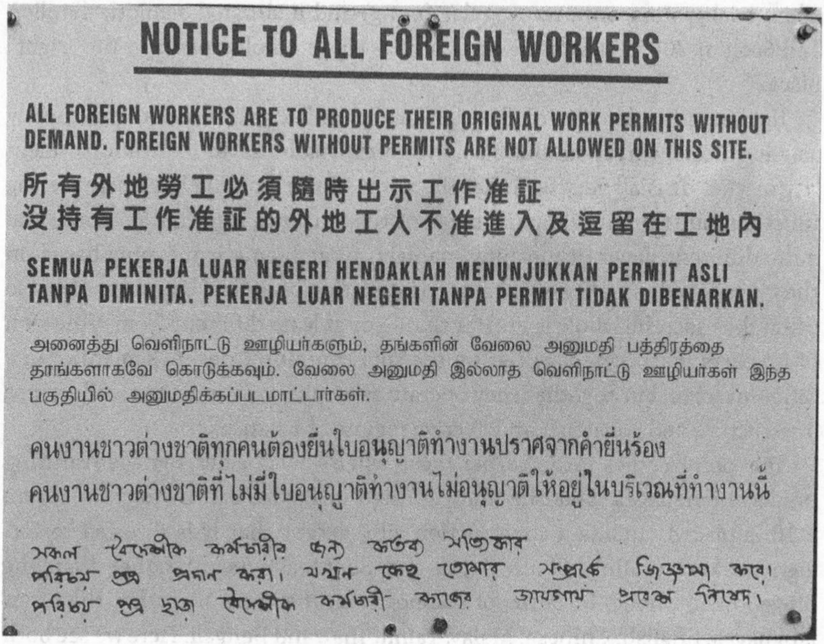

**NOTICE TO ALL FOREIGN WORKERS**

ALL FOREIGN WORKERS ARE TO PRODUCE THEIR ORIGINAL WORK PERMITS WITHOUT DEMAND. FOREIGN WORKERS WITHOUT PERMITS ARE NOT ALLOWED ON THIS SITE.

所有外地勞工必須隨時出示工作准証
沒持有工作准証的外地工人不准進入及逗留在工地內

SEMUA PEKERJA LUAR NEGERI HENDAKLAH MENUNJUKKAN PERMIT ASLI TANPA DIMINITA. PEKERJA LUAR NEGERI TANPA PERMIT TIDAK DIBENARKAN.

அனைத்து வெளிநாட்டு ஊழியர்களும், தங்களின் வேலை அனுமதி பத்திரத்தை தாங்களாகவே கொடுக்கவும். வேலை அனுமதி இல்லாத வெளிநாட்டு ஊழியர்கள் இந்த பகுதியில் அனுமதிக்கப்படமாட்டார்கள்.

คนงานชาวต่างชาติทุกคนต้องยื่นใบอนุญาติทำงานปราศจากคำยื่นร้อง
คนงานชาวต่างชาติที่ไม่มีใบอนุญาติทำงานไม่อนุญาติให้อยู่ในบริเวณที่ทำงานนี้

**Figure 2.16.** A multilingual sign with six languages at a construction site.

Bengali are fully instrumental, conveying a substantive message to their respective language communities; they are meant to be read—what Cook (2013: 68–69) would call "community multilingualism." The ECMT, on the other hand, is fully emblematic here; regardless of the sequence, it is a fetishized entity, meant to be seen more than (if at all) to be read. Functioning as an emblematic, quadrilingual unit, the four languages do not so much communicate information (the message on the sign is relevant only to foreign workers) as replay a recognizable template that calls up the sensibility of official multilingualism.

Equally important is what is *not* seen. Our emphasis thus far has been on what the quadrilingual schema includes, but what it excludes is just as critical. These are the languages or language varieties that fall outside the official matrix: Chinese dialects, Austronesian languages other than Malay (e.g., Javanese, Buginese, and Sundanese), and nonofficial Indian languages (e.g., Bengali, Gujarati, Hindi, Punjabi, and Urdu). The efficacy of the quadrilingual schema is therefore premised as much on the absence of nonofficial/nonstandard languages as on the presence of official ones, the former audible on the streets but systematically silenced on official canvases of multilingualism like public signage.[26]

26. This connects with recent trends in linguistic landscape studies on recuperating that which is suppressed (i.e., on the processes of silencing and erasure) (see Malinowski 2018 and Karlander 2019).

This schema has become such an enduring visual formula in public discourse in Singapore that its very invocation obviates or "rules out" all other competing tongues, eradicating them from official representation. What viewers encounter on a daily basis, then, is a sanitized multilingualism; when repeated over time, the schema sinks in to become a sedimented sociocognitive pattern in local consciousness with a normativizing effect on linguistic behavior. For this reason, the quadrilingual schema as a prescriptive template participates in a systematic practice of verbal hygiene (Cameron 2012),[27] one that streamlines public discourses into cleanly delineated linguistic packages for consumption in conformity with top-down ideals of multilingualism.

## THE AFFECTIVE REGIME OF BALANCE

The institutional dimension of Singapore's semiotic landscape exemplifies a visual choreography that exudes an affect of balance: an emotive value or sensibility embodied in the cognitive–perceptual qualities of equivalence and symmetry and associated with stability and harmony. Wee and Goh (2020) maintain that the concept of affect can be used to appreciate "the activities and goals of urban spaces as these [spaces] try to accumulate various kinds of symbolic capital":

> For example, cities may want to be seen as *convivial* or *business-friendly*, and specific environments or neighborhoods may want to present themselves as *pedestrian-friendly* or *dementia-friendly*. These are less about specific emotions than about encouraging a positive or supportive orientation toward corporate interests or dementia sufferers and their families. They clearly involve attempts at *structuring the semiotic landscape* in ways that, hopefully, come to be construed as possessing *the relevant symbolic capital*. (Wee and Goh 2020: 10 [emphasis added])

According to this view, semiotic landscapes can be considered affective (Jaworski and Thurlow 2010: 4) in that they are structured toward certain states, capacities, orientations, dispositions, resonances, or stances, with a view to gaining the "relevant symbolic capital" for specific interests. In this affective production, language plays an emblematic role in creating an ambience or atmosphere (Wee 2016a: 109; Wee and Goh 2020: 10, *ad passim*).

27. Verbal hygiene is the "motley collection of discourses and practices through which people attempt to 'clean up' language and make its structure or its use conform more closely to their ideals of beauty, truth, efficiency, logic, correctness and civility" (Cameron 2012: vii).

Given its ubiquity, the quadrilingual schema represents a technology of choreography emanating the structured neatness of a politicosemiotic rationality (Inoue 2016). It drives the systematic cultivation of an affective regime, defined as "the set of conditions that govern with varying degrees of hegemonic status the ways in which particular kinds of affect can be appropriately materialized in the context of a given site" (Wee and Goh 2020: 19, based on Wee 2016a: 109). Hence, the quadrilingual signage we have seen so far constitutes a distributed site "structured in ways that are intended to evoke particular dispositions" (Wee and Goh 2020: 19, based on Wee 2016a: 109), where the disposition in question is one that orients the viewer toward a sense of neatness, an affect of balance.[28]

The notions of affect and disposition in respect to semiotic landscapes relate to what Cook (2013: 68–69) calls "atmospheric multilingualism" (as opposed to "community multilingualism"), where the presence of a language serves not primarily to denote meaning but to evoke a feeling or resonance.[29] For example, English words or phrases are often appropriated as fetishized signifiers of chicness on T-shirts and advertisements in Japan, where the comprehensibility of the English texts to target consumers is beside the point (Kelly-Holmes 2014). By the same token, the affective regime surrounding the quadrilingual schema creates an ambience (not substance) of linguistic conviviality, encapsulating the symbolic capital of the institutional dimension of Singapore's semiotic landscape. In this affective regime, the official language constellation functions as a visual–spatial template, abstracting the state's language policy into an instantly recallable trope.

The upshot of this is a translational pattern that activates the specter of neat multilingualism, where the four languages are set in a relation of complementary distribution, placed within a visual–spatial equivalence that

28. Note, however, that the empirical presence of the viewer is not a prerequisite for establishing affect; it is the intention of the sign maker that is paramount. As Wee and Goh (2020: 19, based on Wee 2016a: 109) argue, "[b]ecause an affective regime operates at the level of the site, even in the absence of any particular individual, that is, even when a given site happens to be uninhabited or unoccupied, it is still meaningful to speak of an affective regime associated with that environment. This is because the site itself can be structured in ways that are intended to evoke particular dispositions regardless of whether anyone happens to be present."

29. For example, Chinese is used on bilingual signs in the Chinatowns of some UK cities, serving more to create an aura of "Chineseness" than any informative purposes (see Lou 2016). Blommaert (2010: 29–30) instances the noun *derrière* in the name sign of a chocolate boutique in Tokyo and the preposition "with" conjoining two *kanji* characters on a Japanese phone card. These segments are, respectively, French and English only emblematically, not linguistically. They do not denote meaning so much as index "a complex of associated meanings" (29), in this case an aspiration to chic and globality indexically associated with French and English (see also Järlehed et al. 2018; Vandenbrouke 2016). In the terms used here, these associated meanings are affective values insofar as they are intended to evoke subtle resonances in the target consumer.

threads across a cohesive set of linguistic frames. From this perspective, the quadrilingual schema figures as an ambient "floating signifier," invoking the contours of official multilingualism as part of a "spatial branding" by the authorities (Leeman and Modan 2009: 353). To encounter quadrilingual signs or notices in Singapore on a daily basis, then, is to repeatedly rehearse in one's subconscious the official language policy as a figure of translation.

The quadrilingual schema espouses a categorical neatness to multilingualism, compartmentalizing the four official languages, constructing each of them as monovarietal—hence *prescribing* multilingualism while *proscribing* heteroglossia—and rendering invisible other languages outside that grid. In so doing, it maps the state's language policy schematically onto semiotic spaces, triggering the trope of linguistic conviviality (see Blommaert 2015: 107 on a sociolinguistic understanding of tropes). It outlines a visual rhetoric that structures the semiotic landscape and dovetails public signage centripetally toward an indexical nexus (Blommaert 2015: 109). In this sense, the schema is very much a genre feature (Bakhtin 1981) that manifests in institutional texts, whose panoramic spatial distribution in public spaces confers an iconic façade of legitimacy and authority.

The schema also fossilizes a certain history—that of linguistic legislation and related policymaking in Singapore. That history makes for a meaning potential, a latent ideological substratum undergirding the visual–spatial structure of public texts. To that extent, the quadrilingual schema is a spatial formula pregnant with "invokable histories," one "in which time, space, and patterns of agency coincide, create meaning and value" (Blommaert 2015: 110). Its regularized enactment tells a story: a public narrative on multilingualism in which English, Chinese, Malay, and Tamil coexist as spatially parallel, temporally static identity capsules separated by reified boundaries.

The public dimension of the semiotic landscape, then, is a choreographic site, based as it is on a strategic model aimed at multilingual governance. Under this model, the visual–spatial configuration of languages represents "the calculus of force relationships"—the management of power relations among the four languages—implemented by "a subject of will and power" (de Certeau 1984: xix), in this case the state and its affiliated agencies. This constellation, as already noted, excludes the vernaculars, dialects, and other recognized but nonofficial languages. In so doing, it circumscribes the semiotic landscape into a "proper" (*propre*) based on "standard" languages as defined by a rationalist, purist vision.

By spectacularizing the four official languages with a recurring quadrilingual schema, and in the process marginalizing languages outside that matrix, the choreographed discourse in question projects a totalizing and "geographical" structure of multilingualism. It is visual (taking the form of language displays oriented to the public), panoptic (because iterative and ubiquitous), theoretical (through its exclusion of speech varieties actually spoken on the ground), and geometrical (via a recognizable grid of languages) (de Certeau 1984: 93).

The semiotic landscape thus produced is one in which languages are classified and categorized, stratified, and sanitized. In de Certeau's (1984: xviii) terms, it is a "technocratically constructed, written, and functionalized" site with "prescribed syntactical forms." More precisely, it is governed by "temporal modes of schedules" (e.g., multilingual posters on COVID-19 are put up or taken down in response to exigencies of the health situation and multilingual exhibitions come and go according to schedules prefixed by relevant agencies) as well as "paradigmatic orders of spaces" (e.g., the emplacement of official signage in highly visible public spaces in the city and the segregation of the space on signage into four equal portions, or, as the case may be, with asymmetrical arrangements in favor of English). What ensues is, as de Certeau might have it, a multilingual *place*, an affective regime of balance produced by technologies of choreography from above rather than a multilingual *space* created by spontaneous energies from below.

# CHAPTER 3
# Quadrilingualism as method

*Literary anthologies and other cultural literacy events*

The previous chapter demonstrated how the institutional dimension of Singapore's public landscape is shaped by neat multilingualism, reproduced and sustained by the quadrilingual schema. The quadrilingual schema is an iterative visual–spatial template that serves as a methodology. It streamlines writing in the public sphere by entrenching the visibility of the four official languages as a powerful constellation of watertight categories, existing in parallel with one another and excluding all languages beyond this matrix. It is enregistered as a master signifier that shapes institutional discourses to the official narrative on multilingualism, based on the notion of complementary distribution.

Beyond the semiotic landscape, the quadrilingual schema also structures writing, or rather the representation of writing, in literary and literacy realms. It informs the composition and design of publications and programs with institutional patronage. These publications and programs are often shaped by visual–spatial patterns homologous to those observed on institutional signage, indicating the systematic and pervasive application of neat multilingualism across different genres, modes, and media of writing.

This chapter explores these visual–spatial patterns as technologies of choreography in the context of multilingual literary anthologies that feature creative writing in English, Chinese, Malay, and Tamil, incorporating translation to facilitate cross-language readability. Often supported by state-affiliated bodies and galvanized around the theme of the "nation," multilingual anthologies in Singapore are an "institutional genre of communication" (Agha 2011: 164) whose production unites translation and anthologization in a

*Choreographies of Multilingualism.* Tong King Lee, Oxford University Press. © Oxford University Press 2022.
DOI: 10.1093/oso/9780197644645.003.0003

single artifact.[1] For our purposes, a multilingual anthology is by its nature a translation anthology, even—or especially—if translation appears to be absent. We will also look at extensions of anthologization beyond the book medium, where literary works are experienced in space or rendered interactive via mobile applications, and also at cultural literacy programs structured around the same logic of quadrilingual juxtaposition.

The questions that guide this chapter are: How do multilingual anthologies position different languages in relation to one another by means of translation? What does this tell us about their various formations of multilingualism? How do these formations dovetail with broader ideologies governing the representation of a national literature in Singapore? In attempting to answer these questions, this chapter not only extends the quadrilingual schema's scope to the domain of literature and literacy; it also looks at how the schema participates in broader discursive imaginings of the nation through the structured representation of canonical writing.

## ANTHOLOGIES AS A SOCIAL SEMIOTIC INSTITUTION: TRANSLATION PERSPECTIVES

The anthology is the quintessential form of discursive choreography. It is a genre that entails the selection of texts around designated themes; the arrangement of those texts into a configuration; and their paratextual contextualization by means of titles, cover images, tables of contents, and prefatorial material. Anthologization is often undertaken under individual or institutional patronage and in conformity with prevailing poetics and ideology (Lefevere 1992).[2] In this regard, anthologies "can do for texts what museums do for artefacts and other objects considered of cultural importance: preserve and exhibit them, by selecting and arranging the exhibits, project an interpretation of a given field, make relations and values visible, maybe educate taste" (Essmann and Frank 1991: 66).

It is then possible to say that anthologies, like museums, are curated to project a certain narrative, a poised angle from which a subject matter is represented for readers' consumption. As "configurated corpora," they transmit a literature or culture nationally or globally (Frank 1998: 13) in a semiotic

1. Although translation and anthologization are very different enterprises in terms of their modus operandi, they are both considered modes of rewriting insofar as they involve the partial selection and reframing of preexisting texts (Lefevere 1992: 9).
2. As Lefevere (1992: 8) notes: "Whether they produce translations, literary histories or their more compact spinoffs, reference works, anthologies, criticism, or editions, rewriters adapt, manipulate the originals they work with to some extent, usually to make them fit in with the dominant, or one of the dominant ideological and poetological currents of their time."

package, offering—or imposing—a structure for understanding that literary culture (Essmann and Frank 1991: 67). Depending on the circumstances motivating their production, anthologies can acquire one or more specific functions, as set out in Seruya et al. (2013: 5). Two of these will prove pertinent to the data presented below. The first is preservation, whereby anthologies are "a repository or means of creating a national cultural memory and canon as well as a universal canon"; the second is educational, whereby anthologies have "the explicit purpose of educating taste or [are] associated with the dissemination of mainstream ideological, political, social, ethical, aesthetical, and moral values."[3]

Translation anthologies operate on the same logic, with the additional complication of how original texts and their translations are represented. Just as museums engender particular stories about the subjects they represent by the strategic selection, recontextualization, and spatial arrangement of cultural artifacts (Sturge 2007), so translation anthologies "reflect selection and structuring processes" (Seruya et al. 2013: 1) that produce particular images of a writer, field, literature, or culture (Lefevere 1992: 5). Accordingly, a translation anthology projects an interpretation of a literature and its society through the way it strategically selects, recontextualizes, and spatially configures writing in different languages; in so doing, it perpetuates an image of multiculturalism that embodies particular values.

My approach to translation anthologies is social semiotic. From this perspective, anthologies, as well as cultural literacy events operating within the same semiotic economy, are complex signs. As material artifacts, they are sites of display, or spaces that become "available as medium for the display of text as complex sign" (Bezemer and Kress 2008: 173). Any such display of text or representation of writing is undertaken with reference to social factors by means of semiotic resources (Bezemer and Kress 2008: 174). To read an anthology social-semiotically means to understand how its form and meaning come together in a relation "motivated by the interest of the sign maker" (Bezemer and Kress 2008: 170). The sign maker, in this case the editor(s) of the anthology, is one who uses "available *material-semiotic* resources, *signifiers*, from within specific modes, chosen as *apt* in relation to the *signifieds* of the social group in which the signs are to be made" (Kress 2020: 34 [emphasis in the original]).

3. Other functions proposed by Seruya et al. (2013: 5) include pleasure (to derive aesthetic utility), innovation (to reassess the preexisting canon and introduce new genres), protection (to exhibit literary works written in minority languages), structuring (to afford structure to a branch of culture), accessibility (to offer a selection of literary works to the public), dissemination (to generate literary models for further production), subjectivity (to express the personal orientation of an individual or group), and profit (to derive economic benefits).

Stated conversely, a signifier, "taken together with the history of its prior uses . . . satisfies the *interest* of the sign-maker in finding an *apt* material means of expressing the *signified*" (Kress 2020: 35 [emphasis in the original]). "Interest" relates to the epistemological commitment underlying the anthology, specifically how the social relationship among the four official languages can be realized (see Bezemer and Kress 2008: 170). It is shaped by the social, cultural, economic, and technological milieu within which an anthology is produced and, in turn, "shapes *attention* to a part of the world which is in focus and acts as the *motivation* for (*principles of*) *selection* of that which is to be represented" (Kress 2020: 35 [emphasis in the original]). It is through interest that power enters into semiosis (Kress 2020: 35).

The signifier that concerns us within the material context of multilingual anthologies relates to the visual–spatial form in which languages are configured, and the signified is the concept of multilingualism evinced by such form. This brings us to composition and design. Composition, as we have seen in Chapter 2, refers to how languages are arranged, visualized, and framed in relation to each other. It is the result of a selection motivated by the sign maker's attention to one way of representing multilingualism in Singapore (see Kress 2020). Applying the three principles of composition (Kress and van Leeuwen 2021: 181–82) to the medium of multilingual anthologies, the following questions can be asked:

a. *On information value*: What is the linear sequence of appearance of the four official languages in an anthology, and what is the implication on their relative value in terms of the Given versus the New?
b. *On salience*: Which of English, Chinese, Malay, and Tamil is most salient in an anthology, and how is such salience achieved?
c. *On framing*: Are the literary works in an anthology separated into clearly delineated sections based on their language (strong framing), or do they appear in random linguistic order (weak framing)? What is the implication for the relative values of the four official languages?

These considerations about textual composition and linguistic configuration interact with the overall design concept of an anthology, where design refers to "the practice where modes, media, frames, and sites of display on the one hand, and rhetorical purposes, the designer's interests, and the characteristics of the audience on the other are brought into coherence with each other" (Bezemer and Kress 2008: 174). Design in anthologies includes, for instance, the use of book covers with similar motifs and color schemes across different language-based volumes of an anthology title, which serves the rhetorical purpose of creating visual coherence. It also governs editorial decisions such as whether to include the original text of works subjected to translation, whether to romanize titles and author names in other scripts or orthographies, or whether to acknowledge translators on the book cover.

But the single most important design feature for our purpose is the model of translation. Translation models determine which languages are translated and in what direction(s). Assuming language relations in multilingual societies are seldom symmetrical, such that it might be possible to speak of hegemonic (high prestige) and nonhegemonic (low prestige) languages, there are several possible translation models for multilingual anthologies (based on Lee 2022: 122-23):

a. *Translating a nonhegemonic language into a hegemonic language, but not vice versa.* Works written in a low-prestige language are translated into a high-prestige language, while those written in the high-prestige language stand untranslated. The low-prestige language, as the translated language (it is translated out of), loses agency in virtue of being represented by the high-prestige language; it is voiced over, spoken through. Conversely, the high-prestige language, as the translating language (it is translated into), gains agency by attracting the symbolic capacity to represent, to speak for, the Other.

b. *Translating a hegemonic language into a nonhegemonic language, but not vice versa.* This turns the preceding model on its head by having a low-prestige language translate works written in its high-prestige counterpart, while allowing works written in the low-prestige language to remain untranslated. In a reversal of roles, this model affords the low-prestige language the symbolic capacity to represent—and not be represented by—the high-prestige language, and therefore has the potential to subvert established language hierarchies.

c. *Multilateral translation.* This is an egalitarian model where low-prestige and high-prestige languages mutually translate each other's writing. Each language is translated into as well as out of, and all works manifest in their original language and in translation, resulting in a balanced configuration with no single language having more or less agency than any other.

d. *Nontranslation.* On the other extreme end of the spectrum, translation exists in the negative: all works stand in their original language without translation. The absence of translation silences the imperative to communicate across language borders, highlighting the autonomy of each language to speak only for itself and to its own audience. There is something radical to this model, insofar as multilingual collections are seen as testimony to cultural translatability.

With its focus on design features, this chapter's analysis can be said to be paratextual, where paratexts are "a consciously crafted threshold for a text which has the potential to influence the way(s) in which the text is received"

(Batchelor 2018: 142). The "text" in our case references not the individual literary works included in an edited volume but rather the collection of these works as a whole. This means looking at book covers, tables of contents, and prefaces that provide points of entry into an anthology, "even part-way through someone's encounter with it" (Batchelor 2018: 143). Batchelor (2018) stresses that the main criterion for a paratext is that it must be "consciously crafted." Insofar as this view implicitly construes paratexts as performative thresholds that guide the reader's reception of the text along certain paths, it speaks directly to my conceptual framing of choreography.

What ultimately counts as paratext, however, is determined by the research questions we ask in light of the data at hand (Batchelor 2018: 144). In this regard, I treat the model of translation adopted by an anthology as a paratextual element. Even though it is not a delineated object that one can put a finger on, a translation model influences how languages are distributed across an anthology. This distribution, often reflected in the table of contents, bears directly on how readers visualize the multilingual setup of the collection, which in turn primes them to think of multilingual literature or literacy in Singapore in certain ways.

The model of translation may also impact the materiality of anthologies, for instance, whether an anthology takes the form of a single volume containing works in several languages, or multiple volumes each containing works written in or translated into one language. Looking at translation paratexts from a social semiotic angle resonates with recent developments in translation studies, taking into account the multimodal nature of data sources (e.g., book covers, websites, and transmedia stories) by exploring their grammar of visual design (Batchelor 2018: 174–76, based on Kress and van Leeuwen's work).

With this in view, the following sections examine a series of state-endorsed anthologies published in Singapore between 1985 and 2015.[4] I explain how different translation models shape the compositional pattern of anthologies in distinct ways, conveying different images of written multilingualism. Yet, like the symmetrical and asymmetrical frames of institutional signage discussed in Chapter 2, these models represent variations on the same overarching choreography—one that aligns with official narratives on multilingualism by reinforcing the quadrilingual schema. In shaping the configuration of institutional anthologies whose expressive potential far exceeds that of public signage, these models also become enfolded into constructions of the nation through strategically themed literary and literacy projects.

4. Some of the examples in the next two sections were initially described in Lee (2013) but are reanalyzed here in light of more recent evidence as well as new theoretical perspectives.

## TRIPLE BILINGUALISM: ALL LANGUAGES ARE EQUAL (BUT SOME ARE MORE EQUAL THAN OTHERS)

As a staple of the literary institution in Singapore, multilingual anthologies have a relatively short history dating to the mid-1980s. Possibly the earliest attempt at collating writing in the four official languages is *The Poetry of Singapore* (Thumboo et al. 1985), part of the Anthology of ASEAN (Association of Southeast Asian Nations) Literature series and sponsored by the ASEAN Committee on Culture and Information. Using the vocabulary introduced earlier, this would count as a preservation-type volume, presenting a canon of works to establish Singaporean literature alongside other national literatures in Southeast Asia.

The lead editor was Edwin Thumboo, a pioneer in English-language poetry and an esteemed academic based in the Department of English Language and Literature at the National University of Singapore. Thumboo is very much an establishment figure, having won a series of high-profile national awards, including the first Cultural Medallion for Literature in 1979, the Public Service Star in 1981, and a Meritorious Services Medal in 2006. As a prolific literary editor, he had a palpable influence in shaping the tradition of anthologization in Singapore.

*The Poetry of Singapore* organizes its collected pieces around the by-now-familiar quadrilingual constellation. It is framed in four language-based sections, each prefaced with an introductory essay discussing the literature in one official language. Such arrangement belies the conception of languages as bounded entities in complementary distribution. The sequence in which the sections appear is Malay–Tamil–Chinese–English (MTCE), and the linearity of the book's layout speaks to a design mode for the languages to seen in that order.[5]

The MTCE order projects a left-right syntagm evincing an interest on the part of the anthology editors-as-sign makers (Bezemer and Kress 2010; Kress and van Leeuwen 2021). It is indicative of a political correctness, an editorial sensitivity to the political economy of language (Del Percio et al. 2017) in Singapore. In this sequence, Malay is positioned as Given in nominal recognition of its status as the national language; this is important as the anthology is part of a series of national literatures within ASEAN. English is placed at the

5. Whether or not readers will read the anthology in that order is quite another matter; as Bezemer and Kress (2010: 13; see also Kress 2020: 36) point out, the signs (texts) made by 'makers' (editors), "are never exact replicas when they are re-made by its 'users'" (readers). As mentioned in Chapter 2, what is important is that the language order (Malay first, English last) is presented "*as though* it had that status or value for the reader and that readers have to read it within that structure, even if that valuation may then be rejected by particular readers" (Kress and van Leeuwen 2021: 187 [emphasis in the original]).

end of the left-right trajectory. Bearing in mind that by the mid-1980s English had already become prevalent in Singapore, this end placement creates tension between its relatively low information value (associated with its semiotic placement in the book) and its high symbolic value (associated with its instrumental function in society, see the discussion of Figure 2.2). English can hardly be considered New, though its positioning on the reading path makes it ostensibly so.

Yet Malay's givenness is offset by the translation model adopted in this anthology, under which mother tongue language (MTL) works are translated into English but not vice versa. This is a model of triple bilingualism, a term introduced in Chapter 2. Here, it means that the three MTL sections in the anthology are bilingual, with English appearing as a counterpart to each (Malay/English, Tamil/English, and Chinese/English); in contrast, the English section is fully monolingual. This produces a unidirectional, asymmetrical translation relationship where the three MTLs are translated out of but not into, and English into but not out of.

In positioning English as a clearinghouse through which the other three languages are mediated, the triple-bilingual model is decidedly anglophilic, leading to a preponderance of English in the anthology. A further indication of this can be found in the table of contents, where the titles of MTL works are listed in English translation only, and the names of Chinese and Indian authors are romanized instead of appearing in their original scripts.[6]

Why triple bilingualism? In his general introduction (available in English only), Edwin Thumboo defends "the unique necessity for multilingual representation and translation into English" (Thumboo et al. 1985: 1), in terms of "the imperative to develop the skills and capacities—*best realized through English*—essential to the viability of a small modern republic" (emphasis added). He writes:

> Put briefly, the mother tongue provides social and cultural ballast and ensures the continuity of core traditional values while English performs a number of interlocking roles as the primary language of formal education. In addition to being increasingly the chief linguistic bridge between Singaporeans, English, already the language of international and regional contact, is crucial to training manpower for the financial, industrial, technological, information and service sectors which make up the economy of Singapore. (Thumboo et al. 1985: 1)

Thumboo's rationalization of the economy of language relations is predicated on linguistic instrumentalism, a pragmatic perspective that evaluates

6. In the MTL sections, titles and author names appear in their respective MTL scripts in the source text and romanized in the English translation. The difference does not apply to Malay, which is written in the roman script.

languages in terms of "achieving specific utilitarian goals, such as access to economic development or social mobility" (Wee 2003a: 211). As a piece of metapragmatic commentary, it is consistent with the statal narrative's framing of English as functionally and hierarchically differentiated from the MTLs (see Chapter 1), reproducing the polarized indexical structure that informs state language policies. In this regard, it is worth noting that Thumboo references "mother tongue" in the singular with the definite article, thus grammatically, but also ideologically, conceiving the three MTLs as one functional unit in relation to English.

A homology thus obtains between the perceived functional distribution of languages in the real world and their translational relationship in the discursive realm of *The Poetry of Singapore*. In other words, the anthology's translational design is a simulacrum of the power relation among the four official languages as they are discursively engineered by the state and systematically worked across various scales of text, such as public signage and institutionally sponsored publications. The spatial setup of triple bilingualism specifically recalls the state's language education policy of English-knowing bilingualism (Pakir 1991) or English-based bilingualism (Tan 2021: 162). Just as students in government schools are required to learn English alongside an MTL, so in the anthology, English is coupled with each of Chinese, Malay, and Tamil. This suggests that literary anthologies, though seemingly unrelated to state language policy and planning, can nevertheless corroborate official narratives on language through a choreographed semiotic structure.

A key theme here is the directionality of translation and its crucial role in articulating the differential capital of competing languages in their struggle for space, at once material and symbolic, on the pages of an anthology. As I explained earlier in the previous section, a translating language, defined as the language that translates texts written in other languages into itself, speaks through its own medium but also on behalf of other languages. In so doing, it drowns out and sometimes silences the voices of those represented languages. In contrast, a translated language, the language out of which a text is translated, cedes or loses its voice by ventriloquizing its texts through the translating language. In the case of parallel-text presentation, where the source and target languages appear alongside each other, the ventriloquy is partial, and the translated language retains a degree of identity; in the case where the translated text does not appear, the ventriloquy is total and its language completely submerged.

We must therefore interrogate the ideological value of Thumboo's "multilingual representation" in *The Poetry of Singapore*, constituted as it is by one monolingual English section and three bilingual MTL sections (Malay, Tamil, Chinese), with each MTL work coupled with an English translation. Within each set of parallel texts, an MTL poem appears on the left-facing page with its English translation on the right. This left-right orientation tilts the MTL/

English balancing scale to the former (Kress and van Leeuwen 2021: 185–90), but one is hard pressed to say this semiotic advantage would mitigate the sheer presence of English in the volume.

The repetition of English through translation renders it iterative and hence "weightier" and more salient (Kress and van Leeuwen 2021: 211). This turns English into a connective device that cuts across the modular framing of language-specific sections, insinuating itself iteratively into the space of the anthology. If modular framing constructs the four languages as autonomous elements, then triple bilingualism transforms English into a nexus into which the MTLs must flow. What comes to the fore is the nucleus character of English, which circumscribes the other three official languages by subjecting them to translation while it remains free from the reins of such mediation.

In other words, English constitutes a matrix language in the anthology. It not only holds its own space without penetration by any other language, it also cuts through the material and symbolic spaces framed in the name of the MTLs ("Poems in Malay," "Poems in Tamil," "Poems in Chinese"). On a social semiotic reading, this arrangement suggests a complementary, rather than contrasting, relation between English and the MTLs. It reframes the semiotic space in the book as one that suggests continuity, homogeneity, and nonfragmentation (Kress and van Leeuwen 2021: 221). It neuters the semiotic implication of the sectional divisions based on individual language identities, suggesting that the stability of the quadrilingual schema is ensured by the overarching translational role accorded to English.

Pascale Casanova (2010) uses the term "consecration" to denote a literary dynamic whereby writers working in a dominated language (a language of lesser literary prestige) enter world literature by lending their work to translation into a dominant language (a language of higher literary prestige, especially French and English):

> For a dominated writer, struggling for access to translation [into the dominating language] is in fact a matter of struggling for his or her existence as a legitimate member of the world republic of letters, for access to the literary centres (to the critical and consecrating authorities) and for the right to be read by those who decree that what they read is worth reading. (Casanova 2010: 95)

We might venture to rescale Casanova's (2010) "economy of linguistic exchange" (86) in the global republic of letters to the domestic literary situation at hand, focusing on languages instead of authors. Accordingly, English would play the role of a dominating language and the MTLs that of the dominated languages. Unidirectional translation from the MTLs into English under triple bilingualism can then be interpreted as the institutional consecration of MTL literatures by way of representing them in English, the "Greenwich meridian"

(93, 95) as far as language is concerned in Singapore. Just as MTL works are consecrated, or rendered legitimately readable, by means of being translated into a more visible platform of reception, so English ultimately holds the capacity to consecrate the literature of other languages.

Triple bilingualism naturalizes this act of consecration, essentially a one-way transaction from the MTLs into English. This polarized economy of language relations undergirds the conventional bridge metaphor as activated by Thumboo ("[English] being increasingly the chief linguistic bridge between Singaporeans"), creating a discursive illusion of mutual exchange. Clearly the linguistic exchange is anything but mutual; in Thumboo's words (cited above), it is "best realized through English." But this latter statement is itself the result of an interpellation. As we will see, alternative translation models are available, meaning there is nothing inevitable about triple bilingualism; on the contrary, it is inherently ideological.

Anthologies in the likes of *The Poetry of Singapore* are therefore choreographed into adopting a linguistic configuration that structurally reflects a paradigmatic conception of multilingualism, creating the conditions of possibility for thinking language relations along an MTL/English binary. This binary is a semiotic function of an official narrative, one that normativizes the putative neutrality of English vis-à-vis the MTLs and entrenches their functional complementarity. Yet, as in Thumboo's introduction, it is often projected back onto society as if it were an objective sociolinguistic reality.

### The Fiction of Singapore, Journeys, and Memories and Desires

Triple bilingualism was to become a semiotic prototype for anthologization, as would be attested in preservation-type anthologies throughout the 1980s and 1990s. It was deployed in *The Fiction of Singapore* (Thumboo et al. 1990; in three volumes),[7] published as a counterpart of *The Poetry of Singapore* under the same series and patronage, with Edwin Thumboo again at the editorial helm. This fiction anthology duplicates the sectional framing and language sequence adopted by its poetry predecessor. One difference is that, in the contents page, we see the titles of MTL works in both their original languages and in English translation (with the MTL title placed above the English), although the authors' names still only appear in romanized form.

Overall, however, English retains its status as a matrix language for *The Fiction of Singapore*. This is justified by Thumboo in his general introduction, which extends the same arguments used in his 1985 introduction. Starting

7. The three volumes are numbered (somewhat strangely) II, IIa, and III to signify their continuity with *The Poetry of Singapore*, which is supposed to be Vol. I (although this is not indicated on the cover of *The Poetry of Singapore*).

with the observation that the position of English as a "pivotal, bridge language has strengthened since 1985 when.... *The Poetry of Singapore* appeared," Thumboo maintains:

> As more Singaporeans use it [English] with confidence and sophistication, a greater portion of the Singaporean's experience, of the Singapore experience, will be explored and captured through English. Given its practical value, the perpetual dilemma is how to prevent other mother tongues from weakening. The standard of Chinese for instance, is in danger of declining. And Parthiban in *Gypsies* fears that "When language is forgotten, culture too will go . . . ". (Thumboo et al. 1990: i)

Tellingly, in 1993 *The Fiction of Singapore* was reprinted as a separate, single volume by UniPress (the Centre for the Arts at the National University of Singapore) in conjunction with the Singapore Association of Writers. This latter version combines the three fiction volumes, published in 1990 under the aegis of ASEAN, into one. The language setup of the UniPress reprint is completely different: all traces of MTL are removed, not only from the contents page but also from the text proper, with the MTL texts appearing only in their English translations.

What we have, then, is a monolingual English anthology that purports to be a multilingual representation of Singapore fiction. In other words, the UniPress reprint of *The Fiction of Singapore* is prima facie monolingual but de facto multilingual. The rationale for suppressing the MTLs is possibly logistical and economic: the inclusion of all MTL texts from the three volumes of the 1990 anthology would raise production costs and result in a tome. The change in patronage could also be a factor. The absence of the ASEAN branding in the UniPress edition means the target audience of this 1993 version is primarily local. This may have released the editors from the imperative to represent the works in their original languages as a politically correct gesture to showcase Singapore's multicultural policy to the other ASEAN members.

What is interesting is that this reprint version reproduces Thumboo's introduction in the three-volume *The Fiction of Singapore*, which, despite the asymmetrical directionality in translation, is at least prima facie multilingual. The consequence of this carryover is that in the UniPress version, Thumboo's claim that the experience of Singapore and the Singaporean is "explored and captured through English" inadvertently finds full expression through its blatant erasure of the MTLs. And the "perpetual dilemma," identified by Thumboo (citing Parthiban), of balancing the instrumentality of English against the cultural importance of the MTLs leaves a lingering irony when read against an English-only multilingual anthology.

The next anthology in line was *Journeys: Words, Home and Nation* (Thumboo et al. 1995), in which triple bilingualism continued to figure as a structuring method. This collection, published on the occasion of Singapore's thirtieth year of independence, positions itself as a "stark testimony to the amount of creative energy generated by Singapore poets since the publication of the 'Anthology of ASEAN Literatures: The Poetry of Singapore' in 1985" (Thumboo et al. 1995: xxv). In so doing, it constructs a lineage of literary anthologization of which it is a part. Edited by a multilingual team of scholars, headed again by the indefatigable Edwin Thumboo, *Journeys* further consolidated the tried-and-tested practice of pairing MTL works with their English translations, whilst allowing English-language works to stand on their own. As noted earlier, this results in an encumbrance of the MTLs by English, which as the sole translating (but not translated) language effects a kind of predatory embrace.[8]

To its credit, *Journeys* does foreground translation a touch more than *The Poetry of Singapore* by displaying the names of translators prominently on its cover page. Such overt acknowledgement of translators (never to be taken for granted) arguably goes some way toward recognizing non-English languages and literatures. But any such recognition is offset by the sequence in which the works are lined up. And here the familiar English–Chinese–Malay–Tamil (ECMT) pattern, witnessed frequently on public signage in Chapter 2, resurfaces on a left-to-right reading axis, with the same spectrum of information values as discussed earlier. In contrast to *The Poetry of Singapore*, the ideological pressure to afford Malay premium placement is apparently absent in *Journeys*, as the patron in this latter case is a university-affiliated press, not an ASEAN-sponsored agency. In light of the anthology's function to commemorate Singapore's thirtieth national day celebrations, the invocation of ECMT, together with the adoption of triple bilingualism, entrenches an English-first ideology as the conceptual bedrock for imagining the relationship between language and the nation.

The same setup, implementing both triple bilingualism and the ECMT template, was also followed in *Memories and Desires: A Poetic History of Singapore* (Goh 1998). This volume stresses the idea of a "national topos," sui generis in its "inseparab[ility] from Singapore's sociocultural constituency, its ethnic and religious blend, its colonial history and relatively recent independence" (Goh 1998: xvi). It reifies Singapore poetry into a holistic form that embodies a certain national essence, capable of differentiating from its anglophone (Western) Other. Hence, in his introduction to the volume, editor Robbie Goh speaks of "the relationship between Singapore poetry and national identity, and its difference from the relationship between poetry and culture in many anglophone Western countries" (xvii).

8. The term "predatory embrace" is from Susan Sontag (1969: 74).

Immanent to this presumed distinctiveness of Singapore poetry vis-à-vis poetry in the anglophone West is a smoothing over of the linguistic frames delineating the collected works into English, Chinese, Malay, and Tamil sections. The specific mention of *anglophone* countries in the West also raises the question as to whether Goh had in mind Singapore poetry in general or Singapore English poetry in particular. At any rate, the desire for homogenization under a unifying rubric (a "sociocultural constituency" and "ethnic and religious blend") finds semiotic expression in the univocality of translation. The use of English to represent MTL poetry, while denying the MTLs the same role in respect of English poetry, plays out the tension between the right to translate and the obligation to be translated, ultimately skewing the multilingual space of the anthology toward English.

Yet even as the editor celebrates the homogeneity of Singapore poetry as a distinctive category, he concedes to a fundamental chasm within this category in respect of "the exemplary model of historical consciousness . . . along lines of language, race and culture":

> [I]t is true that the [C]hinese poems, for example, have a slightly different historical sense than, say, the English ones. The comparison is instructive: the English poems often look back with a consciousness that is split between West and East, English and Asian language, rational progressivism and nostalgic pull. . . . In contrast, many of the [C]hinese poems, even in their English translations, speak of the past with the assurance that memory is accessible and immediate . . . which stems from an unhesitating sense of cultural identity. (Goh 1998: xxxi–ii)

Goh's "instructive" comparison perpetuates an essentialist construal of English and Chinese poetry as representing divergent worldviews, with the former embodying a propensity for "rational progressivism" and the latter for "nostalgic pull."[9] This is the Sapir-Whorfian logic at play,[10] only that the focus is literature, not language. It echoes, on the scale of literature, official stereotypes about English (the language of economic progress) and the MTLs (the cultural ballasts) in relation to their functional polarization in Singapore society.

As "a historical project of articulating national identity" (Goh 1998: xvii), *Memories and Desires* embodies the paradox of sustaining discrete cultural

9. I find the phrase "even in their English translations" intriguing. It gives rise to a bifurcated reading, simultaneously suggesting a note of caution (where "even" indicates surprise) and complacency (where "even" implies "nevertheless") on the efficacy of translation in conveying the predisposition of the original work.

10. Also known as the linguistic relativity hypothesis, the Sapir-Whorf hypothesis postulates that languages serve as (more or less) unique prisms through which users perceive their realities. In its strong version, the theory suggests that users of different languages are primed to cognize the objective world in different ways.

identities within an ideological framework premised on linguistic instrumentalism. In public discourse, this is usually encapsulated in much more positive terms, as in "unity in diversity," a clichéd institutional slogan used to negotiate the tension between the de facto heterogeneity of languages in society and a state-based narrative on homogeneity based around identity constructs like Singaporean-ness. Triple bilingualism is a symptom of, but also a prescription for, the articulation of this narrative. In performing an asymmetrical multilingualism within an English-language matrix, it unravels an Orwellian contradiction characteristic of preservation-type anthologies in Singapore: *All languages are equal, but some are more equal than others.*[11]

## MULTILATERAL TRANSLATION: TOWARD
## A HYPEREGALITARIAN MODEL

Although triple bilingualism has proven to be a dominant paradigm of translation in multilingual anthologies, a radically different model emerged with *Rhythms: A Singaporean Millennial Anthology of Poetry* (Singh and Wong 2000). Commissioned by the National Arts Council (NAC), this volume was published to commemorate the thirty-fifth anniversary of Singapore's independence, coinciding with the start of the new millennium.

As with antecedent anthologies, the function of *Rhythms* was preservative, that is, to establish a canon of local poetry as a literary tribute to the nation. But it broke new ground by ushering in the use of a translation model in which all languages translate multilaterally into one another. Thus, a work written in Tamil is translated into English, Chinese, and Malay; one written in Malay is translated into English, Chinese, and Tamil; and so forth. For the first time in literary anthologization in Singapore, English-language works were translated into the MTLs. Tables 3.1 and 3.2 compare this multilateral model with the triple-bilingual model in terms of the number of translation vectors, where a vector is constituted by one direction of translation.

The multilateral pattern signals a departure from the univocal model of triple bilingualism, which positions English as salient in its capacity to represent non-English languages. In the multilateral model, English shares some of this salience by being reciprocally voiced by the other three languages; it is both translated out of and translated into. Such reciprocity offsets the

11. Some noninstitutional anthologies also feature translation from the MTLs into English. Two recent ones include *Living in Babel* (Tan 2017), which anthologizes English translations of literary works originally written in Malay, Chinese, and Tamil; and *Memorandum* (Quah and Hee 2020), a collection of Singapore Chinese short stories translated into English for the first time. The two anthologies are published by independent presses, namely Canopy (an imprint of Select Centre) and Ethos Books, respectively.

**Table 3.1** LANGUAGE MATRIX IN THE TRIPLE-BILINGUAL MODEL WITH THREE TRANSLATION VECTORS

| SL/TL | English | Chinese | Malay | Tamil |
|---|---|---|---|---|
| English | N.A. | N.A. | N.A. | N.A. |
| Chinese | X | N.A. | N.A. | N.A. |
| Malay | X | N.A. | N.A. | N.A. |
| Tamil | X | N.A. | N.A. | N.A. |

SL designates source language (the language from which a work is translated); TL designates target language (the language into which a work is translated); X indicates the occurrence of translation; and N.A. indicates that translation is not applicable or not available.

**Table 3.2** LANGUAGE MATRIX IN THE MULTILATERAL TRANSLATION MODEL WITH TWELVE TRANSLATION VECTORS

| SL / TL | English | Chinese | Malay | Tamil |
|---|---|---|---|---|
| English | N.A. | X | X | X |
| Chinese | X | N.A. | X | X |
| Malay | X | X | N.A. | X |
| Tamil | X | X | X | N.A. |

SL designates source language (the language from which a work is translated); TL designates target language (the language into which a work is translated); X indicates the occurrence of translation; and N.A. indicates that translation is not applicable or not available.

hegemonic position of English, producing an alternative constellation that complicates the MTL/English binary by redistributing the semiotic weight afforded English under triple bilingualism.

There is a visual effect to this reconfiguration of language relations. Each poem in *Rhythms* appears in its original language as well as its translation into the other three languages in a kaleidoscope of successive permutations. The four languages take turns playing the salient role in their respective sections, where poems in their original language are featured in a larger font size and with color-coded titles, occupy more space than the translated texts, and are often framed on a page of their own (with their translations in the other three languages compressed into a single page). Each language section is also decorated with paratextual designs using key words from poetry in that language. With this, the quadrilingual parallel texts spread across the pages create a series of panoramic frames, presenting readers with a dazzling image of linguistic egalitarianism, indeed hyperegalitarianism. They constitute a fetishized display of balanced multilingualism meant as much to be seen as to be read (Kelly-Holmes 2014).

The multilateral model is premised on an implicit critique of triple bilingualism. In their introduction, the editors of *Rhythms* justify their decision to implement "cross/across translations/transcreations" instead of the "one-to-one process" entailed in MTL-into-English translation:

> Because Singaporeans tend to be bilingual it seemed easier to translate/transcreate these creative expressions into English in a one-to-one process rather than attempt the daunting task of cross/across translations/transcreations. . . . For some this would be a project of and for the national agenda, for others *a mammoth realisation that as a people we are capable of communicating across languages and cultural traditions*, and yet for others a wonderful firsthand experience of a poetry going beyond its own linguistic borders. (Singh and Wong 2000: 16–17 [emphasis added])

From this we know that the multilateral translation model was motivated by a desire to produce a certain sensibility on the order of national identity discourse ("as a people we are capable of communicating across languages and cultural traditions"). This "mammoth realisation," as Singh and Wong put it, is also a multicultural fantasy, a utopic vision of symmetrical and reversible language relations (Chong 2010). Multilateral translation is a semiotic instantiation of that vision. It issues from an editorial framework aiming to showcase a vibrant multiculturalism that sets English, Chinese, Malay, and Tamil in perfect equilibrium. Given the commemorative nature of the anthology as part of anniversary celebrations in Singapore, such multilateralism gains performative import in spectacularizing an affect of balance that indexes racial-ethnic conviviality.

The conception of multilingualism in *Rhythms* appears more sophisticated than that of earlier anthologies, acknowledging the pitfalls of cross-cultural mediation rather than uncritically valorizing its instrumentality. It takes into account the "misreading, misinterpretation, misshaping" that may creep into and compromise any act of translation. This is why the editors add their own gloss on translation with the term "transcreation":

> Translations can never be perfect; so we decided we will also use the term transcreation, a term that does not sit easy on many ears. The poem rewritten in another language is always vulnerable to misreading, misinterpretation, misshaping: what is needed is an indulgent, generous spirit which allows for all of these to happen without the reader losing respect for the original creation. (Singh and Wong 2000: 17)

In the context of *Rhythms*, "transcreation" is a misnomer, as the translations do not include radical rewriting of the kind suggested by the term. Nevertheless, the editors' concession of the fallibility of translation and of its possible shading into creative writing indicates a more nuanced view of multilingual transactions than that espoused by Edwin Thumboo. Whereas in earlier anthologies one senses a chauvinistic stance toward translation, such that it is deemed commonsensical for English to translate the MTLs but not the reverse, *Rhythms* rectifies this anglophilic bias by staging a dynamic exchange among the four languages.

## The Read! Singapore series

Multilateral translation as a model of linguistic configuration may have been pioneered by *Rhythms*, a preservation-type anthology, but it was taken up more rigorously by education-type or literacy-oriented anthologies.[12] Between 2005 and 2015, a new species of multilingual anthology emerged in conjunction with Singapore's annual reading campaign, Read! Singapore. Managed by the National Library Board (NLB), Read! Singapore (rebranded as Read! Fest in 2016 and subsumed under the National Reading Movement) is a nationwide, multilingual literacy event that aims to nurture a reading culture. Each year, a constellation of activities is organized around a theme and a list of titles by local and international authors; these activities include book discussions, film screenings, stage performances, meet-the-author sessions, workshops, and reading marathons.[13]

Read! Singapore spawned a series of literary anthologies that bespeak the systematic choreography of quadrilingualism.[14] With each run of the campaign, a handful of pieces originally written in English, Chinese, Malay, and Tamil were translated into the other three languages. What ensues is a complex matrix where every collected piece written in one of the four languages finds another three incarnations. This is the same translation model seen in *Rhythms*, where a work is iteratively and reciprocally circulated across

12. In terms of anthologies, Seruya et al. (2013: 5) define "educational purpose" in relation to "taste" or "the dissemination of mainstream ideological, political, social, ethical, aesthetical, and moral values." The general sense of education is relevant to the reading campaigns (a modality of public education) discussed here. Yet I also tilt the term toward language and cultural literacy; for this reason I use "literacy-oriented anthologies" hereinafter.

13. https://eresources.nlb.gov.sg/infopedia/articles/SIP_2013-06-19_103608.html.

14. Ten anthology titles were published under the Read! Singapore campaign: *Looking In, Looking Out* (National Library Board 2006), *Ties That Bind* (National Library Board 2007), *Home and Away* (National Library Board 2008), *Dreams and Choices* (National Library Board 2009), *Roads Less Travelled* (National Library Board 2010), *Transition* (National Library Board 2011), *Bridges* (National Library Board 2012), *Under One Sky* (National Library Board 2013), *Tenacity* (National Library Board 2014), and *SingaPoetry* (National Library Board 2015). The institutional character of these anthologies is indicated by the effacement of editors' identities on their covers.

languages, accruing a dozen translation vectors compared to just three under the triple-bilingual model (compare Tables 3.1 and 3.2).

Multilateral translation thus effects a translingual neatness lacking in triple bilingualism, exhausting all possible translation directions among the four languages. No one language is more salient than the others in terms of its capacity to translate (as opposed to being translated), thereby creating an impression of equilibrium. The model also generates redundancy, if we compare the number of translation permutations it produces to that under the triple-bilingual model. But such redundancy is precisely part of its specific choreography; it is a semiotic potential built into a calculated performance to create the visual sense that the four languages and their literatures engage one another in perfect communion and multicultural abundance.

What is unique to Read! Singapore is its material framing, in which a literary work is manifested not just across languages but also across book artifacts. Instead of featuring four languages in a single volume (à la *Rhythms*), a Read! Singapore anthology typically comprises separate monolingual volumes, each devoted to one official language and bearing the title in that language.[15] This setup extrapolates the modular framing characteristic of earlier anthologies from within one book to across several books, thereby enhancing the impression of autonomy for each language within the quadrilingual schema.

Such autonomy is further highlighted in the more recent titles, where individual monolingual volumes permutate the ECMT sequence to place their own language up front, thus establishing it as the Given, and also feature one additional piece in that language to render it salient. In the 2013 title *Under One Sky*, for example, the Malay volume sequences the works in the order Malay–English–Chinese–Tamil, with four pieces in Malay and three in each of the other three languages; the Tamil volume pushes the Tamil pieces to the front with a Tamil–English–Chinese–Malay order and gives Tamil four pieces, again one more than that allotted to the other languages; and so forth. Such manipulation of language order and numerical distribution is a clear indication of an overall strategy to render the four languages equally salient.[16]

---

15. This layout pertains to the post-2009 Read! Singapore anthologies. Among the pre-2009 anthologies, we see occasional hybridization between triple bilingualism and multilateralism. *Ties That Bind* (2007) and *Home and Away* (2008) feature a layout recalling triple bilingualism: each comprises a monolingual English volume and three bilingual (MTL/English) volumes. Yet in both cases, translation is multilateral, such that all collected works are available across the four languages.

16. An appendix in *Tenacity* (2014) includes a list of works selected for the Read! Singapore series from 2005 to 2013. Here, the number of short stories listed under each language is notably balanced among the four official languages.

Like other discursive productions conceived under institutional patronage, Read! Singapore anthologies are not merely textual-linguistic entities; they also embody a visual–spatial signification above and beyond the content meaning of the literary works. As artifacts of a literacy campaign, they are certainly meant to be read, but there is also a fetishistic dimension to them, in that they are also choreographed into a sight/site of display. This is evidenced in the consistent visuals shared across the book covers of language-specific volumes under the same title. Figure 3.1 shows examples of these book covers, designed to look like quadruplets with the same physical dimensions, composition, visual motifs, and color scheme. Structurally, this setup recalls the use of quadruple frames in multilingual signage, with each frame featuring one of the four languages while sharing the same information and visual design with the other three (Chapter 2).

The Read! Singapore series is therefore a full-blown manifestation of multilateral translation, where translation pertains not only to the verbal texts but also to the visuality and materiality of language-specific volumes. These volumes are free-standing entities accorded equal visual–spatial resources, while also converging under the same theme, title, substantially similar content, and paratextual packaging. Such convergence comes through strongly in some of the metaphorical titles, which connote the mildly propagandistic idea of togetherness or connectivity (e.g., *Ties That Bind*, *Bridges*, and *Under One Sky*).

**Figure 3.1.** Examples of Read! Singapore anthologies in four-volume sets. Clockwise from top left: *Transition* (2011); *Bridges* (2012); *Under One Sky* (2013); *Tenacity* (2014). Courtesy of National Library Board, Singapore.

Multilateral translation therefore offers a different take on the slogan "unity in diversity" than triple bilingualism. It proffers an alternative pattern for instituting neat multilingualism in which English relinquishes its privilege as regards information value and salience and sits as an equal partner of the MTLs. The model operates as a semiotic technology to project a hyperegalitarian image of multilingualism by translating symmetrically across the four languages and framing those languages individually in separate books, while still encompassing them under a homogeneous visual–thematic rubric.

## THE RETURN OF TRIPLE BILINGUALISM

Although multilateral translation is a later development and is more sophisticated in terms of its linguistic configuration, it has not displaced triple bilingualism. On the contrary, triple bilingualism has continued to maintain a strong presence in subsequent anthologies, particularly those of the preservation type. This is in no small part due to Edwin Thumboo's enduring influence in the local literary field.

These anthologies include *Fifty on 50* (Thumboo, Kamari, et al. 2009), an NAC-supported anthology published in celebration of the city-state's fiftieth year of self-governance. This publication's commemorative nature and state patronage underpin the conservative tone of Thumboo's editorial preface, which at the outset invokes the long-standing CMIO (Chinese, Malay, Indian, Others) formula:

> 1959 was a most significant year in our politics and history. The cornerstones for the foundation of a modern, multi-racial nation that took into account the factors of her survival, development, progress, and emergence in strength and unity, started to be laid. The overwhelming challenge was how to bring together Chinese, Malay, Indian and Eurasian, many new citizens, to live in harmony. (Thumboo, Kamari, et al. 2009: 7)

With its emphasis on racial harmony in the context of "survival, development, progress, and emergence in strength and unity," this 2009 editorial preface forms a consistent narrative with the prefaces written by Thumboo in 1985 (*The Poetry of Singapore*), 1990 (*The Fiction of Singapore*), and 1995 (*Journeys*). Like these previous anthologies, the publication of *Fifty on 50* was occasioned by a milestone event, namely, the anniversary of Singapore's attainment of self-government in 1959, and is thus part of higher-level discourses related to national identity construction.

In relation to this national discourse, triple bilingualism proves to be a central, though not exclusive, paradigm of multilingualism. As is characteristic of this model, in *Fifty on 50*, English-language works are left untranslated while MTL works are translated into English; within parallel texts printed on facing pages, the MTL work appears to the left of its English translation (coming before the translation in a left-to-right syntagm), thus assuming the information value of Given. Translators in the anthology are explicitly acknowledged (in earlier anthologies this was not consistently done); and the titles of MTL works, though not the names of their authors, are available in their respective languages, both in the table of contents and in the main text.

The new development in *Fifty on 50*, however, lies in its eschewing of the usual framing principle under which anthologized pieces are paradigmatically siloed into four language-based modules. Under its new spatial setup, literary pieces appear in no particular linguistic order. The usual paradigmatic structure dissolves into a syntagmatic one, creating a dynamic sequence rather than a static quadrilingual division. The editorial rationale for this is that "after 50 years it would be invidious to segregate them [literary works] linguistically" (Thumboo, Kamari, et al. 2009: 7). This latter statement, no doubt penned by Thumboo as the lead editor, is a metalinguistic commentary on the lineage of anthologies conceived under his editorship. It retrospectively constructs the modular framing of quadrilingual writing, so characteristic of earlier anthologies, as undesirable, because highly divisive ("invidious").

Yet this supposedly more polyphonic and less "invidious" structure does not conceal the fact that English is still the only translating language in *Fifty on 50*, functioning as a salient thread that weaves the MTL pieces together. Nothing has fundamentally changed insofar as the MTLs do not get to translate the English pieces; the language bias is covertly intact, even if the dynamic sequencing appears to be more liberal because less divisional. In fact, quadripartite sectioning at least has the semiotic effect of pronouncing the autonomy of the MTLs by framing them separately. This effect is compromised in *Fifty on 50*, which arguably disadvantages the MTLs by collapsing them into an English-dominant matrix.

The same translation model and compositional structure are adopted in another anthology published in the same year, entitled *Reflecting on the Merlion* (Thumboo, Yeo, et al. 2009), this time with MTL pieces flushed to the right side of facing English/MTL parallel texts. The implication here, as per Kress and van Leeuwen (2021), is that even within English/MTL couplings, English is the Given (the point of reference) and MTLs, the New (the point of contention). Once again, the MTLs are marginalized in terms of information value (they are right-placed in a reading syntagm), salience (they are translated languages only and so figure less pervasively than English), and framing (they are deprived of their own linguistic frames). This is exacerbated by the fact that the MTL titles and author names appear in the table of contents only in English translation.

Even more recently, triple bilingualism has come up in *Contour*, an NAC-supported anthology published by Poetry Festival Singapore (formerly National Poetry Festival), a literary collaborative whose advisor was Edwin Thumboo. As with *Journeys* and *Fifty on 50*, a historical event undergirded the publication, in this case marking two hundred years since the nation's founding in 1819 (according to official history). Hence the anthology's aim to "[chart] the lyric imagination of our people in Singapore's bicentennial year" (Ng et al. 2019: 1). Using the MTL/English parallel structure, the anthology also inserts itself into the tradition of anthologization in Singapore by having Edwin Thumboo (then retired) write an endorsement on its book jacket. It echoes Thumboo, Kamari, et al. (2009: 7) in justifying the removal of linguistic framing, stating that a dynamic sequencing "offers a far more polyphonic portrait of Singapore's poetic voices than the hitherto typical English-Mandarin-Malay-Tamil division" (Ng et al. 2019: 4).

## QUADRUPLE MONOLINGUALISM AS MULTILINGUALISM

The two primary models of multilingualism exhibited by literary anthologies in the three decades since 1985 embody different language ideological stances.[17] Triple bilingualism foregrounds the prerogative of English to function as a mediating nexus across the official languages in a one-to-many relation (English/Chinese; English/Malay; English/Tamil). It creates an asymmetrical platform where English obtains salience through its iterative presence and its power to translate, and where the MTLs are stripped of their agency by having to perform as a perennial other—always translated but never translating. Multilateral translation, by contrast, operates on a reciprocal economy of exchange in which the four official languages crisscross in a many-to-many relation. The ensuing platform is symmetrical, with a contrived sense of neatness,

---

17. Beyond triple bilingualism and multilateralism, a model that we might call mono-multilingualism also appears intermittently. This is where a multilingual anthology is published entirely in English, meaning MTL works do not appear in their original languages. We came across a version of this model with the 1993 reprint of *The Fiction of Singapore*, which flattened a quadrilingual anthology into a monolingual one *sans* the MTLs. More recently, the NAC-published, Thumboo-edited collection *& Words* (Thumboo 2010), although purporting to be about "poems Singapore," comprises predominantly English-language poetry, relegating MTL works to a section titled "Singapore poems in translation." There is no parallel text presentation, resulting in the erasure of the MTLs from the pages. In two other anthologies, *SG Poems 2015-2016* (Valles et al. 2016) and *SG Poems 2017-2018* (Ng et al. 2018), published under the atronage of the National Poetry Festival and supported by the NAC, not only is the (uni)direction of translation MTL-into-English, the original MTL texts are excluded. With these cases, we are reverted to the paradox of representing multilingualism monolingually, representing an extreme, fully asymmetrical model of translation that ironically cancels out multilingualism.

as semiotic resources are carefully choreographed to achieve a hyperegalitarian representation of all four languages.

Each of these models tells a slightly different story and has a different purpose. Triple bilingualism is an instrumental model that affords English discursive license over the MTLs, structurally resonating with Singapore's official language policy and bilingual education policy. It is more typical of preservation-type anthologies with a commemorative function, wherein the aim is to articulate a literary canon that contributes to macrolevel discourses of nation-building and identity formation. The multilateral translation model, in contrast, is an idealist one, evoking a utopian universe where all languages are equal, with none more equal than others. It belongs more properly to the domain of literacy-oriented anthologies, an insulated realm of reading in which realities of language power can be reconstituted.

Yet these categorizations of anthologies are not watertight. We have seen, for instance, that *Rhythms*, as a commemorative anthology, adopts the multilateral model, whereas some literacy-oriented anthologies under the Read! Singapore series (*Ties That Bind, Home and Away*) also lapse into triple bilingualism. This indicates that triple bilingualism and multilateral translation should be seen as alternative but coexisting models that together shape Singapore's literary landscape. Although different in the ways they configure languages and organize discursive space, both models are paradigmatic of a top-down strategy, an institutional order. The NAC and NLB patronage behind these anthologies, as well as the lineage of anthologization marked with Edwin Thumboo's editorial signature, attests to such an order.

According to this view, triple bilingualism and multilateral translation are specific choreographic techniques within the taylorist production of literature. Like the quadrilingual schema governing the composition of public signage, these translation matrices perpetuate an institutional framework within which multilingualism is imagined; they embody a methodology that interpolates readers into an official narrative of multilingualism. More specifically, they prescribe a quadruple monolingualism, which foregrounds the identity of individual languages but also their boundedness and complementary distribution. Complementary distribution construes the four official languages as delineated repertoires, as homogeneous monolingual slates (Heller 2002: 48; see also Heller 2003), which also entails the proscription of nonofficial and nonstandard languages from the matrix.

As with public signage, asymmetries among the four languages typically lean toward English. Malay occasionally gets premium status, but this is by virtue of its national language status, and is therefore strategic rather than incidental (the fact that Chinese and Tamil never come first in terms of information value in single-volume multilingual anthologies testifies to this). It is through such strategic choreography that institutional anthologies entrench Singapore's de jure multilingualism, streamlining the messy heteroglossia of its de facto multilingualism (Tan 2021: 163) into neatly classifiable and manageable categories.

## EXEMPLARS FROM SG50

Having reviewed the development of anthologies and their key semiotic features, we now turn to two 2015 publications to further exemplify the ideological character of these institutionalized productions. The anthologies at issue are *Singathology* (Gwee et al. 2015) and *SingaPoetry* (National Library Board 2015), respectively commemorative (preservation-type) and literacy-oriented (education-type) anthologies. The two volumes are good cases for us because both are SG50-related. As mentioned in Chapter 1, SG50 was an iconic event celebrating the fiftieth anniversary of Singapore's independence. The two anthologies therefore arose within the same significant moment of public nation-making, participating in a rich array of discourses in the lead-up to the high-profile celebration. As signaled by the *Singa-* prefix in their titles, they are imbued with ideological importance from the outset. Comparing the two anthologies can therefore point us to the choreographic apparatuses surrounding literary constructions of the multilingual nation at a critical historical juncture.

Both anthologies appeal to the canon. The subtitle of *Singathology* reads "50 new works by celebrated Singaporean writers," positioning itself as an elite volume authored by past recipients of prestigious literary honors in Singapore, namely, the Cultural Medallion and the Young Artist Award. In a similar vein, the blurb for *SingaPoetry* tells us that the selected poems were "endorsed by a selection committee chaired by Professor Edwin Thumboo— a noted academic and one of Singapore's finest living poets" (National Library Board 2015: back cover). We witness again the lingering specter of Thumboo, whose name is invoked as a signifier of authority even after his retirement. Although Thumboo has a more symbolic role in *SingaPoetry* (i.e., that of endorsing selected poems rather than actually selecting poems), his name is nonetheless coopted to lend canonical weight to the volume.

### *Singathology*: Canonizing the nation

*Singathology* comprises fifty works in two volumes. The number is of course not accidental but strategically pegged to the SG50 theme (see also *Fifty on 50*, discussed previously, which plays with the same number in relation to the fiftieth anniversary of Singapore's self-government). In terms of their language of composition, the works are distributed as follows: twenty-two in English, fourteen in Chinese, six in Malay, and six in Tamil. The disparity in numbers could be partly attributed to the differential quantity of writing available in each language. That is, due to uneven demographics, there are fewer authors writing in Malay or Tamil than in English or Chinese.

Yet, as mentioned earlier, the number of pieces allotted to different languages in multilingual anthologies acquires a symbolic meaning in relation to their relative power. Without stretching the point too far, I suggest that the numerical alignment of Malay and Tamil works is striking enough to indicate a degree of calculated planning, possibly motivated by an imperative to avoid an overt imbalance between these two MTLs. By the same token, the uneven distribution gives the anthology a strong anglophone bent, with Chinese, being less dominant than English in terms of symbolic capital but more pervasive than Malay and Tamil in terms of number of users, coming in second place.

Where translation is concerned, *Singathology* adopts the triple-bilingual model, where Chinese, Malay, and Tamil works are followed by English translations, but not the reverse. Recapitulating my earlier discussion, although the MTL works appear in their original languages and on the left side (the position of the Given) of each set of parallel MTL/English texts, English gains salience as a dual medium: of writing (for English-language works) and of translation (for works in the MTLs). The anthology follows more recent anthologies in not framing its collected works separately by their language of composition. However, it installs a section titled "Notes on Singapore Literature" to introduce the literature written in the four languages. These are set out in separate subsections, each written by a literary specialist in one official language, but, crucially, they are all written in English. The will to stratify languages into a quadruple monolingualism is therefore still operative, despite a simultaneous gesture to remove such framing and offer the impression of a heterogeneous mix.

One might again speculate on the relation between the anthology's semiotic features and the broader context of its production. In his introduction to *Singathology*, the editor ruminates on the significance of the number fifty, explicitly referencing the golden jubilee: "A country at fifty stands at a symbolic threshold it wishes that it understands in view of some fated awakening. At fifty, a key part of a nation's self-image tends to fall away. . . . Inching towards its own jubilee, Singapore encountered its grave loss too when its most beloved Founding Father departed" (Gwee 2015a: 9). In light of its connection to SG50, *Singathology* can be interpreted as a showcase of the nation's literary profile, featuring a host of institutionally recognized authors. Describing his anthology as a "monumental two-volume work" that seeks to "commemorate the living Singapore," the editor articulates the relation between writing and nation as follows:

> A nation is here being laid open for your scrutiny through fifty works by writers who have all been conferred one of Singapore's two highest accolades: the Cultural Medallion and the Young Artist Award. These writers have been invited

to help commemorate the living Singapore in their own ways, in any medium of their choice, and this anthology is the outcome. Together, the pieces expose not so much a sense of who we Singaporeans are as what we give to ourselves, through our writers, as being about us. (Gwee 2015a: 13)

The editor's foregrounding of the "two highest accolades" conferred upon the contributors to this "monumental" collection reveals the anthology's alignment with the literary establishment: the discursive authority to represent the nation during the benchmark year of 2015 is bestowed upon award-winning writers.

The anthology's appeal to the canon and to nationhood (the latter evidenced in frequent references to the nation in the editor's introduction) befits its SG50 agenda, and it is against this authoritative self-positioning that we can interpret the meaning potential of its multilingual model. As with other anthologies based on triple bilingualism, *Singathology* dovetails with the official narrative on multilingualism, yielding symbolic significance in the context of this commemorative volume. Its maintenance of structural equilibrium among the four official languages, the discursive privilege given to English as its exclusive translating language, and its reinforcement of quadruple monolingualism are well-attested traits of the institutionalized literary landscape, speaking to a top-down linguistic branding of literary Singapore.

### *SingaPoetry*: An exemplar of nontranslation

*SingaPoetry*, however, paints quite a different picture. Eighty-two poems are divided into four sections according to their language of composition. As usual, we have the four official languages,[18] although this time, there is no translation. We have seen in the triple-bilingual model that it is not unusual for English to stand on its own, but for the MTLs to do the same is a marked practice. This nontranslation model, together with a modular organization of works into language-based sections, exudes an egalitarian ethos by removing the ground of English mediation, allowing all languages to stand their own ground. In so doing, the model foregrounds the salience of the MTLs by dislodging them from the encumbrance of a translating language and preventing their discursive spaces from being shared out through translation.

The difference between *Singathology* and *SingaPoetry* is again attributable to their functional persuasions. Although both anthologies revolve around SG50, *Singathology* is more clearly commemorative. This arguably predisposes

18. There is, however, a self-professed Singlish poem: Angeline Yap's "Landowner's wife to building contractor (a conversation in Singlish)," (National Library Board 2015: 49) a rare exception in institutionalized anthologies.

the anthology to alignment with the prevailing statal narrative on multi-lingualism at the critical time of the golden jubilee celebrations. Hence the anthology's triple bilingualism, where all four languages are equal, but English more equal than the MTLs. *SingaPoetry*, by contrast, has a strong literacy goal, as it was published under NLB's flagship reading campaign. Its nontranslation model may thus be linked to the educational nature of that campaign, whose aim is to encourage reading in all four official languages.

That said, as a high-profile production supported by a major institution, *SingaPoetry* offers a radical conception of multilingualism in Singapore. Prima facie, the nontranslation model is diametrically opposed to the multi-lateral model characteristic of other literacy-oriented anthologies published by NLB. Yet these two approaches are also united in their mitigation of the default impulse to underscore English as an overarching medium, and in enabling the MTLs to articulate themselves free from the asymmetrical constraints of triple bilingualism. In contrast to triple bilingualism, these approaches are manifestations of the symbolic capital of the MTLs against an environment where the practice of foregrounding English has long been taken for granted.

But this is not to say that *SingaPoetry* espouses an antiestablish-ment language ideology. Thumboo's introduction (National Library Board 2015: 8–13) again offers paratextual evidence of the alignment between po-etry and ideology. Positing that poetry can help answer the questions "What is Singaporean? What is Singapore?," Thumboo delves into "the decisive matter of official languages" in a laudatory tone: "Singapore retains Bahasa Melayu, Chinese and Tamil for good reason" (9), that is, for ethnic preservation, polit-ical stability, and social cohesion. The word "retains" is loaded, suggesting that the three MTLs might have been eradicated from the linguistic landscape, as if their existence were somehow precarious.

Thumboo then constructs English as a kind of salvation language, protect-ing Singapore "[a]gainst the trend and tide of linguistic chauvinism sweeping across Asia and our region," regurgitating the familiar official line on the im-portance of English "as a means to link the communities and serve as the main conduit to the world" (9). At this critical juncture, English is metaphorized as "a hyphen, engendering the growth of a shared identity, but enduringly Singaporean in content and thrust" (9).

Tying the institution of English as a common language to identity-building imperatives, this strategic metaphorical intervention leads to a conclusion that is ironically replete with a linguistic chauvinism like that meant to be resisted in the first place: "When seen in its totality, our poetry in English reflects this larger, evolving vision, at times taking up specific moments and themes. . . . As English grew in importance, more wrote in this language, though there were and still are few [*sic*] Malay poets" (National Library Board 2015: 9).

In fact, Thumboo's introduction is punctuated with frequent mentions of poetry *in English*, beginning with the declaration that "[a]s we celebrate 50 years of nationhood this year, our poetry in English is equally deserving of attention as the other successes we have achieved" (National Library Board 2015: 8), branding English poetry an exemplar of success while eliding MTL poetry. In another instance, he speaks of Singapore's history being "in our poetry. Through its own making, poetry in English has surely arrived" (8).

This emphasis on English-language poetry within the context of a multilingual anthology is both symptomatic and problematic: symptomatic, because it corroborates the numerical superiority of English works—twenty-eight pieces, as opposed to eighteen each in Chinese, Malay, and Tamil; problematic, because it inadvertently deconstructs the multilingual setup of the anthology. In this regard, it is interesting to note the equal number of works included in each of the MTL sections. This numerical equivalence is a clear sign of choreography, implicitly constructing the three MTLs as parallel units standing in contrast to English.

Yet Thumboo is cautious not to sideline the MTLs completely. In discussing how poems "arch back into our memory banks to crucial issues of colonialism, nationalism and nation" (11), he cites one poem from each of the four languages. Set against Thumboo's valorization of English poetry in the preface, this measured and politically correct gesture, while affording the MTLs cursory acknowledgement, also points to a delicate balance between English and the MTLs that must be consciously maintained by the institution in constructing its idea(l) of the multilingual nation.

In sum, *Singathology* and *SingaPoetry* represent two anthology prototypes with different translation patterns. But it is important to recognize that, in each case, the model of translation adopted is the semiotic consequence of curation; that is, it is installed to align with the purpose of the project at hand, and always within the parameters of official language policy. Hence, dialect and vernacular registers have no place in these state-supported publications. This point will come into greater relief in Chapter 5 when we consider anthologies in noninstitutional domains.

## BEYOND THE PAGE: MULTIMODAL CHOREOGRAPHIES

The two SG50 publications also bring to the fore a new development that affords a multimodal dimension to multilingual anthologization by remediating print texts into embodied events. Both anthologies received high-end patronage from statutory boards, namely, the NAC in the case of *Singathology* and the NLB in the case of *SingaPoetry*. Such patronage afforded the publications ample funding but also significant profile on nationwide dissemination platforms beyond the book medium. *Singathology*, for instance, was launched at a premium venue, the City Hall Chamber of the National Gallery. Reading events and meet-the-authors sessions were organized around it during the 2016 Singapore Writers Festival; and in that same year, it won the honor of runner-up for Book of the Year at the Singapore Book Awards. In 2019, the anthology received an informal endorsement from Singapore's prime minister in his Facebook post written for World Book Day 2019.[19]

*SingaPoetry* is an especially good case in point, illustrating the complex inter-textualities involved in taking multilingual writing across modes and media. The book was published in conjunction with an exhibition at a downtown train station (City Hall Mass Rapid Transit, or MRT) called Poetry on Platforms, which ran from July 16 to August 13, 2015. In that exhibition, selected poems featured in the anthology were printed without translation on colorful post-ers and displayed on train platform doors, where commercial advertisements would normally be expected (Figure 3.2). Unsurprisingly, poems from all four official languages were selected for display, staging a vibrant visuality of neat multilingualism—specifically, quadruple monolingualism.

*SingaPoetry* was therefore an anthology-cum-exhibition, conceived as part of Read! Fest 2015. An incarnate of Read! Singapore, Read! Fest is choreog-raphy par excellence, where the idea of performativity becomes literal in, for instance, a series of promotional videos produced by the NLB for the event,[20] some of which are in the style of commercial music videos.[21] Other spin-offs included a poetry contest ("Be a Poetry on Platforms Star Poet Contest"), a book talk at the National Library, and audio recordings of collected poems recited in their original languages and made available on the official website of Read! Fest.

With these extensions, we see how the multilingual structure of an an-thology can be performed beyond the page. Print anthologies, then, can be located within a constellation of networked events and artifacts across lan-guages, modes, and media, representing a burgeoning methodology in mar-keting multilingual writing to a wider (lay) audience. This goes beyond mere translating of texts, which print anthologies have always done. What we are witnessing here is a multimodal approach to multilingual literature, where

19. In his post, the prime minister introduced *Singathology* as follows: "A collection of writings by Singapore authors for the SG50 year. Many different genres—poetry, prose, plays, and in different languages too. We often pick up books by foreign authors, but we should remember that there is lots of good Singapore writing too!" https://www.facebook.com/leehsienloong/photos/a.344710778924968/2405610962834929/?type=3&theater.

20. See, for instance, the promotional video for Read! Fest 2018: https://www.youtube.com/watch?v=sAehkFyPQdQ&t=26s) and Read! Fest 2019: https://www.youtube.com/watch?v=UXmjeXVY0kA.

21. See, for instance, "Book at the Beach," https://www.youtube.com/watch?v=8MtJkpezYFE&t=19s, and "I'm Gonna Read a Book Today," https://www.youtube.com/watch?v=Bam2TB2pb0s.

**Figure 3.2.** Poetry on Platforms (July 16–August 13, 2015, City Hall MRT Station, Singapore). Courtesy of National Library Board, Singapore.

works written in the four languages are taken beyond the verbal plane and distributed into multiple modalities of engagement. Each of these modalities foregrounds different experiential aspects of literature. For example, audio-books and reading events offer an oral–aural experience, whereas poetry exhibitions and other participatory events entail visuality and embodiment. Such development from multilingualism to multimodality stretches the semiotic potentiality of literary anthologies (and their collected works) across a range of material and technological platforms, thereby extending their reach.

As anthologies, *Singathology* and *SingaPoetry* are therefore significant precisely because they are more than anthologies; they bring into view the systematic extrapolation of languages and literatures into an intersemiotic, ambient multilingualism. Events such as these transform the nature of literature and literacy, turning reading and writing from private, discursive activities into complexes of public relations events, dovetailing with statal constructions of the nation. In doing so, they also point to higher-level architectures operating behind the scenes, as in Poetry on Platforms, which involved collaboration between the NLB and Singapore Mass Rapid Transit Corporation. Such mediation is a process of resemiotization (Iedema 2003), which often entails sophisticated planning in the form of well-coordinated institutional programs. It belies the power of institutional patrons in choreographing financial, spatial, logistical, technological, human, and other resources in the representation of multilingual writing in concert with prevailing language ideologies.

Mobile technology offers further opportunities for the multimodal articulation of literature. One example is Text in the City, a mobile application developed by The Arts House and made available for free on the Apple App Store and Google Play in 2014–2015.[22] The app opens a virtual space in which literature interfaces with digital technology, with the aim to "take local poetry out of classrooms and bookstores and place it directly in the hands of Singaporeans," as described by William Phuan, then-director of The Arts House.[23] The app is designed as an interactive map (Figure 3.3) that uses a cartographic theme, mapping one hundred poems by fifty writers onto Singapore's virtual terrain. Given that the app was launched in the lead-up to SG50, the number fifty is again weighted with a symbolic value that resonates with nation-building discourses, with the hundred poems projecting a sense of wholeness.

The featured poems are classified into six color-coded geographical zones (Figure 3.3, top left) and three "poetry trails," namely The Civic District, Chinatown, and Bras Basah. This represents the synthesis of anthology and geography on an interactive platform. Users tap the colored zones on the app to access poems written about specific districts or neighborhoods. In Figure 3.3 (top right), for example, we see poems about Serangoon Gardens and Lorong Chuan in the North-East zone, visually supported by a virtual map indicating the location of those places. Alternatively, users can use the search function to filter poems about specific locations or landmarks, such as the Merlion (Figure 3.3, bottom right).

Each poem is accompanied by an audio recording in its original language as recited by the poet, a brief introduction to the poet, as well as images of and historical information about the neighborhood or landmark central to the piece. Figure 3.3 (bottom left) is a screenshot of the app's interface with an English poem on Chinatown's Amoy Street by the veteran poet Lee Tzu Pheng. As with *Singathology*, poems from Singapore's four official languages are represented, with MTL works accompanied by English translations. Here again the translation is asymmetrical, reinforcing the role of English as a common denominator cutting across the ethnic languages while still maintaining a façade of quadrilingualism.

The alignment of literature and literacy, already evident in the Read! Singapore series, takes a mobile turn as the app makes Singapore poetry "readily available for users to read or listen to anytime, anywhere."[24] The

22. The Arts House is Singapore's national center for the literary arts, run by Arts House Limited, a public company under the NAC.

23. https://www.theartshouse.sg/media-centre/showmediacentre/singapore-poetry-goes-mobile-in-text-in-the-city.

24. Quote from William Phuan, Director of The Arts House: https://www.theartshouse.sg/media-centre/showmediacentre/singapore-poetry-goes-mobile-in-text-in-the-city.

**Figure 3.3.** Screenshots from the Text in the City mobile application. Clockwise from top left: (a) geographical zones, (b) poems in the North-East zone, (c) search-by-location function, (d) an English-language poem by Lee Tzu Pheng. Courtesy of The Arts House, Singapore.

interactive platform also transforms the dynamic of literacy campaigns, encouraging users not simply to read but also "to write and contribute to our canon of written Singapore works,"[25] thereby creating a more participatory and embodied mode of literacy. Although this injects a dose of egalitarianism into the literary canon, one should remember that all writing represented on the app still falls safely within the boundaries of the quadrilingual schema.

25. Quote from William Phuan, Director of The Arts House: https://www.theartshouse.sg/media-centre/showmediacentre/singapore-poetry-goes-mobile-in-text-in-the-city.

The usual linguistic framework governing institutional expressions is very much intact.

Text in the City is more than a piece of interactive media technology. Attesting to the contemporary postmedium condition (Krauss 2006), it remediates itself across platforms and genres, generating short ambient films around some of the works featured in the app. Choreography takes on a literal sense here, with these professionally made films combining poetry, music, and moving images to lyricize a sense of nostalgia tied to the local heartland and places of long-standing interest.[26] The app also spawned a range of participatory events, moving poetry from virtual into physical spaces.[27] These include

a. *poetry workshops, talks, and performances.* These were coordinated and publicized events that included a parent–child workshop with "master storyteller" Kamini Ramachandran, in which children were taught to craft poetry by playing games; a bilingual (Malay/English) recollection of *kampung* ('village') life in 1950s Singapore by Cultural Medallion poet Mohamed Latiff Mohamed; and a poetry slam by Singapore Literature Prize winner Joshua Ip (who also appears in Chapter 5) and spoken word artist Jennifer Anne Champion.

b. *roadshows and meet-the-poet sessions.* At these events, poets read their work to audiences, and books by local writers were made available for sale in booths. Notecards with handwritten poems were distributed to audiences. At library roadshows, children were given worksheets with questions to guide them in writing rudimentary "place-based poems." One question asked children to write a "sense poem" by filling in blanks within the structure: "(Place) looks like/sounds like/smells like/tastes like/feels like (Object)." Another asked them to illustrate their poem in the given space. Parents could submit their children's work to the Text in the City poetry writing competition. These tools of engagement point to a logistical micromanagement, under which activities relating to literary-literacy events are meticulously planned and executed.

c. *literary-heritage tours.* Itineraries were created around the Text in the City app, specifically its three poetry trails, and depicted on maps where poems were "assigned to" particular places or landmarks. Under the curatorship of trained guides from the Singapore Heritage Society, participants would visit sites of cultural or historical significance along the designated trails.

26. See, for example, "Finding Enlightenment in the HDB Heartland," by Alvin Pang: https://www.youtube.com/watch?v=4mRSH9N395s, and "MacRitchie Reservoir: A Memory," by Lee Tzu Pheng: https://www.youtube.com/watch?v=6mcZt4KsrzE.
27. An official video by The Arts House shows the myriad activities revolving around the Text in the City app: https://www.youtube.com/watch?v=LeHdRnjoOIg.

While taking in the sights, the app would orient visitors to specific references in poems titled after or based on those places, creating a text-city symbiosis through mobile technology. For instance, on the map of the Civic District Trail, the iconic sculptural landmark Merlion linked to Thumboo's "Ulysses by the Merlion" and Alfian Sa'at's "The Merlion." The two poems were to be read when the tour group stopped by the Merlion sculpture.[28] This station connected with four other place-poem couplings, producing a clearly directed, counterclockwise reading-walking trajectory forming a closed loop on the map.

d. *Text in the City poetry writing competition.* Organized as an offshoot of the app, this competition invited individuals to submit their own poems to win prizes. Speaking to one of the project's slogans, "Discover Your Inner Poet," it exemplifies a commodification of writing, attaching literary creativity to a price/prize tag. Submissions were restricted to the four official languages, reflecting a compliance with the strictures of language policy.

Together, these artifacts and activities accrue into a writing-related program that is thematically coherent, logistically sophisticated, paradigmatically managed, and amply funded. As such, they are part of a spectacular production (de Certeau 1984: xii) on the part of state-affiliated arts institutions. This precipitation of writing into a coordinated program of public relations events involves the resemiotization (Iedema 2003) of literary discourse, as suggested above. Text in the City is further an instance of mediatization (Agha 2011) in its transformation of a mediated act of communication (poetry) into a commodity (a mobile application) or commoditized activity (e.g., poetry contest). Writing and multilingualism, in the context of anthologies and literary campaigns, are repackaged and remediated into event complexes for public consumption, stretching far beyond the perimeters of the codex book.

## CULTURAL LITERACY PROGRAMS

With the discontinuation of the Read! Singapore series, public events of this kind are expected to replace traditional print anthologies in the performance of multilingual writing. The well-structured nature of these events points to a

28. The juxtaposition of Edwin Thumboo and Alfian Sa'at is intriguing. While Thumboo is an establishment figure, Sa'at is a well-known activist-writer with a clear antiestablishment position. Although similarly titled, their poems had opposing ideological dispositions: Thumboo's "Merlion" appeals to an official imagination of the nation via the figure of the Merlion, while Sa'at's "Merlion" is critical of that imagination. The Thumboo–Sa'at juxtaposition thus introduces a strain of self-deconstruction that complicates the dyadic place-poem coupling, although it is unclear if such a self-deconstructive stance was intended by the organizer.

logistical sophistication, exemplified by the balanced and complementary distribution of activities conducted in the four official languages. They are part of a broader choreography, that is, the systematic mediatization of the affect of neat multilingualism. These events need not be specifically literary but can extend toward a more general multicultural literacy.

A case in point is a 2019 cultural literacy exhibition entitled "Let's Rojak Interculture Playstreets," supported by the Singapore Wellness Association and the Harmony Fund administered by the Ministry of Culture, Community and Youth. This is a mobile exhibition circulating across public libraries in Singapore with an objective to "inspire [viewers] to surprise one another with a few greetings in Chinese, Malay, and Tamil, to recognise the many beautiful holy buildings we may have passed through countless times and to have an intimate conversation with our neighbours about our faiths" (Banner text).

The exhibition clearly targets a younger audience, as indicated by the playful, childlike tone in the title. Couched under its heritage education objective is a subtle language policy agenda, aiming to inculcate in younger viewers a particular narrative of multiculturalism by means of the quadrilingual schema. So, although the words "*rojak*" (a Malay term denoting a local salad made of mixed vegetables and fruits) and "interculture" in the title might suggest the celebration of multiculturalism, this is, to put it oxymoronically, a streamlined cultural heterogeneity in alignment with official language policy and the CMIO. A series of pull-up banners of equal dimension and coherent design show the deft even-handedness with which the four official languages and their associated cultures are represented in the exhibition. Figure 3.4 shows a set of four banners, themed "How to say it in English, Chinese, Malay & Tamil" and introducing six basic words ("how are you," "thank you," "sorry," "yes/no," "goodbye," "welcome") in the four official languages.

The subject matter here cannot be more trivial, but the language ideological value underlying the visual–spatial pattern is anything but. The banner displays are set up in a linear (left-to-right) fashion, with one banner assigned to each official language, an enactment of quadruple monolingualism. The six words are presented laterally as parallel translations across the four languages, framed within a similar design template and pegged at roughly the same height across the four banners.[29]

29. Connecting back to the analyses of Chapter 2, one might notice that the title banner (far left in Figure 3.4) lists the four languages in the ECMT sequence ("How to say it in English, Chinese, Malay & Tamil"). In view of Chapter 2's discussion about the pervasiveness of ECMT, this would not be an accident. Departing slightly from the ECMT sequence, the Malay banner in the image comes before (to the left of) the Chinese one. As noted in the previous chapter, this minor permutation does not shake up the quadrilingual schema: it is nonetheless the English banner that takes the leftmost position, semiotically construing the language as a Given.

**Figure 3.4.** A set of four banners at the "Let's Rojak Interculture Playstreets" exhibition at a public library.

The texts in the four languages are matched with images of people representing the corresponding ethnicities. The banners are therefore multimodal entities that pigeonhole the four official languages into their corresponding ethnic stereotypes, with a further inflection with heteronormative gender relations. From left to right, we see a lineup of standard pairings: English language/Caucasians, Malay language/Malays, Chinese language/Chinese, and Tamil language/Indians, in each case coupling a man and a woman as models. The installation, then, accomplishes more than just introducing simple expressions in the four languages; it also cultivates in young viewers an ethos of balance, with implications of racial harmony and linguistic conviviality, by naturalizing a parallel series of language-ethnic (as well as male-female) matchings.

Here we see the same cautious balancing among the four official languages, with asymmetries leaning toward English, as in the anthology examples above. Notice, for instance, that the words on the MTL banners appear in romanized script. The motivation for this is of course to enable viewers to pronounce non-English words, but this orthographic decision also entails erasure. Except for Malay, which in Singapore adopts a romanized script, romanization is tantamount to domesticating nonalphabetic scripts like Chinese characters and the Tamil *abugida* script, subsuming them into a visual economy associated with Western languages in general and English in particular.[30] The issue could have been easily circumvented by using two script forms (the original and the roman script) on the Chinese and Tamil banners; the space on the banners would seem to allow for that. The absence of these nonalphabetic scripts may thus be interpreted as a conscious decision; their resemiotization into the roman script creates a typographical coherence, producing a visual consistency across the quadruple frames.

The "Let's Rojak Interculture Playstreets" represents a very basic literacy setup targeting young viewers, but full-fledged cultural literacy programs are also designed around similar multicultural motifs. Two examples from The Arts House suffice to demonstrate the point. These are events orchestrated under prescribed, macrolevel themes ("Building Identity," "Love and Loss"), mobilizing all four official languages as they choreograph literary art into a multilingual, genre-shock, and transmedia spectacle.

The first of these is *LumiNation*, held annually in conjunction with National Day. The scripting of the event's name to embed the word "nation" already shows its connection to institutional discourse. This comes through particularly clearly in its 2019 theme, Building Identity, which aimed to place "personal relationships with the nation in conversation with communal narratives and histories, as well as [explore] the relationship of self, place and space in creating a fuller sense of belonging."[31] The event boasts an extremely rich, multimodal program in which all cultures associated with the official languages have a presence, although traces of vernacular culture are also visible.[32]

Another event, *Textures*, follows a similar though more aesthetic agenda. Branding itself as "a signature program . . . celebrating Singapore literature and those in the literary arts industry,"[33] its 2019 itinerary features plays based on local literature; multimedia exhibitions combining poetry and sketching; art song (poetry-and-music) performances in different languages; and workshops, sharing sessions, and panel discussions on collaborative comics, writing and journaling methods, adaptation techniques (e.g., from the written

30. Notably, the romanization uses a conventional notation; for example, the Chinese words are transliterated using the Pinyin system based on Mandarin, a notation system taught in schools.

31. https://www.theartshouse.sg/programmes-details/the-arts-house-presents/lumination-2019.

32. Activities include, for instance, photography exhibitions on past and present places of interest; talks on Singapore's history and identity through the lens of literature, postwar novels, and place histories; animated shorts, films, and documentaries on themes informed by local society and folk culture; multimodal renditions of classic Malay songs with poetry recitals; and performance forums on the content and aesthetics of lyrics in Malay drama serials.

33. https://www.theartshouse.sg/programmes-details/the-arts-house-presents/textures-2019.

word to theatre, storytelling, or visual art), Malay musical genres, Tamil storytelling, and Chinese illustrated books.[34]

Through these activities, the promotion of cultural literacy becomes a platform for the subtle reiteration of statal narratives on multiculturalism, in turn premised on a quadruple monolingualism. Like anthologies, literacy events are therefore cultural choreographies. Mirroring the CMIO, they continually shape an established profile of multilingual Singapore in the public imagination, articulating it to thematic concerns related to national identity and belonging. Literature and culture, as practiced by the institution, are never just themselves; they speak to and play out a latent script that governs the underlying semiotic structure of their manifest products.

## A LITERARY "PROPER"

This chapter has presented examples of multilingual cultural productions with institutional patronage. We started with literary anthologies showcasing Singapore's four official languages in several strategic formations—triple bilingualism and multilateral translation in the main, but also monomultilingualism and nontranslation. Each of these formations undergirds a different orientation toward negotiating the delicate power relation among the four languages. As iterative visual–spatial structures, they function as formulaic expressions seeking to either sustain a hyperegalitarian balance among the official languages or to foreground the nexus role of English in harmonizing the MTLs.

To the extent that these translation models operate within the parameters set down by official language policy, their structures can be said to "conceal beneath objective calculations their connection with the power that sustains them from within the stronghold of its own 'proper' place or institution" (de Certeau 1984: xx). From print anthologies, we proceeded to look at cultural literacy programs characterized by the same choreographic neatness. Like anthologies, they constitute sites of a streamlined multilingualism that draws on quadruple monolingualism. One can think of anthologies and literacy events as representing a grid or map, a literary "proper" via de Certeau's characterization of *place* and strategy (1984: 36), as follows:

a. They compress time (into the discursive space of a codex book) by selecting and consolidating separate works, written over a temporal span, into a corpus, thereby exercising "a mastery of time through the foundation of an autonomous place."

34. https://www.theartshouse.sg/programmes-details/the-arts-house-presents/textures-2019.

b. They create the impression of wholeness, that is, a comprehensive, hence panoptic, view of the local literature, turning literary pieces into "objects that can be measured, and thus control[ling] and 'includ[ing]' them" within the scope of official multilingualism.

c. They exhibit the "power of knowledge" in relation to the literary canon, by transforming "the uncertainties of [literary] history into readable spaces." More accurately, we can identify in the discursive and semiotic strategies of anthologization "a specific type of knowledge," sustained and determined by institutional power, to construct an ideal multilingual *place* with neat borders and a balanced structure.

Anthologies and cultural literacy programs therefore exemplify a strategic modality of multilingual governance in Singapore that systematically works the quadrilingual schema into public discourse. In entrenching a semiotic motif homologous to that witnessed on public signage, they reinforce complementary distribution as the reigning ideology of multilingualism, under which clear-cut boundaries are drawn among the four official languages as well as between official and nonofficial languages. Where such literary and literacy-oriented writing is themed around national identity, we see how neat multilingualism on the level of discursive texts or embodied activities fosters higher-level discourses or, conversely, how the institutional articulation of identity implicitly rides on the structure of quadruple monolingualism. In the next two chapters, we turn to a diametrically different type of multilingual choreography that has arisen in response to such institutional articulations— one that eschews the neat stratification of languages, celebrates heteroglossia, and promotes a resistant cultural politics in writing.

# CHAPTER 4
# Ludifying English

## Singlish as ideological critique

In the last two chapters we looked at institutional practices of multilingualism that tend to reify language identities and boundaries, producing models of neat multilingualism that preclude linguistic syncretism and code-mixing. This chapter and the next examine alternative choreographies of multilingualism that both complement and articulate against institutional practices. These choreographies, taking the form of metalinguistic Singlish writing and vernacular-oriented poetry, can be said to release the heteroglossic energies of multilingualism from below (Pennycook and Otsuji 2015: 9–13). Emergent and resistant in disposition, they are grassroots practices illustrating what Pennycook and Otsuji (2019a) call "mundane metrolingualism," a term that highlights the "translinguistic ordinariness" (75) of urban multilingualism as well as "local contexts of everyday diversity" (178). This is a multilingualism in the city that, rather than being abstracted into systemic methodologies, is grounded in the quotidian and the worldly (176).

Singlish, an evolving, heteroglossic vernacular that blends resources from English and various local languages, best exemplifies mundane metrolingualism in Singapore. What I am interested in exploring in this chapter, however, is not Singlish as it is used in the streets—as is Pennycook and Otsuji's concern—but rather Singlish as it is rhetorically delivered through metadiscursive writing. Here, an unmarked speech variety associated with the mundane in the popular imagination becomes highly marked when performed as a stylistic locale-specific register in writing. Therein lies the performative and transgressive value of Singlish writing: just as social styles can be activated through "creative, design-oriented processes" in talk (Coupland 2007: 3), so

*Choreographies of Multilingualism.* Tong King Lee, Oxford University Press. © Oxford University Press 2022.
DOI: 10.1093/oso/9780197644645.003.0004

Singlish-as-style (Wee 2016b) can be mobilized in writing to creative and critical ends.

Creative-critical Singlish writing can take on metalingual, poetic, and metacultural functions when agitating against dominant language ideological narratives: metalingual, because its very discourse constitutes the topic it expounds on; poetic, because it foregrounds the phono-orthographic and morphosyntactic features that mark the discourse (see Bauman and Briggs 1990: 73, drawing on Jakobson's typology of language functions); and metacultural because it embodies "the potential to define the culture in which it functions" (Coupland 2012: 4).

By virtue of these functions, Singlish as a speech register can be seen as entextualized (Bauman and Briggs 1990: 73): it is "lifted out of its interactional setting," turned into an "extractable" rhetorical resource, and emplaced in a different mode and discourse (e.g., a written text) to evoke grassroots sensibilities and project an egalitarian stance. In other words, for Singlish to be usable as a stylistic resource, it needs to be decontextualized from its conversational settings and recontextualized, and specifically resemiotized (Iedema 2003), in new material-semiotic frames (e.g., a printed book or a Facebook page), while carrying "elements of its history of use" (Bauman and Briggs 1990: 73) into those new frames. The result of such entextualization is "a highly reflexive mode of communication" (Bauman and Briggs 1990: 73) constituting a discursive performance, where Singlish coils unto itself precisely to launch a critique of the perceived hegemony of Standard English. Hence, discursive practices that tactically deploy Singlish illustrate "the dialectic between performance and its wider sociocultural and political-economic context" (Bauman and Briggs 1990: 61) in Singapore.

My case in point in this chapter is a 2018 book by Gwee Li Sui, *Spiaking Singlish: A Companion to How Singaporeans Communicate*. A cross between a popular expository text and a Lonely Planet-style guide, the book curates forty-five terms and expressions from the Singlish repertoire and explains their meanings in sociocultural context. What is the motivation for writing such a book on Singlish? What social, political, and linguistic debates around Singlish was he responding to? In what follows, I introduce the characteristics of the book, in particular how it reinvents English with a view to challenging prevailing linguistic hierarchies. This is followed by a review of sociolinguistic developments that led up to Gwee's brand of written Singlish, including the Speak Good English Movement (SGEM) and the counterdiscourses it has provoked, in particular the Speak Good Singlish Movement (SGSM). Finally, we interrogate the ethics of creative Singlish, and ask whether the writing practices of highly educated Singaporeans fluent in both English and Singlish do not foster an implicit elitism while making claims to linguistic egalitarianism.

As its title suggests, *Spiaking Singlish* is a primer dedicated to Singlish, but one with a playful, metalinguistic twist. Marketing itself as "possibly the first book on Singlish written entirely in Singlish,"[1] the book flaunts its performativity in the title itself: *spiaking* is the Singlish variant of "speaking," an exaggerated mimicry of the way the word is presumably pronounced by Singaporeans. Whether such a pronunciation is empirically attested is quite beside the point;[2] it is the slippage between received and parodied pronunciations that is the source of earthy humor.

*Spiaking Singlish* is more than just an introductory text as to how Singlish is spoken by Singaporeans. Rather, as a blurb on the publisher's website suggests, Singlish is foregrounded here as a register for styling:

> *Spiaking Singlish* doesn't just describe Singlish elements. . . . Rather, it aims *to show how Singlish can be used in a confident and stylish way to communicate*. Gwee Li Sui's collection of highly entertaining articles shares his observation of how Singlish has evolved over the decades. To appeal to the "kiasu" nature of readers, each of the 45 pieces comes with a bonus comic strip. There is also a Singlish quiz at the end of the book for readers to test their grasp of Singlish![3]

The motivation behind the "companion" is therefore nonpedagogical. Its primary intent is not to educate readers on Singlish in any prescriptive manner. Nor is it meant to be merely descriptive of how Singlish actually sounds; the first sentence in the blurb above makes this clear. The real intent of the book is rather the ludification of English as it is used in Singapore.

## LUDIFICATION OF ENGLISH

Ludification denotes playfulness in respect of all aspects of culture. Raessens (2014) maintains that play

---

1.    https://www.marshallcavendish.com/marshallcavendish/genref/Spiaking-Singl ish_B1106_Singapore.aspx.

2. *Spiaking* is arguably quite off the mark from the Singlish pronunciation of "speaking" today, where the duration of the diphthong *-ea* would normally be clipped. The spelling of *spiak* could have originated from the phrase *no spiak* (nəʊ spiːˈjʌk), which, according to the *Dictionary of Singlish and Singapore English*, is a corrupted form of "no speak," referring to someone "dumbfounded or flabbergasted, or has nothing to say" (see http://www.mysmu.edu/faculty/jacklee/singlish_N.htm). Notwithstanding its provenance, I continue to view *spiaking* as an orthographic aberration in line with the generally playful disposition of the book.

3.    https://www.marshallcavendish.com/marshallcavendish/genref/Spiaking-Singl ish_B1106_Singapore.aspx (emphasis added).

is not only characteristic of leisure, but also turns up in those domains that once were considered the opposite of play, such as education (e.g. educational games), politics (playful forms of campaigning, using gaming principles to involve party members in decision-making processes, comedians-turned-politicians) and even warfare (interfaces resembling computer games, the use of drones—unmanned remote-controlled planes—introducing war à la PlayStation). (94)

Just as education, politics, and warfare can be ludified (rendered playful), so can language. *Spiaking Singlish* underscores the ludification of language, where English is made light of, punctured as it were, by creative Singlish interventions.

The best place to start is the book's introduction, which professes itself to be a "Cheem Introduction," where *cheem* means sophisticated (as in depth of knowledge). Here the (mis)alignment of a vernacular with sophistication points to a self-mocking, tongue-in-cheek perspective that informs the entire work. Tellingly, Gwee (2018: 13) does not shy away from self-praise with conscious irony: he lauds his book as *sibeh kilat* (more than excellent), "hands-down the cheemest Singlish book in print ever or at least to date"—where *cheemest* instances Singlishism (Wee 2016b: 53) by inflecting *cheem* with an English superlative suffix. It demonstrates the creative dynamism of stylized Singlish practices, where words of non-English origin are often meshed into English morphologies to create contingent formations (see Lee and Li 2020).

A former faculty member of the Department of English Language and Literature at the National University of Singapore, Gwee does not miss a chance to take a pointed swipe at academia. He positions his book as superior (the term used is *lagi steady poon pee pee* "more competent") to the academic publications of "cunning linguists" that the author claims *catch no ball* (fail to understand). All of this seemingly justifies the Singlish imperative that kickstarts the introduction—*Dun siow-siow* (lit. don't fool around), meaning to take someone or something seriously—whereby readers are enjoined to treat the book in earnest. As with the numerous quips found throughout the book's pages, that imperative is meant to be taken ironically; indeed, to read the book in all seriousness is precisely to undo its intent. What the intense self-reflexive humor in Gwee's writing requires is rather a ludic reading, an irreverent playfulness on the part of the audience.[4]

4. On this note, it is of interest that Gwee Li Sui is also the author of several volumes of ludic poetry, such as *Who Wants to Buy an Expanded Edition of a Book of Poems?* (Gwee 2015b), *The Other Merlion and Friends* (Gwee 2015c), and *Haikuku* (Gwee 2017). The playful character of these books can be gleaned from Gwee's combination of Singlish and satire in his poems, the highly graphical book covers, and the seemingly light-hearted titles. "Haikuku," for instance, comes from the conflation of "haiku" (a traditional Japanese poetic form) and "*kuku*," an onomatopoeic word that mimics the sound of birds, extended to reference the male sexual organ in Singlish.

Take, for example, the book's first entry on the word *anyhowly*, the Singlish variant on "anyhow." In explaining why Singlish would appropriate an existing English word without changing its meaning substantively, Gwee takes the opportunity to propose his own linguistic "law":

> Here's a good time for me to share one typical way I fewl [eye-dialect spelling of "feel"] Singlish as a language develops. To be sure, "anyhow" is a sibeh tok kong ["extremely potent"] word for the Singaporean mind, which is always stuck between a love of freedom and a fear of luanness ["disorder": *luan*, a transliteration from Hokkien/Mandarin + the English suffix *-ness*]. It's macam ["as though"] God made this word for us one! [Singlish structure] But, when a Singlish term kena [passive marker] used a lot, something I call Gwee's First Law of Singlish Dynamics kicks in. This law states that a frequently employed expression tends towards a *rhyme*. (Gwee 2018: 28 [bracketed translations and explanations added])

The so-called Gwee's First Law of Singlish Dynamics is a nonce creation given to the author's personal observation of a Singlish pattern; it is deliberately cloaked in pseudoacademic nomenclature, with the "Family Name + First Law of . . . Dynamics" structure parodying the labels of famous scientific theories (e.g., Newton's First Law of Motion and the Second Law of Thermodynamics). No reader is expected to ascribe any intellectual intent to this "law," which is meant to create a disjunct between the apparent triviality of Gwee's observation and its heady title and a jarring gap between the nonofficial status of Singlish and its grandiose appellation. This kind of nonserious language belies the more aggressive stance of mocking the lofty rhetoric of the establishment, including academia. The wry humor that arises here is reflexively and metadiscursively captured by Gwee himself in the same entry, in what he calls his Second Law of Singlish Dynamics: "a frequently used expression tends towards *humour*" (Gwee 2018: 30 [emphasis in the original]).

The ludicity or playfulness of *Spiaking Singlish* lies in part in the way it defamiliarizes Singlish. Although the individual terms introduced in the book are themselves unmarked, they are collocated with such intensity as to give rise to a hyperbolic display of multilingualism. The following metacommentary on the history of Singlish illustrates my point:

> Singlish has long-long history one! [Singlish structure] Dun listen to some people talk cock sing song ["utter nonsense"] and anyhow say this, say that [Singlish structure]. These who suka ["like"] talk cock—that is, engage in nonsensical or idle talk—we call talk cock kings. They say got no Singlish before Singapore was independent [Singlish structure]. They say last time only got [Singlish existential verb] Melayu ["Malay"] and cheena ["Chinese"] dialects campur-campur ["to

mix"] but no England ["English"] because people bo tak chek ["did not study"].
Lagi ["even"] worse, they say Singlish only became tok kong ["potent"] when
Singaporeans felt rootless and buay tahan ["unable to tolerate"] Spiak Good
England Movement ["Speak Good English Movement"]. Wah piang [Hokkien
answer to "Oh my god"] eh [Singlish interjection]! No lah! [sentence-final par-
ticle]. (Gwee 2018: 80 (bracketed translations and explanations added))

In code-switching terms (Myers-Scotton 1997), one might identify English as
the matrix language in the above passage, and Malay and the Chinese dialects
(mainly Hokkien) as the embedded languages. Yet here, the degree of heteroglossia (as indicated in my inserted glosses) is so high that such a characterization may not be very helpful at all. As Li Wei (2018a) maintains in respect
to a similar example from naturally occurring Singlish conversation, it may be
counterproductive to attempt to identify and count the languages or language
varieties Singlish speakers are using as if they were discrete. In this regard,
"[a] classic code-switching approach would assume switching back and forward to a single language default, and it would be the wrong assumption to
make about this community of multilinguals" (14).

In this light, the metadiscourse of *Spiaking Singlish* aims to disturb the identity of English as the matrix language underlying Singlish. It evinces a high
performativity (Coupland 2007) based on an ironic parody of the mundane
performativity of everyday Singlish interactions. More specifically, Singlish
words and phrases are decontextualized from their ordinary conversational
settings and recontextualized within a self-styled Singlish "companion." In
other words, the formal features of an everyday spoken language are entextualized (Bauman and Briggs 1990: 73) and resemiotized (Iedema 2003) as
resources for playful, metadiscursive writing.

So, let us take stock of the rhetorical transformation of Singlish from street
vernacular to ludic style in *Spiaking Singlish*. In the terms of Bauman and
Briggs (1990: 75), based in turn on Goffman's (1974) theory of framing, the
book's companion genre and format constitute a "metacommunicative management" of the text. The entextualization of vernacular Singlish terms within
the semiotic-material frame of a putatively lexicographical genre creates tension between the perceived difference between the oral and the written, the
prosaic and the (pseudo-)scholarly. This tension generates humor while hint-
ing at the potential of Singlish to function as a written language in its own
right. In this regard, the book's paratextual features—its self-naming as a
"companion," the alphabetical ordering of entries as per dictionaries or glossa-
ries,[5] or the Singlish "quiz" at the end modeled on the familiar multiple-choice

5. This companion/dictionary format is nontrivial. As Schneider (2003: 252)
observes, dictionaries of native varieties of English are "a characteristic trait" of endonormative stabilization.

question (MCQ) format used in examination papers—should be interpreted as part of an ironic frame that is evocative of a language orthodoxy and subverted from within with Singlish as the metalanguage.

In terms of form (Bauman and Briggs 1990: 75), the recursiveness involved in explaining Singlish in Singlish creates a self-sufficient, endonormative loop that results in locale- and register-specific linguistic entertainment, spurring laughter for "in-group" Singlish speakers "in the know." Such metadiscursivity calls attention to the form of the discourse itself, that is, the entextualized Singlish formulations, including their morphological flexibility (e.g., non-English words inflected as though they were English words), orthographical contingency (many Singlish words have no fixed spelling), and multilingual composition.

Finally, the function (Bauman and Briggs 1990: 75–76) of the seemingly lighthearted metadiscourse is an ideologically charged one. It is to establish the autonomy of Singlish by "elevating" it from a spoken vernacular to a written medium; to convey the message that Singlish is not to be evaluated with reference to the exonormative (from the vantage of Singlish) criteria of Standard English. In this regard, Gwee's suggestion that Singlish possesses a "dynamics" governed by its own "laws" (quoted above) speaks to the politics of writing Singlish within a language ideological regime that systematically militates against it. In doing so, he also demonstrates how style is a surface manifestation of and a "shorthand" for stance (Kiesling 2009).

## FROM STYLE TO STANCE

The whimsical style of *Spiaking Singlish* coheres with the perceived informal, bottom-up character of Singlish and foregrounds the book's antiestablishment stance. This stance is evident in several passages in the book's introduction, in which the author explicitly argues against the government's (always playfully [mis]spelled as *Gahmen*, with a capital G) view on Singlish. In one exemplary instance, he declares that government efforts to "blame social immobility on Singlish and then try to kill Singlish" are "smart" (in an ironic sense) but futile. He then dishes out his admonishment: "Whack Singlish for fiak since you cannot stop people from anyhowly?" (Gwee 2018: 22)—roughly translating into: "Why the f*ck are you censuring Singlish since you can't stop people from messing up their language?"

Singlish is thus more than just a tongue; it is loaded with signification in relation to language politics. As Gwee wryly notes, "Singlish is different [from the four official languages]: it gets no love from the Gahmen" (Gwee 2018: 14). The iconoclastic stance here cannot be more obvious: Singlish "gets no love" from the establishment. The eye-dialect orthography emblematizes a resistant discourse—*Gahmen* is an eye-dialect variant of "government" inflected with a distinctively Singlish accent. By imparting a contingent written form to a word rooted in orality, Gwee does not revert to the discursive authority he seeks to transgress but rather deconstructs such authority by attaching a spurious Latin transcription to a vernacular that does not possess its own script. Given that Singlish is rooted in the patois, the use of eye-dialect in words like *spiaking* in the title and *Gahmen* here is per se a point of transgression.[6] It contingently transforms the oral–aural transience of a spoken variety into the visual–verbal fixity of a language equipped with an apparent orthography.[7] The resistant nature of the Singlish orthography is especially striking in the present example, where the word in question happens to be *government*.

Such invented spellings first appeared in the *Goondu* (stupid) series by veteran writer Sylvia Toh Paik Choo (Toh 2011)[8] and gained traction as a practice during the early days of text messaging and online chats among Singaporeans. They are a highly performative gesture, mimicking spelling errors and spelling words in idiosyncratic ways to reflect their accented pronunciations in local vernaculars (see Tagg 2012 on such creative orthography as an online practice). For Blommaert (2008: 7), such misspellings manifest heterography, the "deployment of graphic symbols in ways that defy orthographic forms."

Heterography is a characteristic feature of "grassroots literacy," or aberrant forms of writing produced by individuals who do not have access to advanced literacy resources. In *Spiaking Singlish*, however, heterography becomes a tool to choreograph the "look," or poetics, of a grassroots literacy, one indexically associated with Singlish-using heartlanders (see the discussion of the heartlander/cosmopolitan divide in Chapter 1). According to this view, what is significant about *Spiaking Singlish* is the identity work it does through Singlish. As suggested earlier, Singlish as rhetorically articulated in the book, with its disproportionately high concentration of Singlish-inflected syntax as well as lexis from Malay and Chinese dialects, is something of a caricature of Singlish as it is spoken on the streets. Gwee's metadiscourse, therefore, does not so much represent as it enregisters (Agha 2003, 2007; Johnstone et al. 2006) Singlish, weighting it with the noncosmopolitan, hence egalitarian, values that it is perceived to index, and standing it in diametrical opposition to Standard English, weighted with the "elitist" values of the establishment.

---

6. Other instances of invented transcriptions in the book, loosely based on Singlish pronunciation, include *fewl* (feel), *liddat* (like that), *lumber* (number), and *nemmind* (never mind).

7. I say the orthography is "apparent" because Singlish words have always been spelled according to convention (if they need to be spelled at all), and there are words for which the spelling remains unstable.

8. Sylvia Toh's *Goondu* series was a pioneer collection of colloquial, multilingual words commonly used in Malaysia and Singapore, published in two volumes in 1982 (as *Eh, Goondu!*) and 1986 (as *Lagi Goondu!*). The two volumes were combined and published as *The Complete Eh, Goondu!* by Marshall Cavendish in 2011.

The enregisterment of Singlish as a spoken vernacular to a heartlander ethos did not start with Gwee, whose intervention lies in capturing and accentuating the already enregistered value of Singlish in a *written* performance. The emergent indexical connection between Singlish and "local" identity has been noted in the literature. Alsagoff's (2010) cultural orientation model (COM) goes some way toward elucidating this connection. COM explains that acrolectal speakers in Singapore often vary their speech style between Singlish and Standard English to index their self-positioning within a local–global continuum. Identity work is performed "by negotiating and exploiting the multidimensional space defined by the contrast between these two contrapuntal cultural perspectives" (Alsagoff 2010: 343).

On the one hand, the use of linguistic resources indexically associated with Singlish "indicates a symbolic movement towards a local(ist) orientation that stresses sociocultural capital," invoking such values as "rapport, familiarity and intimacy" on the individual level and "group membership and the framing and positioning of community identity" on a collective level (Alsagoff 2010: 343). On the other hand, the use of features indexically associated with Standard English "indicates a symbolic shift towards a global(ist) orientation, stressing economic capital"; it represents "formality, authority and distance" on an individual scale and "institutionalism and economic power" on a collective scale (Alsagoff 2010: 344).

Alsagoff's COM thus postulates that the Singlish–English continuum correlates with the local–global continuum, where "[t]he degree to which features of each of the referential varieties is focused on depends on the degree to which speakers wish to signal these values or practices" (Alsagoff 2010: 344). Leimgruber (2013, following Eckert 2008) extends the COM toward an indexical model, reimagining "local" and "global" orientations as indexical fields comprising various stances. For example, the local is affiliated with such attributes as "closeness," "community membership," "friendly," "informal," "rude," and so forth, while the global signals such values as "important," "serious," "distance," "formal," "authority," and so forth (106).

Unlike the COM, the indexical model does not assume that Singapore English utterances are identifiable as leaning toward either the Singlish or the Standard English side of a continuum. Rather, it considers features prototypically associated with Singlish or Standard English as resources that can be mobilized in tandem to index certain stances in response to contingent circumstances. Hence, in producing an utterance, a speaker would first determine the stance they wish to express, then locate relevant features from the available linguistic resources that match the chosen stance, and finally mobilize these features in the act of speaking to perform the stance (Leimgruber 2013: 107). According to this view, one can invoke specific features in speech as performative resources to project particular stances.

What these two models reveal for us is that it no longer suffices to simply see Singlish and Standard English as being in a static diglossic relationship, where the two are functionally labeled low and high varieties, respectively (Gupta 1994), or to understand them as sociopragmatically distributed according to differential levels of proficiency in English and degrees of formality (Pakir 1991). Rather, we must think of language use as a nuanced indexical operation pointing to gradations of cultural orientations and social stances on the part of its users. More specifically, formal features from the Singlish–English spectrum can be consciously or subconsciously activated as resources for identity work on different scales. Moving from speech to writing, the brand of grassroots literacy witnessed in *Spiaking Singlish* has the same performative potential, where linguistic resources from demotic idioms are stylized into a rhetorical register indexing a decidedly localist, noncosmopolitan stance.

**Enregistering Singlish: Indexical orders**

On the question of indexicality, Johnstone et al.'s (2006) study of Pittsburghese, a dialectal variety frequently used in southwestern Pennsylvania, provides a comparative case. Drawing on Silverstein's (2003) indexical orders, Johnstone et al. investigate several layers of social meaning generated by Pittsburghese, postulating three indexical orders. First-order indexicality comes into being when formal features of speech become associated—by linguists, not by the speakers themselves—with sociodemographic identity. For example, the monophthongal /aw/ is found to be an "indicator" (Labov 1971) of speech variation among working-class men from Pittsburgh.

The correlation between linguistic form and social meaning on this first order can then be abstracted to form a second-order indexical. This is where speakers themselves begin to interpret formal features in their speech as "markers" (Labov 1971) of ascribed social meanings or to perform (or refrain from performing) those features to enact their attendant social meanings. For example, given the first-order indexical that the monophthongal /aw/ is associated with working-class males (as specified by linguists), speakers from Pittsburgh may employ this phonetic feature more audibly to play up a working-class ethos, or less audibly to portray a more cosmopolitan outlook (Johnstone et al. 2006: 83).

Most important for our purpose is third-order indexicality, which comes about when people make conscious connections between formal features typically associated with a language variety and a locale-specific identity. In the case of Pittsburghese, the monophthongal /aw/ turns into a third-order indexical when "it gets 'swept up' into explicit lists of local words and their meanings and reflexive performances of local identities, in the context of widely circulating discourse about the connection between local identity and local speech" (Johnstone et al. 2006: 84).

On this third indexical order, features from Pittsburghese are proactively appropriated, often "in ironic, semiserious ways" (Johnstone et al. 2006: 83), for their entrenched connections with a place, in this case Pittsburgh. This has resulted in metadiscursive practices and artifacts "that have enregistered local speech in the local imagination as unique and unchanging," reinforcing, indeed stereotyping (Labov 1971), "the ideological links between local speech and place" (Johnstone et al. 2006: 94). These include, for example, articles in local newspapers describing phonological, lexical, and grammatical features seen as distinctive to Pittsburghese, with a view to piquing "local curiosity about local speech" (95). Further developments included attempts to construct an aura of legitimacy around Pittsburghese by coopting expert testimonies from dialectologists. Also witnessed were the rise of vernacular publications, including folk dictionaries like *Sam McCool's New Pittsburghese: How to Speak Like a Pittsburgher* (96) and websites like www.pittsburghese.com, devoted to engaging young adults in "folk-lexicographic activity" pertaining to Pittsburghese (97).

The sociohistorical background against which Singlish has evolved is very different from that surrounding Pittsburghese. Yet the two share the common destiny of being enregistered to index locality (and to some extent, a working-class identity), leading to their commodification in marketing contexts, as exemplified in both Pittsburghese and Singlish T-shirts (see Chapter 6). *Spiaking Singlish* can be seen as a "folk-lexicographic activity" participating in such commodification, similar in nature to Sam McCool's folk dictionary. Johnstone et al.'s analysis thus offers a useful framework to postulate the indexical trajectories navigated by Singlish. Table 4.1 summarizes the three indexical orders of Singlish modeled on the case of Pittsburghese, although such comparison in no way suggests that their historical paths are parallel.

As a first-order indexical, Singlish has long been studied as a linguistic curiosity, with scholars (some of whom are nonspeakers of the variety) undertaking fine-grained analysis of its formal features.[9] Early studies (Platt 1975, 1977) tend to see these features as intrinsic to the hybrid language situation in Singapore and as emblematic of the relatively low levels of education and disadvantaged socioeconomic status of its speakers. On this order, the potential of Singlish to index sociodemographic attributes (i.e., relatively less educated or cultivated Singaporeans) is established as a matter of intellectual

9. These include, inter alia, studies on phonetics/phonology (e.g., consonant clusters [Anttila et al. 2008]; monophthong vowels [Deterding 2003], or consonant deletion [Starr 2019]); prosody (Deterding 2001; Lim 2009b); grammar/syntax (e.g., reduplication of nominal modifiers [Wong 2004]; the Singlish passive *kena* [Bao and Wee 1999]; see also Bao 2015; Lim 2004); lexis (e.g., *until* [Bao and Wee 1998], *must* [Bao 2010]; *ownself* [Wee 2007]); and pragmatics (e.g., particles [Wee 2003b, 2010], and in particular, sentence-final particles [Wee 2002, 2009; Wong 2005]). For a comprehensive bibliography on these aspects (up to 2009), see Lim et al. (2010: 288–96).

**Table 4.1** INDEXICAL ORDERS: PITTSBURGHESE AND SINGLISH COMPARED

| Pittsburghese (based on Johnstone et al. 2006: 82–83) | Singlish |
|---|---|
| **First-order indexicality** | **First-order indexicality** |
| Variant features of English are found to have sociodemographic correlations, namely, that their speakers are predominantly working-class males from southwestern Pennsylvania, and especially from Pittsburgh. Such correlations represent an unmarked way of speaking, and are not discernible to the "socially nonmobile speakers in dense, multiplex social networks." | Certain phonological, lexical, or morphosyntactic features of speech come to be recognizable—by linguists, for instance, but not by speakers themselves—as correlated to speakers from Singapore. At this early stage, Singaporeans do not perceive their own speech features as marked, because they do not come into frequent contact with variant ways of speaking English due to relative immobility, both socially and geographically. |
| **Second-order indexicality** | **Second-order indexicality** |
| Speakers from Pittsburgh begin to appreciate the distinctiveness of their variety. They attribute social meaning to formal features perceived to evoke Pittsburghese and are able to manipulate their speech styles to produce identity effects (e.g., community membership with working-class males). These effects should be seen in relation to "ideologies about class and correctness." Pittsburghese "can also be linked with locality by people who have had the 'localness' of these forms called to attention." | Formal features of Singlish are recognized by speakers to be evocative of a place- or class-based identity, as distinct from Standard English. Those features are activated in speech to tactically perform social work, as when acrolectal speakers of English deliberately shift into a colloquial register to index distance from the cosmopolitan and camaraderie with the heartlander; or, especially when overseas, to create affective bonds with fellow Singaporeans. At the same time, Singlish is enregistered by authorities as an inferior variety of English that results in social immobility. |
| **Third-order indexicality** | **Third-order indexicality** |
| People draw on "the increasingly widely circulating idea that places and dialects are essentially linked (every place has a dialect)" to proactively construct and essentialize the correlation between Pittsburghese and local identity. Highly codified lists of linguistic features associated with Pittsburghese exist and are appropriated by Pittsburghers and non-Pittsburghers alike to "perform local identity, often in ironic, semiserious ways." | Speakers and writers capitalize on the correlation between Singlish and local identity (established on the second indexical order) to produce rhetorical, ludic performances of Singlish. The object of such performances is to disrupt the hegemony of English by foregrounding the autonomy of Singlish as a stylized, not aberrant, way of speaking or writing. |

interest. That potential has not been taken up by the speakers themselves (i.e., the persons-in-the-culture) to actively instantiate a place- or class-based identity.

On the second order of indexicality, phonological and lexicogrammatical features associated with Singlish on the first order are taken up by speakers to mark their identity as "locals," thereby delineating ingroup/outgroup membership. Thus, as Alsagoff's COM and Leimgruber's indexical model tell us, speakers slide between Singlish and English to express an orientation along the local–global spectrum and, more specifically, mobilize formal features associated with Singlish (and in contrast to Standard English) to index particular stances—for instance, attaching Singlish particles to the end of their utterances to index friendliness or intentionally "relaxing" their spoken grammar to tune in to informal settings (Pakir 1991).

Yet on this order of indexicality, Singlish departs from Pittsburghese in that it is concurrently stigmatized by the state as a "broken" variety of English (Wee 2016b: 49), one that impairs children's acquisition of Standard English and interferes with the nation's participation in the global economic order. Language labels such as "broken English" are markers of enregisterment (Møller and Jørgensen 2011). Thus, by systematically labeling Singlish "broken English," official discourses enregister Singlish as a low-proficiency version of English and a hindrance to the nation's path toward globalization.

On the basis of second-order indexicality, third-order indexicality emerges in metadiscursive practices and artifacts that appropriate Singlish, often in jest, to reflexively flaunt a place- or class-based identity. These practices and artifacts stereotype formal features of Singlish, stabilizing and essentializing their indexical potential in connection with an imagined construct of "Singaporeanness" in opposition to a cosmopolitan Singaporean identity espoused by the state. On this order, Singlish can be invoked to activate "a nostalgic sense of belonging and a youthful sense of urban hipness," as Johnstone (2010: 399) says of Pittsburghese. Such valorization of Singlish as metonymic of an "authentic" Singaporean identity is often performed with ironic intent, as with *Spiaking Singlish*, serving as a ludic corrective to state discourses that censure Singlish as an aberrant version of English.

### Singlish as fetish

Referring to Table 4.1, *Spiaking Singlish* can be seen as operating on the third indexical order: it is a rhetorical deployment of Singlish based on its preexisting use (on the level of second-order indexicality) to index mundane, as opposed to cosmopolitan, sensibilities. In other words, prior usage of Singlish as the default medium to encode a heartlander ethos is reinscribed to articulate a metacultural discourse on a higher order of indexicality.

That discourse, as mentioned earlier, is resistant and antiestablishment and agitates against official language policy by amplifying the distinctiveness and autonomy of Singlish. This critical stance is premised on a two-pronged enregisterment on the second indexical order. On the one hand, Singlish is invested with the perception of rustic vitality thanks to the many colloquialisms in its repertoire—mostly sourced from Hokkien, Singapore's most dominant Chinese dialect. According to this account, it bears a strong association with an imagined authenticity based on what is perceived as "low-brow" culture. On the other hand, as we will examine in more detail below, official narratives have maintained the consistent line that Singlish is the inferior cousin of Standard English since at least the late 1990s. Due to its enregisterment by the authorities as "broken" English, Singlish is driven underground, as it were, effaced from official representations of multilingualism and branded a subterranean variety indexing unsophisticated personalities and noncosmopolitan outlooks. In this regard, Singlish parallels Pittsburghese, where "the same features that are in some situations, by some people, associated with uneducated, sloppy, or working-class speech can, in other situations and sometimes by other people, be associated with the city's identity, with local pride and authenticity" (Johnstone 2009: 160).

It is on this basis that we should appreciate *Spiaking Singlish* as a language ideological intervention on the third indexical order. As an ostensible "companion to how Singaporeans communicate," it is Singapore's answer, in terms of its folk-lexicographic genre, to Johnstone et al.'s (2006: 96) example of *Sam McCool's New Pittsburghese: How to Speak Like a Pittsburgher*. Like the "highly codified lists" that exist in respect of Pittsburghese (Johnstone et al. 2006: 83), *Spiaking Singlish* seeks to acquire legitimacy for Singlish by creating an impression of consistency regarding its words, sounds, structures, and orthography (see Johnstone et al. 2006: 96). As Gwee clarifies, part of the contribution of his book is "to see whether Singlish can be written long-long [in long form] and with intelligence anot ['or not']" (Gwee 2018: 15) by attending to standardizing, spelling, and sentence structures.

Gwee's moves should not be interpreted as a metadiscursive regimentation (Makoni and Pennycook 2007: 2) of the vernacular, that is, as the consolidation of a "grassroots" tongue to a binding framework. Indeed, that kind of regimentation is precisely what *Spiaking Singlish* is pushing against.[10] His tactics, including his uptake of the term "Singlish" rather than, say, "Singapore English," in the book title, need to be understood as the enregisterment of

10. Pennycook and Otsuji (2019b: 90) argue that the notion of enregisterment allows us to appreciate the flexible uptake of language labels by ordinary speakers in ways that often diverge from how linguists use the same labels. They therefore call for linguists to "be wary of assuming that such labels necessarily imply degrees of fixity" and "not to make top-down assumptions about the meanings behind language labels."

Singlish to romanticize an egalitarian identity and codify a nonconformist stance. They are conceived to subvert the more powerful frame of Standard English (and, as a corollary, the government's definition of Singlish as "broken English"), which has long served as an official point of reference from which to evaluate Singlish. Hence, to turn Singlish into a lexicographic project is to undertake a radical, experimental response to the normativizing force of Standard English, in order to *potong a way to a lagi tok kong Singlish* "to carve out a path toward a more potent Singlish" (Gwee 2018: 15).

With his stylized, scripted, and metalinguistic performance of Singlish, Gwee can be said to position himself as a "legitimate contributor," as opposed to a "passive consumer," of English as it evolves in the Singapore context (Wee 2016b: 58). To borrow Bauman and Brigg's (1990) formulation, Gwee is affording himself the authority to perform Singlish "such that [his] recentering of it counts as legitimate" (77). Drawing on the Singlish lexicon as a resource to project a locale-based identity and to engage official language discourses in a provocative way, he effectively transforms Singlish from a spoken variety through a social language (Gee 2001) into a discursive style (Wee 2016b: 51). Singlish, in other words, becomes a fetish, its oral–aural idiosyncrasies (rather than its visuality; Kelly-Holmes 2014) objectified into a curiosity for voyeuristic interest and into an affective register invoking grassroots sensibilities.

In this regard, Gwee demonstrates what Wee (2018: 79) calls "linguistic chutzpah"—a linguistic "confidence that is backed up by meta-linguistic awareness and linguistic sophistication, giving the speaker the ability to articulate, where necessary, rationales for his or her language decisions." More precisely, Gwee embodies Wee's (2016b: 58) ideal user of English in Singapore, who can "confidently engage in informed metadiscourses about evolving linguistic standards and appropriateness which may serve as a fundamental resource for contesting the hegemonic construct of the traditional native speaker."

Yet Gwee goes even further: he rejects outright the proposition that Singlish is even a variety of English, claiming that Singlish and English are only occasionally similar: "The two are, in fact, macam ['as though'] apples and oranges—and becoming more and more so" (Gwee 2018: 16). This apples-and-oranges theory overstates the autonomy of Singlish, but that overstatement is itself telling of the book's militancy vis-à-vis language doxa. It corroborates Gwee's performance of an *extreme* Singlish, a radical version of what might be called empirical Singlish—that which is used on the streets.

It is here that Singlish, in my view, has a more political edge. The articulation of an extreme Singlish essentializes the correlation between (vernacular) language and (grassroots) identity. It makes an oral–aural fetish out of Singlish and uses that as a sardonic response to the state's long-standing enregisterment of Singlish as an aberrant offshoot of multilingualism and its valorization of Standard English as an orthodox language. Hence, the agenda of *Spiaking Singlish* is not merely to provide infotainment; it is to scandalize the language bureaucracy represented by Standard English by way of a marked Singlish, which exoticizes a street tongue into a transgressive counterlanguage. All delivered in a nonserious tone, as part of an overall ludic choreography that mocks the technocratic standoffishness of Standard English.

## THE POLITICAL ECONOMY OF WRITING SINGLISH

*Spiaking Singlish* is more than just an exemplar of linguistic iconoclasm. The entextualization of Singlish resources in a written performance speaks to wider contexts of engagement between Singlish proponents and the language establishment. Bauman and Briggs (1990: 76) maintain that an account of textual performativity entails "the political economy of texts" with an eye to illuminating "problems of broader concern." At issue is how entextualization raises questions of power and legitimacy:

> To decontextualize and recontextualize a text is thus an act of control, and in regard to the differential exercise of such control the issue of social power arises. More specifically, we may recognize differential access to texts, differential legitimacy in claims to and use of texts, differential competence in the use of texts, and differential values attaching to various types of texts. All of these elements, let us emphasize, are culturally constructed, socially constituted, and sustained by ideologies. (Bauman and Briggs 1990: 76)

As noted earlier, the vernacular choreography of *Spiaking Singlish* decontextualizes Singlish resources from their everyday environments and recontextualizes them in a stylized discourse. In so doing, its author is claiming a legitimacy in his Singlish writing, based on his linguistic chutzpah, in a way that promotes its efficacy as a medium of written communication. As we will see in the next section, this legitimacy has not gone unchallenged, notably by the establishment, which holds a completely different set of values in respect of Singlish. Herein lies the discursive contestation over who—the institution or the individual—controls the social valuation of Singlish. But we also have to ask what kinds of individuals can write *in* Singlish, and what kind can write *for* Singlish (see Wee 2018: Ch. 4).

### Gwee's polemic

To appreciate the political economy of *Spiaking Singlish*, we need to draw out several layers of backstories, unraveling the tensions around vernacular languages in general and Singlish in particular. The first of these involves a polemic between Gwee and the press secretary to Singapore's prime minister.

On May 13, 2016, two years before the publication of *Spiaking Singlish*, Gwee published an op-ed in the *New York Times* (NYT), titled "Politics and the Singlish language," later retitled (for unknown reasons) in its online version as "Do you speak Singlish?" (Gwee 2016). The original title signals the antiestablishment intent of the piece, alluding as it does to George Orwell's 1946 essay "Politics and the English language" and pronouncing Singlish as a "language" (without scare quotes), which, in the Singapore context, is to strike the nerve of official language policy at its core.

Although Gwee is against Singlish being turned into "Singapore's most political language" and seeming "to thrive on codifying political resistance" (Gwee 2016: n.p.),[11] he also partakes of this alleged politicization through his response to the establishment. The NYT op-ed manifests how Gwee himself intentionally positions Singlish against the government's language policy, making a case for Singlish to be vindicated from the negative press it has received from the establishment. The piece opens provocatively with a war metaphor: "Is the government's war on Singlish finally over? Our wacky, singsong creole may seem like the poor cousin to the island's four official languages, but years of state efforts to quash it have only made it flourish. Now even politicians and officials are using it" (Gwee 2016: n.p.). Here, in his characteristic self-deprecatory tone ("wacky, singsong creole" and "poor cousin"), Gwee sets the stage by positioning Singlish as an underprivileged, victimized language that proliferates in the face of state oppression. Such positioning belies and reifies the dichotomy between Singlish and the state, which Gwee is purportedly against.

Further witness how Gwee systematically entrenches the war metaphor in his arguments (Gwee 2016):

> Singlish, now *an enemy of the state, went underground*. But unlike the *beleaguered* Chinese dialects, it had *a trump card*: It could connect speakers across ethnic and socioeconomic divides like no other tongue could. . . .
>
> Singlish's status grew so powerful that the Chinese dialects *took refuge in it* to re-seed themselves.
>
> *The government's war on Singlish* was doomed from the start: Even state institutions and officials have nourished it, if inadvertently. The compulsory national service, which brings together male Singaporeans from all walks of life, has only underlined that Singlish is the natural lingua franca of the grunts. (n.p. [emphasis added])

11. In *Spiaking Singlish*, Gwee (2018: 21) complains about "how Singlish ownself ['itself'] kena politisai ['is politicized'], made to seem anti-Singapore or anti-Gahmen ['anti-government']."

Conceptual metaphor theory (Lakoff and Johnson 2003) tells us that metaphors provide us with a schematic frame within which we cognize our reality through ontological mappings and epistemological extensions. Thus, Gwee's war metaphor ontologically figures the Singapore government as an aggressor and Singlish as a guerrilla force ("an enemy of the state" that "went underground"). The epistemological implication is that Singlish is a democratic language of the masses ("the natural lingua franca") that needs to keep fighting to prevent itself from being "beleaguered" by the oppressive bureaucracy.

I stress the metaphoricity of Gwee's argument to underline the rhetorical nature of his polemic. It does not follow, however, that the general point he is making is untrue. The government has indeed installed structural policies and campaigns to discourage the widespread use of Singlish. Yet to say that this is tantamount to a war on Singlish is to evoke a pointed metaphor evincing a specific language ideology. That same metaphor is not attested in official discourses on Singlish; it is part of a rhetorical praxis. It discursively produces an asymmetrical and irreconcilable relationship between Singlish and the language establishment, with a view to eliciting empathy from readers for the former, construed by the establishment as an object of stigmatization.

This stigmatized status can in turn be leveraged and transformed into a resource for popular appeal. This is where Gwee expressly indexicalizes Singlish by imputing a countercultural value to it, resignifying it from a spoken vernacular into an ethical stance: "the more the state pushed its purist bilingual policy, the more the territory's languages met and mingled in Singlish. Through playful, day-to-day conversations, the non-official composite quickly became a formidable cultural phenomenon" (Gwee 2016: n.p.). Moreover, a generational element is introduced to reconfigure the act of speaking Singlish into an act of youthful defiance of authority: "And in the eyes of the young, continued criticism by the state made it the language of cool" (Gwee 2016: n.p.).

With this, Gwee turns Singlish into an emblem of the heteroglossic, young, vibrant, and chic; by implication, he also constructs the state's language policy as signifying the monoglossic, traditional, stifling, and out of sync. This imbues Singlish with a new set of indexical meanings to counteract those inherited from official discourses, a line Gwee would later take up in lexicographical form in *Spiaking Singlish*. In his effort to qualify Singlish as "a formidable cultural phenomenon" against institutional discourse, Gwee resignifies the perceived incorrectness of Singlish—with reference to Standard English, as always—into a *political* incorrectness, thus rendering the question of Singlish political through and through. For him, the fact that politicians and officials use Singlish is evidence that even the establishment cannot but succumb to the vibrancy of the vernacular, with the implication that the people's tongue must ultimately prevail: "Now even politicians and officials are using it"; "The tourism board can't help but showcase it as one of Singapore's few unique cultural creations"; "Finally grasping that this language is irrepressible, our leaders have begun to use it publicly in recent years" (Gwee 2016: n.p.).

The most political moment in the op-ed comes at its denouement, where Gwee cites what he calls a "blunder" made by none other than the prime minister himself. The blunder in question—ironically described as "a precious contribution to the [Singlish] lexicon"—was the prime minister's invocation in a national address of the putative local dish *mee siam mai hum* (Malay vermicelli noodles without cockles). As Gwee correctly points out, the noodle dish *mee siam* is never served with cockles to start with.[12] With this anecdote, Gwee presses the point that Singlish is unstoppable: the governing elites too, are coopting Singlish, albeit for instrumental reasons such as to enhance solidarity with a grassroots audience during election rallies; yet in so doing they amply demonstrate their failure to engage with language realities on the streets, hence leading to the prime minister's alleged Freudian slip, which (for Gwee) "happily became Singlish for being out of touch."

## The establishment hits back

The Prime Minister's Office was not amused. On May 23, 2016, ten days after Gwee's op-ed was published, Chang Li Lin, then press secretary to the prime minister, retaliated with her own op-ed in the NYT, titled "The reality behind Singlish" (Chang 2016). Chang's profile meant her opinion represented the position of Singapore's highest office, with local media reporting the controversy the following day.[13]

In her short rejoinder, Chang first maintains that Gwee's article "makes light" of government efforts to promote Standard English among Singaporeans, insisting that there is "a serious reason" behind such efforts, implying the frivolity of Gwee's argument. Chang then proceeds to explain the importance of Standard English to Singaporeans' livelihoods and to effective communication among Singaporeans as well as between Singaporeans and the global community of English speakers. Taking a pedagogical line, she maintains that learning English requires "extra effort" on the part of the majority of Singaporeans, for whom English is not a mother tongue, and that Singlish may further impede such efforts (a template argument used by the authorities

12. It could be that the prime minister meant to reference *laksa*, another local delicacy usually served with cockles; alternatively, he could have intended to say *mee siam mai hiam* (Malay vermicelli noodles without chili), mispronouncing *hiam* as *hum*.

13. Rachel Au-Yong, "PM's press secretary rebuts NYT op-ed on Singlish," https://www.straitstimes.com/singapore/pms-press-secretary-rebuts-nyt-op-ed-on-singlish; The Independent, "Sharp sting from poet's op-ed—PM Lee's press secretary responds," http://theindependent.sg/sharp-sting-from-poets-oped-pm-lees-press-secretary-responds/.

since the late 1990s). The piece concludes with a sarcastic statement targeting Gwee: "Not everyone has a Ph.D. in English Literature like Mr. Gwee, who can code-switch effortlessly between Singlish and standard English and extol the virtues of Singlish in an op-ed written in polished standard English" (Chang 2016: n.p.).

What Chang points out in her closing remark is the paradox of Gwee's position, or the ethical dilemma of his promotion of Singlish. I mentioned earlier that Gwee resignifies Singlish into a wayward medium by weighting it with countercultural values ("the language of cool"). The underlying assumption is that Singlish speakers in general have the ability to maneuver the language in "day-to-day conversations" with such dexterity as to render it "playful" and "cool" (Gwee's words, cited earlier). Yet there is nothing inherently "playful" or "cool" about Singlish per se; those qualities are ideological constructs, manifested as rhetorical style (as in *Spiaking Singlish*). They do not inhere within the lexis or structures of the register as such but are performed into being; often it is only highly educated individuals who possess the metapragmatic knowledge and metalinguistic skills to perform Singlish as a third-order indexical.

This brings us to the question of who uses Singlish. Two groups of Singlish users can be identified (Wee 2016b: 49; Wee 2018: 15, 58, 85). One group comprises monolectal Singlish users who have little or no access to a comprehensive repertoire of Standard English, due to, inter alia, relative lack of education. The other group consists of highly educated individuals who can code-switch easily between Singlish and Standard English, whom Wee (2018: 101) calls the "Singlitterati": "a relatively closed circle of well-educated creative and artistic individuals who enjoy playing around with Singlish words and phrases and are keen to promote Singlish." Members of this latter group are able to deploy linguistic features conventionally associated with Singlish for identity work, such as to establish solidarity with the heartland, or, as in *Spiaking Singlish*, for metadiscursive work, such as to critique language policies.

In this regard, it is interesting to read Chang's sarcastic statement about Gwee's paradox against what Wee (2016b) says about the government's undifferentiated approach to Singlish users:

> By using the label "Singlish" in this manner [as "bad" or "broken" English], *the government is either unable or unwilling to distinguish* speakers who have little or no competence in Standard English (and thus speak a largely ungrammatical variety as their only variety of English) from speakers who are competent in Standard English (and who code-switch into a colloquial variety for strategic interactional purposes). (49 [emphasis added])

By stating that "[n]ot everyone has a Ph.D. in English Literature like Mr. Gwee, who can code-switch effortlessly between Singlish and standard English and extol the virtues of Singlish in an op-ed written in polished standard English," Chang disproves Wee's point: the government does in fact distinguish between these two groups of Singlish users. Indeed, Chang shows that the government is well aware of the importance "not to lose sight of the fact that speakers who confidently manipulate linguistic resources to perform . . . Singlish are socio-linguistically distinct from those who speak what might be categorized as ungrammatical English because they lack the ability to do otherwise" (Wee 2018: 85).

At issue here is the ethics of using Singlish from different ideological vantage points. Whereas Gwee seeks to articulate the use of Singlish toward a heartlander ethics, Chang advances the alternative ethical position that Singlish advocates, themselves highly competent users of Standard English, may lead less-proficient users of Standard English astray by distracting them with Singlish. This is the "interference claim" (Wee 2018: 84–88), a point of contention in Singlish debates.

Wee (2018: 11) observes that "[t]he rhetorical emphasis on Singlish as a builder of solidarity across all Singaporeans seems to ignore or at least downplay those cases of Singaporeans who are either unable or unwilling to speak Singlish." This seems to be the case with Gwee. In his bid to challenge government policies on Singlish, he assumes that Singlish users can generally deploy Singlish to ludic ("playful") effect or for countercultural purposes ("cool" by virtue of official censure). This disregards the fact that not all Singlish users operate on the third order of indexicality; monolectal speakers, in particular, use Singlish as a practical medium of communication, and it would be presumptuous to think of this group of Singlish users as consciously using Singlish rhetorically as "the language of cool" or to project a ludic, rebellious stance.

Given that Gwee celebrates the vernacular creativities and presumed egalitarianism of Singlish, his vision of Singlish is paradoxically romantic and elitist, premised as it is on users having a sufficiently high proficiency in English to proactively appropriate resources from Singlish to enact identity or political stances. His resignification of Singlish in the op-ed is therefore mythical in the Barthesian sense (Barthes 2012): it renders values such as playfulness and coolness apparently natural to the language itself when they are in fact ideological.

Gwee did not miss the opportunity to ride the wave of his own controversy. In *Spiaking Singlish*, he references the incident and cites Chang's rebuttal, self-derisively speaking of himself as *kena buak gooyoo* (being reprimanded; usually by someone in authority) for *sayanging* (caring for) Singlish (Gwee 2018: 20). In this light, *Spiaking Singlish* should be interpreted as an extension of the NYT op-ed episode. By making Singlish a metalanguage in his book, Gwee nullifies the paradox of "extol[ling] the virtues of Singlish" in a "polished standard English" in his op-ed, as alleged by Chang in her counter op-ed. The use of Singlish to sustain a book-length commentary about Singlish highlights its capacity to operate as a language "proper": just as Standard English can be used to represent the linguistic features of the English language in reference texts, so Singlish can be used in "talk about talk" as a full-fledged language, contrary to its officially imputed status as a subterranean tongue. According to this reading, the mischievous tone of the prose is crafted to match its meta-cultural intent; it affords the problem of Singlish a deliberately ludic touch, as though ironically alluding to Chang's charge that Gwee "makes light" of government efforts to promote English.

## Solidarities of Singlish

The NYT episode created ripples on social media, prompting like-minded individuals to write commentaries in support of Gwee in the aftermath[14] and others to rally behind the government.[15] Particularly striking is a blog post titled "Singlish vs Standard English: I say, RELAK, lah!" by Law Kim Hwee. In this post, Law comments on the NYT op-ed incident and embeds her riposte to Chang's op-ed. This riposte is stylistically distinctive and hence worth reproducing in full (Law 2016: n.p.):[16]

14. See, for instance, Bertha Henson, "Singlish/English: for peace and harmony," http://themiddleground.sg/2016/05/24/singlishenglish-peace-harmony/ Accessed June 2020; Nicholas Yong, "Gahmen, don't like that leh," https://sg.news.yahoo.com/comment-gahmen-dont-like-that-leh-090524923.html; Andrew Loh, "PA celebrated Singlish as part of national identity," http://theindependent.sg/pa-celebrated-singlish-as-part-of-national-identity/; Michael Cyssel Wee, "Singlish is not the enemy," http://themiddleground.sg/2016/06/03/singlish-not-enemy/; Benjamin Goh, "Singlish is recognized, but not by Singapore," https://www.theonlinecitizen.com/2016/05/30/singlish-recognized-not-singapore/; SM Ong, "Singlish debate redux: Dr Gwee Li Sui is the new Phua Chu Kang sia," https://smong.net/2016/05/singlish-debate-redux-gwee-li-sui-is.html; Limpeh Foreign Talent, "Don't use Singlish as the scapegoat!," http://limpehft.blogspot.com/2016/05/dont-use-singlish-as-scapegoat.html.

15. See, for instance, Marietta Koh, "Singlish must not be allowed to displace Standard English," https://www.straitstimes.com/forum/letters-in-print/singlish-must-not-be-allowed-to-displace-standard-english; G Joslin Vethakumar, "Singapore Right in Rebutting NYT Piece on Singlish," https://joslinv.wordpress.com/2016/05/24/singapore-right-in-rebutting-nyt-piece-on-singlish/.

16. My English rendition (square-bracketed notes added):

Hello, Ms Chang, why are you like that? Don't behave like shit [note: KNS stands for *kana sai* 'like shit']. Relax.

If you have something to say, couldn't you say it nicely? We can't tolerate government officials reprimanding our brother, okay? Do you think the government is so powerful? We are all Singaporeans. We can talk nicely.

You know, we are "one people, one nation, one Singapore" [note: alluding to a phrase from the chorus of a national song]. Do you know how we can be "one"? It's easy. If you are abroad, you can detect Singaporeans without a doubt based on their Singlish accent and their obsession with food.

Eh, hello, Ms Chang, why so liddat one? Don't be KNS, leh. Relak, lah!

Got something to say, say nicely, can or not? We no can tahan gahmen people tekan our bro, okay? Why? You think you gahmen so you are tok kong, ah? We all Singaporeans. Can sui sui talk one.

You know, huh, we one people, one nation, one Singapore. How we are "one", you know or not? Simple lah, you go outside country, when you hear how we talk (yah lah, yah lah, I mean our accent), the Singlish we spiak and oso siow about food—you know, cannot chabot. that one sure Singaporean!

So, when Lao Lee and the cheng hu talk and talk about "pledge ourselves as one united people," we the people already ourselves make our own way to become "one united people"—with SINGLISH!

Why not you gahmen so clever, make use of what we the people alleady doing to make us more united? But you, what they call you now—ELITE ah (ha! KNS!)—want to kill Singlish. Worse ah, now our hawker food all become so expensive, liddat we sure die, we sure cannot unite one!

You talk liddat in your letter, we go pengsan liao! Bo sui, bo sui!

So, please hor, Ah Lian (eh, your name Li Lin almost same like Li Lian), I say, RELAK, lah.

Here Law constructs an imagined community of Singlish proponents rallying against the government's denunciation: *We no can tahan gahmen people tekan our bro* (We cannot tolerate government officials reprimanding our brother). And within this imagined community, in which Gwee is defended as a "brother" (a comrade), Singlish serves as more than an idiosyncratic styling resource: it fosters a political solidarity.

Law expressly disagrees with Chang in particular and with the government that Chang represents more generally, but it is ultimately the materiality of the register that performs. This comes into relief when we consider that Law's piece, written in a stylized Singlish, is framed within and stylistically detached from a broader text, written in Standard English. The intentional contrast of registers creates a jarring effect, performing a visual–aural rupturing of an English discourse by Singlish from within.

Law's code-switching on the level of discourse could be meant as a critical response to Chang's point that "[n]ot everyone has a Ph.D. in English

Lee Kuan Yew and the government speak of "pledge ourselves as one united people." The fact is that we the "people" already have our own way of making ourselves "one united people"—with SINGLISH!

Why won't the government use what the people already have to make them "one united people"? Instead, you, the so-called ELITE (my foot!), want to kill Singlish. Worse, the food sold at hawker centres have become so expensive. At this rate we will surely die and not be united.

The way you write your letter makes us faint. It's not very nice at all.

So please, Ah Lian! (well, your name "Li Lin" sounds almost like "Li Lian") [note: Ah Lian means female gangsters in Hokkien/Singlish]. I say, relax!

Literature like Mr. Gwee, who can code-switch effortlessly between Singlish and standard English." Further evidencing this point, within her relatively short post, Law mentions twice that she does not possess a PhD in English Literature, showing her intent to answer Chang's sarcastic remark. More than that, it serves as a discursive metaphor for how bottom-up sensibilities can surreptitiously undercut top-down policy structures.

Yet, to my mind, Law does not at all resolve Chang's sarcasm. In fact, as someone who has "interacted and communicated with many colleagues and customers across USA, Europe and Asia" over a thirty-year career, and who "speak[s] and write[s] fairly decent English—and communicate[s] in Singlish as and when" (Law 2016: n.p.), Law clearly is a representative of the Singlitterati with a cosmopolitan outlook. Her eloquent code-switching act in the post may in fact bolster Chang's charge that Singlish advocates are promoting Singlish in disregard for people who may not have an adequate grasp of Standard English or be able to switch back and forth between the two registers.

For our purposes, what is important about Law's rejoinder is that it aligns with *Spiaking Singlish* in terms of rhetorical tactic, enabling us to contextualize Gwee's project within a larger constellation of Singlish-based practices. *Spiaking Singlish* is therefore not a singular instance of Singlish being enregistered for identity work; it is part of a counterhegemonic praxis within which Singlish becomes a method for social engagement. It represents a "cultural model of action," "functionally reanalysed" from an assemblage of "diverse behavioural signs" (Agha 2007: 55) that we have come to call Singlish. This transformation from linguistic signs to social action was triggered by a further layer of ideological context: the SGEM.

## THE SGEM AND ITS COUNTERMOVEMENTS

The SGEM marked a threshold event in Singapore as far as language is concerned. It is Singapore's answer to Britain's "great grammar crusade" in the late 1980s (Cameron 2012: 78–115), hence an exemplification of verbal hygiene. The genesis of the movement can be traced back to a 1999 National Day rally speech by then-Prime Minister Goh Chok Tong.[17] In a section of that speech devoted to English use, Goh argued for the promotion of English over Singlish on several interrelated grounds, which I summarize as follows:

a. *Pedagogy*: that learning Singlish will get in the way of learning English, such that students "may end up unable to speak any language properly, which would be a tragedy."

17. National Day rally address by Prime Minister Goh Chok Tong on August 22, 1999, https://www.nas.gov.sg/archivesonline/speeches/record-details/773bbd69-115d-11e3-83d5-0050568939ad.

b. *Career opportunities*: that Singlish limits the career opportunities of individuals. This is the heartlander/cosmopolitan divide (Tan 2003: 758–59)
mentioned in Chapter 1, where Singlish is explicitly indexed as the language of the heartlanders and associated with occupations such as "taxi-
drivers, stallholders, provision shop owners, production workers and
contractors"; this stands in contrast to English: the language of the cosmopolitans, associated with the domains of "banking, IT, engineering, science
and technology."

c. *Global communications*: that using Singlish would impede communications between Singaporeans and the rest of the world, to whom Singlish is
"quaint but incomprehensible."

d. *National economy*: that by virtue of the perceived impenetrability of
Singlish, Singapore "cannot be a first-world economy or go global with
Singlish."

In this speech, Goh specifically targeted the sitcom figure Phua Chu Kang,
first mentioned in Chapter 1. Phua Chu Kang became hugely popular at the
time for his earthy humor and slangy Singlish talk, his most famous, and
most emulated, expression being *don't pray pray* (based on "don't play play"
or "don't fool around"). Goh turned Phua Chu Kang into a negative model of
what Singapore students should not aspire to be, maintaining that the character "has made the teaching of proper English more difficult." Goh said he had
asked the media company to "try persuading Phua Chu Kang [note: the character, not the actor himself, who speaks excellent English] . . . to improve his
English" by enrolling in English-language classes offered by the government.
It is unclear if Goh's last statement was meant in all seriousness, but the rec-
ommended change did happen: the sitcom subsequently altered its script to
have Phua Chu Kang learn English as part of the storyline. This move is liable
to interpretation as an act of self-correction on the part of the national media
in the face of pressures to fall in line with top-down language imperatives.

Phua Chu Kang will appear again in Chapter 6, but at this juncture I want to
point out a somewhat surprising parallel between Phua Chu Kang and Gwee
Li Sui. Both are competent English users; both perform Singlish in a stylized
and entertaining manner, albeit on different media; and both have been subject to criticism by a person of authority for allegedly promoting Singlish. In
this context, we can hypothesize that Gwee's writing is responding not just to
Chang Li Lin's op-ed in particular but also to a larger language ideological milieu defined by the SGEM more generally.

Prime Minister Goh's 1999 rally speech set the stage for the official launch
of the SGEM on April 29, 2000. In his speech at the launch ceremony,[18] he

18. Speech by Prime Minister Goh Chok Tong, at the launch of the Speak Good
English Movement on Saturday, April 2, 2000, at the Institute of Technical Education

rehashed the same arguments against Singlish, though in a slightly more acute rhetoric. Singlish was now defined as "a corrupted form of English" and indexicalized as a marker of lesser intelligence or competence. The goal of the SGEM was thus to enable the younger generation to "get a good grounding in English" so as not to be "condemned" to "a similar fate" as monolectal Singlish speakers from an earlier generation. Singaporeans are admonished not to see Singlish as "cool," or "to feel that speaking Singlish makes them more 'Singaporean.'" On the contrary, Singlish purportedly "reflects badly on us [Singaporeans] and makes us seem less intelligent or competent." In this connection, competent speakers should set a good example of using good English, for "[i]f they speak Singlish when they can speak good English, they are doing a disservice to Singapore."

Here again, it is interesting to read Gwee against Goh to appreciate the language ideological thrust of Singlish practices and discourses within wider statal narratives. Prime Minister Goh's exhortation against perceiving Singlish as a cool language and an emblem of local identity is flatly contradicted by Gwee—recall in particular his op-ed statement that "in the eyes of the young, continued criticism by the state made it the language of cool" (Gwee 2016: n.p.). Goh's statement that competent users of English would be "doing a disservice to Singapore" if they deliberately chose to use Singlish is echoed in Chang Li Lin's ironic statement that not every Singaporean is consummate in both Singlish and English.[19] And *Spiaking Singlish* exactly exemplifies the "disservice" that Goh speaks of, as though Gwee is offering himself up as the precise target of Goh's speech.

For over two decades, the SGEM has promoted English through a range of activities and artifacts (see Sim 2015 for an overview), with evolving themes targeting different sectors of society. During its initial years, the movement pitched Singlish as the diametrical opposite of English, with an objective "to help Singaporeans move away from the use of Singlish," according to an early mission statement on its official website (cited in Lim 2015: 264). This produced a zero-sum relation between Singlish and English that precluded any possibility of coexistence (Lim 2009a: 58). With this objective, the SGEM set itself up for failure, because, for the movement to be considered successful, Singlish would need to be wiped out from Singaporeans' repertoire—an impossibility (Wee 2018: 62).

(ITE) headquarters auditorium, https://www.nas.gov.sg/archivesonline/data/pdfdoc/2000042904.htm.

19. The same point is reiterated in several statements made by other senior politicians, notably Lee Kuan Yew, the first prime minister of Singapore, who in 1999 described Singlish as "a handicap we must not wish on Singaporeans," advising that "[t]hose Singaporeans who can speak good English should to help create a good environment for speaking English, rather than advocate, as some do, the use of Singlish . . ." (cited in Wee 2018: 80).

The SGEM has since changed its tack: according to its current mission state-ment, the SGEM now "recognizes the existence of Singlish as a cultural marker for many Singaporeans," while aiming to "help those who speak only Singlish, and those who think Singlish is English, to speak Standard English."[20] This milder and more nuanced position narrows the movement's target to mono-lectal users of Singlish. In so doing, it circumvents competent English users who appropriate Singlish as performative resources and avoids being doomed to failure at the outset by squaring off the promotion of "good English" with the annihilation of Singlish (Wee 2018: 62). SGEM's altered stance also sug-gests that the language authorities are both able and willing to differentiate these two categories of Singlish speakers (compare Wee 2016b: 49).

Be that as it may, Singlish is still an undesirable element for SGEM's over-arching aim to "create an environment of good English in Singapore,"[21] such that the dichotomy of Singlish versus Standard English remains very much intact. It is thus no surprise that the SGEM has stirred controversy since its inception.[22] It has also triggered resistant choreographies of multilingualism in Singapore, to which *Spiaking Singlish* is affiliated in form and spirit.

## TalkingCock.com

One prominent example is the online portal, TalkingCock.com, established by Colin Goh in August 2000, just a couple of months after the SGEM was inau-gurated. TalkingCock.com was Singapore's "first full-bore satirical website"[23] that published Singlish-based commentaries on local news and current affairs, with a strong countercultural slant. The website thus thrives on a linguistic chutzpah that plainly contradicts the aims of the SGEM, similar to that dem-onstrated by Gwee in his NYT op-ed and in *Spiaking Singlish*.

Several offshoots from the website are noteworthy for their transgressive intent. The most important of these is *The Coxford Singlish Dictionary* (here-inafter *Coxford*) by Colin Goh and Yen Yen Woo. *Coxford* is a portmanteau of "Oxford" and the Singlish word *cock* (ridiculous, stupid). The parody is multi-modal: the book cover shows an image of a cock (the animal) and an invented coat of arms in the shape of Oxford University's but inserted with images of a cock and a computer, among other things.

Originating on TalkingCock.com as a crowdsourced endeavor to gather definitions and illustrations of Singlish usage, the dictionary was published

20. https://www.languagecouncils.sg/goodenglish/about-us.
21. https://www.languagecouncils.sg/goodenglish/about-us.
22. For critiques of the SGEM, see Rubdy (2001), Chng (2003), Bokhorst-Heng (2005), Lim (2009a), Gupta (2010), Bruthiaux (2010), and Wee (2005, 2018: 61–64, 72n.1).
23. http://colingoh.com/project/talkingcock-com/.

in hardcopy by Angsana Books in 2002, with a second edition in 2009. Marketed as the "funniest and most complete guide to Singaporean vernacular English available" (book cover), it prides itself as the first attempt to "[catalogue Singlish] in a systematic manner," to "document the constantly-evolving patois, as well as provide a comprehensive guide to its usage in a way that celebrated, rather than condemned, it" (Goh and Woo 2009: xiv). It recalls the folk-lexicographic activities associated with the enregisterment of Pittsburghese (Johnstone et al. 2006: 97) and was a generic precedent for the form that *Spiaking Singlish* would eventually adopt.[24]

The main section of *Coxford* is written dictionary-style (A–Z) with numerous items from the Singlish lexicon, each with a pronunciation guide in mock-IPA (International Phonetic Alphabet) style, a definition or explanation (in Standard English), and an example sentence with an English gloss. To illustrate, the following is the entry for *cockanaden*, to which the title of the book is etymologically related:

> **cockanaden** | kok-ker-nah-duhn | A somewhat vulgar way of describing someone as very stupid or addled. Although the word is a combination of "cock" (see above) and "naden" (a common pronunciation of the Tamil name "Nathan"), its use is not restricted to any particular race.
>
> *Ah Beng: "Eh, where to find the Lim Peh Ka Li Kong column in the TalkingCock website, ah?" (Hey, where can I find the Lim Peh Ka Li Kong column in TalkingCock. com?)*
>
> *Ah Seng: "Under 'Columns' lah, you cockanaden!" (Under "Columns", you moron!)*
> (Goh and Woo 2009: 69)

By explaining what *cockanaden* means in Singlish (with reference to the root word *cock*), the entry reveals the ludicity of the book's title, with the example sentence taking a metadiscursive turn on the TalkingCock website to which the dictionary is affiliated. Also featured is a "Singlish for the Traveller" section that parodies tourist guides in providing handy Singlish words for a range of purposes ("Meeting and Greeting," "At the Hawker Centre or Coffeeshop," "At the Doctor's," "Romance," and so forth).

The second edition injects an additional dose of mischief with a "P.S.L.E.: Powderful Singlish Language Examination" appended at the end, playing on the acronym of the Primary School Leaving Examination familiar to all Singaporeans. The semiotics of this mock exam give rise to what may be called "subversive nostalgia" for Singaporeans of older generations. Written in a basic, typewriter font on a tinted, coarse-looking paper, this "exam

---

24. *Coxford* was not the first book in this genre. It was preceded and probably inspired by Sylvia Toh Paik Choo's *Goondu* (stupid) series, published in 1982 and 1986 (Toh 2011).

paper" mimics the materiality of test papers of yesteryear, complete with the standard format comprising MCQs and cloze passages. The nostalgic form is fully subverted by the content, with the personal information section asking for "secret society" and "kind of tattoo" (playing on how Singlish is indexically linked with a low level of education and cultivation in the public imagination); ludic instructions to candidates written in Singlish (*This booklet got many pages; You better follow what we say. If not skarly you get jilo, then you know!*); and all the questions written in Singlish and testing one's proficiency in Singlish vocabulary and grammar (for instance, a grammar cloze passage tests the use of sentence-final particles *hor, lah, meh, man*, etc.).

At this point we should note the generic similarities between *Coxford* and *Spiaking Singlish*. Gwee's companion features longer commentaries for fewer items, but in terms of its formal features (e.g., the lexicographical setup and the Singlish quiz) and ludic concept, it may have been influenced by *Coxford*, especially given that its authors are named by Gwee in his book as his admired predecessors in Singlish writing (Gwee 2018: 13).

TalkingCock.com also saw the birth of an initiative called the Society for the Preservation of Authentic Singlish (SPAS), which came with a manifesto challenging the government's premises for prohibiting the use of Singlish in TV programs. The SPAS was probably triggered by the Phua Chu Kang incident in 1999, which led to the state-affiliated media's self-correction over their liberal use of Singlish in the sitcom.

Turning the tables, the SPAS manifesto asks: "Why not ask the ang-mors ['Caucasians'] to speak like us? What makes them so atas ['snobbish']?." Suggesting that TV characters who use Standard English are *bleddy chia'h kantang* drama club types (bloody Asians speaking with a fake Western accent, typical of those who enrol in drama clubs in schools) who do not speak "like normal people," it comes to the conclusion that the authorities are ultimately more interested in selling TV shows to foreign markets than in serving a local audience. The manifesto then proceeds to defend Singlish, drawing parallels with Cockney in respect of Londoners and Scouse in respect of Liverpudlians, stating that "Singaporeans are not so stupid that we cannot tell the difference between the kind of language acceptable in casual settings and the kind expected in business or official correspondence." The question is then raised as to why Singlish is censured in the local media while TV shows from the United States featuring Americanisms continue to be imported, with the insinuation that such double standards indicate a lack of self-confidence and a self-imposed colonialism. The manifesto ends with a call to arms: "Singlish is a language that is unique to us and we should celebrate it."[25]

---

25. The manifesto was originally available on TalkingCock.com but is no longer accessible. A transcript of the manifesto is cited in Mullany and Stockwell (2015: 172–73). Bracketed translations and explanations are mine.

The SPAS is part of a campaign called Save Our Singlish! (SOS), initiated under the aegis of TalkingCock.com on April 27, 2002, as a bottom-up response to the perceived siege of Singlish by the SGEM. In his speech at the campaign's launch, Colin Goh recapitulated the arguments made in the SPAS manifesto but used a more serious diction in calling for action from the authorities.[26] At the outset, he claimed that the SOS is "not the Speak Good Singlish campaign. It's the SAVE our Singlish campaign" (cited in Wee 2005: 59 [capitalization in original]). (The invocation of "Speak Good Singlish," as a then nonexistent theme, uncannily heralds the SGSM, which appeared eight years later; see discussion in the next section, The Speak Good Singlish Movement.) The SOS campaign proceeded to emphasize that it is not against SGEM objectives. "We are NOT anti-English. We completely support the speaking and writing of good English," Colin Goh declared in his speech, adding that his campaign sought to become a complement to rather than adversary of the government's pro-English movement (Wee 2005: 59 [capitalization in original]). This move was intended to preempt accusations that the SOS is "anti-English."

The SOS is thus geared toward a Singlish defensive, and only as far as mainstream media is concerned: "We're not asking you to switch to teaching Singlish in school as a subject. We're just saying, don't try to wipe out our culture by preventing it from being depicted on TV or radio" (Goh, cited in Wee 2005: 59). Distinguishing between Singlish and "broken English"—though the boundary between the two is not as clearly delineated as he makes it out to be—Colin Goh insists that Singaporeans "are intelligent enough to know we don't write formal letters in Singlish. When was the last time you typed out, 'Eh, give me a job, leh!' And we try not to speak Singlish to our foreign friends because we instinctively know that they might not understand" (cited in Wee 2005: 59). This takes us back to the ethics of promoting Singlish, where the existence of Singlish users who do not have the requisite linguistic resources to speak English at a proficient level often goes unacknowledged.

Underlying Colin Goh's statement is a crucial assumption: all Singlish users are also Standard English users. Bundled under the rubric of "Singaporeans," they are perceived as generally capable of code-switching between the two registers fluently. To his credit, Goh does make a qualification to the effect that if Singaporeans do mix up the two registers, that is, if they use Singlish in circumstances that require English and vice versa, "it's not because Singlish exists, but that we may not have been taught proper English" (cited in Wee 2018: 59–60). Still, this assumes a priori a speaker's ability to code-switch, which should not be taken as a default position across the board. Notwithstanding this, the SPAS and the SOS campaign represent a milestone in language advocacy in

26. Part of this speech appears in slightly reworded form in Colin Goh's introduction to the first edition of *The Coxford Singlish Dictionary*, published with Y. Y. Woo.

Singapore, directly critiquing official policies and making pointed recommendations in respect of Singlish.[27]

## The Speak Good Singlish Movement

A second milestone was made several years later by the SGSM, a Facebook initiative established on September 11, 2010, immediately after the launch of the 2010 run of the SGEM (Wee 2018: 81). Compared to the SOS campaign, the SGSM has a broader remit. Not restricted to mainstream media, it pursues a more ambitious tactic in not simply asking for official restrictions on Singlish to be relaxed but in also proactively using Singlish performatively in social media as an antagonistic counterpoint to SGEM discourses. In doing so, the SGSM sets itself diametrically against the state's verbal-hygienic framework.

In its manifesto, aptly written in Singlish, the SGSM claims that it does not set itself against the SGEM.[28] Rather, it seeks to demystify popular misconceptions about and misappropriations of Singlish, namely, that Singlish is frequently equated to broken or bad English and associated with crassness and lack of education. Defending Singlish as a language "full of culture, of nuances and wordplay" that "pulls together the swee-ness [the Hokkien word for 'beauty' suffixed with the English -ness] in the grammar, syntax, and vocabulary of so many languages," it chides Singlish haters for branding the language as "simple, shallow, and useless" while remaining ignorant about "the subtle rules of this natural evolving language."[29]

Despite the claim that it is not against the SGEM in principle, the SGSM is in fact a countermovement. As the founder said in an anonymous online interview, the Facebook group "is a result of that frustration with the regular raid on Singlish and its stigmatisation" (The Online Citizen 2010). The SGEM, at least in its early runs, surely represents a "raid on Singlish" with its anti-Singlish rhetoric. In an introduction to its website posted in 2009, the SGSM clearly shows its linguistic chutzpah: "Our Gahmen ['government'] has been damn siao on ['overly enthusiastic'], trying to tell us to speak good engrish ['English'], good chinese [sic]. This is the Facebook Singlish Speaker's Corner, let it all out my friends. Don't be paiseh ['embarrassed']."[30]

27. Namely, that "Singlish be allowed in TV, radio, films and all publications as a natural reflection of our dialogue"; and "the same censorship standards be applied to English and other language programmes as they are to Singaporean ones" (Colin Goh, cited in Wee 2005: 60).

28. In an interview with The Online Citizen, the founder of the SGSM states that "The Speak Good Singlish Movement isn't against the intentions of the Speak Good English Movement" (The Online Citizen 2010).

29. The quoted fragments here are taken from SGSM's manifesto as cited in Wee (2018: 82). The original manifesto is no longer accessible.

30. https://www.facebook.com/Speak-Good-Singlish-Movement-128281041371/.

In addition to the use of the pejorative term *siao on*, which denotes excessive efforts in undertaking an endeavor, the allusion to Speaker's Corner is important. This refers to a well-known, though underused, space in Singapore's Hong Lim Park, the first and only spot in the city where people can publicly voice their opinions—especially those that run counter to received wisdom or mainstream discourses—on social issues in a relatively free manner. SGSM's self-branding as a virtual Speaker's Corner thus suggests its propensity to weigh against official lines.

From this, one might ponder Gwee's connection to SGSM, whose founder has been in perpetual anonymity. According to Wee (2018: 82–83), "[e]xactly who the founders of the SGSM are is not clear," though he surmises that they probably had training in language studies or literature. Indeed, many of the posts on SGSM's Facebook site valorize Singlish, occasionally *in* Singlish, hence signaling "a high degree of self-conscious playfulness" (Wee 2018: 82). This is evident in the many postings on SGSM's now-archived Facebook site. It is here that we can see the metalinguistic performance in *Spiaking Singlish* as continuing a tradition of "talking about talk" on new and social media.[31]

In this light, it might be interesting to do a comparative reading of the introduction to *Spiaking Singlish* and two extant interviews with the anonymized SGSM founder, one with the e-news portal The Online Citizen (2010) and the other with the blogger Ms Demeanour Singapore (2011). Table 4.2 lays out several excerpts in which striking similarities (marked in bold) between the interview transcripts and the introduction to *Spiaking Singlish* can be identified in terms of rhetorical thrust and imagery (the "fishing village" reference is especially telling). The two sets of discourse are pegged at different registers, with the two online interviews transcribed in largely Standard English with a sprinkling of Singlish, and the introduction (as we already know) fully written in a stylized Singlish; the juxtaposition of relevant excerpts in Table 4.2 suggests that they can be read as parallel, intralingual translations.

Perhaps the anonymity of SGSM's founder is meant to put a veil of mystery around the vernacular movement to enhance reader interest. Given the sensitive (because it is stigmatized) position of Singlish within the language policy setup of Singapore, such anonymity could add a dramatic touch to the political incorrectness of pro-Singlish discourses, constructing them as potentially censorable. At any rate, what is important here is not the real face behind the anonymity of SGSM's founder but the discursive continuities between vernacular projects: SGSM continued the mandate of TalkingCock.com (and related projects) and set a fundamental tone for subsequent critical engagements around

31. Gwee's commentaries in *Spiaking Singlish* found their beginnings in the sociopolitical online portal *The Middle Ground* (https://themiddleground.sg/) accessed July 30, 2020, now defunct.

| Interviews with SGSM founder | Introduction to *Spiaking Singlish* |
|---|---|
| "Firstly, there is this crazy recurring idea that Singlish is guilty for the **drop in written and spoken English in Singapore**. Please lah OK! If English standards are down, isn't it more logical to **look to the schools?** If English is taught well, people will know how to use proper English and **can tell when they are speaking Singlish and when not**. By knocking Singlish, you still won't be improving anyone's English what [Singlish structure]! And it is not even that the rules of Singlish and the rules of English are same-same ['the same']. They are so different that **blaming poor English on Singlish is as good as blaming it on, say, Malay!**" (Ms Demeanour Singapore 2011) | "Then came the dark days once the Gahmen noticed how general **England proficiency got more and more kena sai** ['deteriorated']. I dunno whether **it relooked at teaching in schools** anot ['or not'], but a link was soon established between Singlish's huatness ['prosperity'] and England's lack of." (Gwee 2018: 18) "But, if you campur ['mix'] England ['English'] and, say, Melayu ['Malay'], **you can still tell what is England and what Melayu** because you *know* from school what each involves. So **why cannot** [Singlish structure: 'can't we'] **do the same for Singlish** ah?" (Gwee 2018: 22) |
| "Surely, you **improve someone's English proficiency by teaching the language to him or her better**. And, if the schools have been doing this job well, then there is nothing to fear from its speakers' casual code-switching. **They will do it anyway; if there were no Singlish, it would be Manglish, Hokkien, American slang**, J-pop, K-pop, Indi-pop, what have you." (The Online Citizen 2010) | "It seems obvious to unker ['uncle', here used as a first-person reference] that, **for England to huat** ['prosper'], **the sure way is to teach it better**, Whack Singlish for fiak ['f*ck'] since you **cannot stop people** from anyhowly ['doing this their own way']? **Without Singlish, they can still turn to other open colloquial forms such as street Hokkien or Melayu, American England** ['American English'], and internet lingo." (Gwee 2018: 22) |
| '[T]he gahmen ['government'] still runs around insisting that **the more Singlish you speak**, the worse your English becomes, and then **the economy will suffer. We may become a fishing village again**." (The Online Citizen 2010) "For them, if you speak Singlish, your English will automatically suffer . . . and, **in the long run**, [you will have] **helped throw Singapore back to a fishing village**." (Ms Demeanour Singapore 2011) | "For example, got those jokers ['ignorant people'] who think . . . **[t]he more Singlish is used, the more Singapore's international business climate will suffer** . . . **and then, ten years down the road, we're a fishing village again**." (Gwee 2018: 16 (ellipsis in original)) |

*Table 4.2* CONTINUED

| Interviews with SGSM founder | Introduction to *Spiaking Singlish* |
| --- | --- |
| "Secondly, to hold to the 'one language only' idea seems pretty bizarre, especially when it is coming from the same guys who brought us **institutional bilingualism** in Singapore. In fact, you can easily make a case for Singapore's bilingual policy being what turns Singaporeans into expert **code-switchers**." (The Online Citizen 2010) | "If you have multiculturalism and you have **institutionalised bilingualism**, then cannot stop languages from **chum-chumming** ['getting together'] liao." (Gwee 2018: 22) |
| "Those who complain that Singaporeans are uptight and **have no sense of humour** are also those who **aren't too excited about Singlish**." (The Online Citizen 2010) | "People who say Singaporeans **lack humour** and cannot ownself laugh at ownself ['laugh at oneself'] therefore **dunno or dun speak Singlish well lah**." (Gwee 2018: 21) |

Singlish, culminating in *Spiaking Singlish*. Within this lineage, the SGEM turns into a metonym for taylorist language apparatuses, against which intellectuals develop counterdiscourses through anti-SGEM initiatives.

In this context of the SGEM and its discontents, we can appreciate a figure that concludes the introduction to *Spiaking Singlish* (Gwee 2018: 26). Here Gwee, a graphic artist by profession, hijacks the SGEM logo and slogan to create an equivalent visual–verbal rubric for the fabricated "Spiak Good England and Singlish Movement." This is an instance of what Naomi Klein calls culture jamming, "the practice of parodying advertisements and hijacking bill-boards in order to drastically alter their images" (Klein 2000: 280), a practice seen by Baker (2019: 94) as "[p]erhaps the most radical form of genre-based subversion of dominant narratives." This figure taps into the same visual motif (a boxed slogan with scare quotes on a diagonal axis) and verbal formula (Speak XXX Movement) of the SGEM to "hack into a corporation's own method of communication to send a message starkly at odds with the one that was intended" (Klein 2000: 281).[32] In so doing, it evokes a fantastical scenario where Singlish

32. This is not the first instance of culture jamming in respect of SGEM's logo. Earlier attempts see "Singlish" being superimposed over "English" on the SGEM slogan; see https://www.theonlinecitizen.com/2010/09/17/"please-stop-hum-tumming-singl ish-just-leebit-alone"/ (accessed July 30, 2020). More recently, in 2019, a teenage blogger designed a series of mock posters parodying the SGEM theme, "Let's Connect" with the hashtagged #LetsKonek (where *"koneck"* approximates how "connect" is typically pronounced in Singlish) and also appropriating the SGEM logo into a SGSM logo. The posters feature a series of alliterative slogans referencing local neighborhoods, institutions (e.g., national service), personality types (e.g., gangsters and expatriates), and phenomena (e.g., prostitution): *Talk Cock from Clementi to Choa Chu Kang; Ah Bengs from Yishun to Yew Tee; Chao Keng from Tekong to Tengah; Ang Mohs from Farrer Road to*

is publicly promoted as a "movement" or campaign, while ironically meshing the notion of speaking good English (or *spiak England* in Singlish) into a Singlish-inflected frame. The outcome of this intersemiotic parody is a ludic—because impossible—counternarrative in which Singlish displaces English.

## CITIZEN SOCIOLINGUISTICS IN SINGAPORE

*Spiaking Singlish* traces a lineage of counterdiscourses emerging in response to top-down language management discourses, as epitomized by the SGEM. These counterdiscourses accrue into what Rymes (2020) calls *citizen sociolinguistics*. This term refers to online participatory practices where any individuals, with or without an academic background in sociolinguistics, converge on new or social media platforms to discuss the nitty-gritties of their patois or to comment on how people use the language. As the term "citizen" might suggest, citizen sociolinguistics emphasizes public participation and the agency of laypersons in talking about language matters based on their own practice, subjective observations, language intuition, and unique repertoire, although expert linguists are not excluded. This kind of networking is afforded and enhanced by social media, within which citizen sociolinguists exchange their views on linguistic features of interest to them. As a result of such interaction, which includes people posting videos on the pronunciation of street names or on the use of gender-neutral pronouns, "a diversity of viewpoints emerges, and disagreements tease out issues of genuine curiosity and concern" (Rymes 2020: 22). This fosters connectivity and community, though it can also lead to stereotyping and contestation.

In the case of Singapore, new and social media portals such as TalkingCock.com, the SGSM, and various blogs have given rise to proliferative Singlish-themed writing practices. Many of these practices are undertaken by individuals motivated to defend Singlish against institutional encroachment; they are "scaling practices in everyday discussions of language" (Rymes and Smail 2021: 441) that dovetail with critical, bottom-up narratives against official movements or campaigns. I do not mean to say that citizen sociolinguists necessarily adopt resistant ideologies. Hypothetically, there is nothing to prevent Singlish haters from starting a social media platform to discuss the faults of Singlish, in which case they can also be considered citizen sociolinguists.[33] Generally speaking, however, much of the new and social media

---

Holland Village; *Piak Piak from Geylang to Orchard Towers*. See https://thekopi.co/2019/08/03/speak-good-singlish-2019/.

33. By contrast, Chang Li Lin, for instance, cannot be considered a citizen sociolinguist as she published her NYT op-ed in her capacity as the press secretary to the prime minister, not in her capacity as a language user.

writing revolving around Singlish does bear an antiestablishment strain, although there have also been occasional pieces written in support of the government's stance.

In recent years, many citizen sociolinguistic forums have been shut or have fallen into disuse. TalkingCock.com was retired in 2010; the SGSM Facebook page seems to have become inert.[34] It is against these developments that we can see *Spiaking Singlish* as inheriting and extrapolating the citizen sociolinguistic tradition in Singapore. Although *Spiaking Singlish* is published as a hardcopy book (it originated in an online portal), its personalized style, reflexive metadiscursivity, and keen interest in idiosyncrasies qualify it as a citizen sociolinguistic specimen. In the terms of Rymes and Smail (2021), its metacommentary "scales down" discussions of Singlish to the level of the everyday.

In this connection, the Singlish interventions of *Spiaking Singlish* and the broader imagined community of Singlish advocates fit with de Certeau's (1984) sense of everyday practices creating dynamic, ever-evolving *spaces* out of, but still within the framework of, institutionally imagined *places*. They are "multiform, resistance, tricky and stubborn procedures," which "an urbanistic system"—in our case, an official language policy privileging Standard English—"was supposed to administer or suppress" (96). Yet, "far from being regulated or eliminated by panoptic administration," that is, the top-down language policy and language educational system, these Singlish practices have "reinforced themselves in a proliferating illegitimacy, developed and insinuated themselves into the networks of surveillance" (96). According to this reading, we might characterize Singlish practitioners as "[u]nrecognized producers, poets of their own affairs, trailblazers in the jungles of functionalist rationality" (96). Operating within a language ideological bureaucracy, they exercise "surreptitious creativities" within and against "discourses of the observational organization," hence practicing with recalcitrance "an individual mode of reappropriation" vis-à-vis a "collective mode of administration" (96).

In writing against the establishment, members of the Singlitterati perform an alternative choreography that seeks to champion grassroots literacy in Singapore. They endeavor to represent their lesser-educated counterparts in

34. The original link (www.facebook.com/MySGSM/info) to SGSM's Facebook page leads to nonexistent content. Wee (2018: 82) reports that SGSM's Facebook page registered 37,384 "likes" as of December 5, 2016, while an archived page from SGSM's site (https://archive.vn/20121215015056/http://www.facebook.com/MySGSM, accessed July 30, 2020) reports 3,140 members as of December 2012. There is another SGSM Facebook page (https://www.facebook.com/Speak-Good-Singlish-Movement-12828 1041371/) that currently registers only 280 likes, with only scattered and dated postings. Apparently, the current version of SGSM's Facebook page is not the same as the former version, which was likely retired several years earlier.

intellectual debates on Singlish. But precisely because they are choreograph-ing (not transcribing) everyday Singlish, they also shape it into a rhetorically elaborate register, such that, in the final analysis, the kind of literacy that emerges from their writing is not so representative of the grassroots after all. This returns us once again to the ethics of valorizing Singlish, in particular the question of voice: when monolectal speakers of a vernacular language are rep-resented by their Singlitterati counterparts who can switch between vernac-ular and standard registers at ease, the former slip into the subaltern: "spoken for, spoken about, but never directly speaking" (Wee 2018: 109). And the ver-nacular that is purportedly celebrated, when mobilized at the scale of creative and metadiscursive writing, can paradoxically become inaccessible to its lay speakers. Mundane multilingualism, it turns out, is not mundane at all.

Such is the ethical dilemma that arises when a marginalized variety is ar-ticulated beyond its immediate indexical order in pursuit of politico-ideolog-ical work. Laudable as *Spiaking Singlish* is in terms of the egalitarian values it espouses, one needs to ask whether a Singlitterati representative who shuttles fluently between Singlish and Standard English can legitimately speak on be-half of Singlish users in general by means of a performative version of Singlish. As noted earlier, an arguably elitist assumption underlies the Singlitterati's position on promoting Singlish, namely, that English-speaking Singaporeans can generally code-switch between the colloquial and the formal. Hence the argument that Singlish and English are not mutually exclusive because they are flexibly activated in different situational contexts. This latter view over-rates the standard of English beyond the Singlitterati circle and implicitly excludes Singlish users who do not have the resources in their repertoire to readily switch into the formal register.

In celebrating the dynamic energies of Singlish, it is important to recognize that the ability to code-switch between English and Singlish is a privilege—I agree with Chang Li Lin on this specific point. For monolectal Singlish users, Singlish is a survival tool, not some curious resource for self-styling or a cre-ative site for fetishizing a heartlander identity against cosmopolitan impera-tives. *Spiaking Singlish* pivots its writing unequivocally toward the heartland while choreographing a highly performative brand of Singlish replete with hu-morous rhetorical feats, which ironically bespeaks an elite cosmopolitanism. Such practices risk romanticizing the language-identity nexus and turning Singlish from a rich, naturally occurring vernacular into the empty signifier (à la Roland Barthes) of a nebulous "local consciousness."

That said, *Spiaking Singlish* remains admirable as a stylistic experiment with the transgressive potentialities of the vernacular in Singapore. Gwee, however, cannot go it alone in his enterprise of celebrating Singlish as a local resource. With the closure or inactivity of Singlish-themed portals like TalkingCock.com and SGSM, citizen sociolinguistics in Singapore may have encountered a bottleneck, with only individual efforts sustaining the practice. Citizen sociolinguistics, as Rymes and Smail (2021: 442) tell us, thrives "on an ever-growing context of commentary" from a community of language users. For Singlish to thrive as a true vernacular, there need to be more citizen sociolinguistic platforms as well as vibrant exchanges on those platforms from Singlish users with different repertoires. Only then can Singlish generate "an incessant cycle of feedback loops," cultivate "a dynamic discourse community through iterations of interactions," and foster diversity within itself "from the ground up, from the scaled-back level of the grass roots" (Rymes and Smail 2021: 442).

# CHAPTER 5
# Multicultural fantasies from below

## *SingPoWriMo and citizen poetry*

Moving on from the folk lexicography and metadiscursive commentaries in Chapter 4, we now turn to a very different domain, that of creative literature, with an eye to how a localist brand of poetry based on social media affordances is shaping up as an emerging mode of multilingual choreography in Singapore. In Chapter 3, we looked at literary anthologies as semiotic configurations of canonical texts, focusing on how power relations among the four official languages are conceived along the neat contours of quadrilingualism and mediated through translation. This chapter offers a contrasting case by examining a participatory writing platform. In focus here is not how writing is translated between languages but instead how it is always already translational by way of heteroglossia—the incorporation of a diversity of voices within its constitution.

Recent years have witnessed heteroglossic writing maturing into a critical practice, one that self-consciously pursues iconoclastic agendas by transgressing literary form and linguistic boundaries. Edgy in content, aberrant in style, and critical in disposition, such practices may be described as choreographies from below to the extent that they are initiated by individual authors and distributed by independent presses or on social media, often with a strong identity stance at their core. Located outside the institutional apparatus, they are grounds for cultivating a grassroots ethos rooted in the vernacular, set against the scaffolding of neat multilingualism and generic literary conventions.

If neat multilingualism indexes compliance with and reproduction of a prescribed language order, heteroglossia performs a recalcitrance to such order, the dispersal of writerly agency, and the sustenance of entropy. In de

*Choreographies of Multilingualism.* Tong King Lee, Oxford University Press. © Oxford University Press 2022.
DOI: 10.1093/oso/9780197644645.003.0005

Certeau's (1984) terms, heteroglossia represents tactical practices that "produce without capitalizing, that is, without taking control over time" (xx). Bottom-up writing practices are deliberately provincial; they make no claims to the panoptic representation of the literary landscape. Such panoptic representations are the business of top-down literary architectures, as embodied by multilingual anthologies that seek to delineate the canon—a "circumscribed community" (xx) of literature, often defined by temporal landmarks (e.g., the millennium, fifty years of self-government, and the golden jubilee). Into this circumscribed community, tactical writing practices introduce random contingencies, "a Brownian movement" (xx), subtly destabilizing a literary ecology shaped by top-down language policies.

To be sure, there is nothing new about adding a dash of local accent to English-language cultural productions, which "signals the author's intention to evoke local associations and represent local speech habits in naturalist terms" (Patke and Holden 2010: 38). Among Singaporean authors, early attempts at such code-mixing were experimental and intermittent, generally falling short of a systematic practice.[1] In more recent years, developments along this trajectory have gained new momentum, in part due to rising identity consciousness among the educated citizenry, and to the disseminative capacities of social media.

A generation of Singaporean poets are now breaking new ground in harnessing the disruptive potential of heteroglossia and stylizing it into a tactical register in their work. Fully capable of writing in Standard English, these writers tend to hijack the official language using the vernacular, creating linguistically raw and formally heterogeneous texts that would be considered amateurish or outright unliterary by orthodox standards. Through their writing, these young poets perform an emerging aesthetic of hybridity and earthiness, espousing an alternative vision of multilingualism that implodes the myth of plural monolingualisms. This leads us to my case study for the present chapter, a social media writing platform that harnesses the creative contributions of citizen poets to democratize literature and perform the carnivalesque potentialities of the vernacular.

---

1. Theater appears to be an exception, probably because the dramatic medium calls for what Patke and Holden (2010: 41) describe as "sustained linguistic ventriloquism" of how characters from different ethnic or dialect backgrounds speak, resulting in a "selective and deliberately constructed 'fidelity' to the multilingual and not-always-mutually-comprehensible dimension of social reality." Here language mixing tends to be deliberately pursued, not just as a mimicry of street talk but as a discursive means to forge a grassroots identity eschewing official categories of multilingualism (St. André 2006b). This is demonstrated in the multilingual plays of Stella Kon and Kuo Pao Kun (see Patke and Holden 2010: 41–42, 130–35).

In Chapter 3, I argued that a distinctive feature of multilingual representations from above is a categorical neatness with respect to Singapore's four official languages. This is evident, as we saw, in multilingual literary anthologies published under the aegis of institutional patronage, where multilingualism is configured as a set of discrete monolingual frames in the four official languages. Works written in each of these languages are generally airtight in their linguistic constitution: there is little by way of mixing or switching across language boundaries, and seldom if ever do texts feature languages or speech varieties excluded from the quadrilingual framework, notably Singlish. Playing an instrumental role in this dynamic of neat multilingualism is translation, which sustains a structure of reciprocity by iterating the same texts across different languages and producing a visual–verbal affect of balance.

The quadrilingual setup that characterizes these literary anthologies is a function of what Chong (2010) calls "multicultural fantasies" on the part of the state. According to this "fantasy," multiculturalism is conceived as a neatly packaged ideal type performable in tangible sites, such as in the arts and culture. The ideal type in question is one in which the four official languages and their associated cultures can be stereotypically invoked by a range of materialities, such as apparel (e.g., the Chinese *qipao*, the Malay *sarong kebaya*, or the Indian *sari*), musical instruments (e.g., the Chinese *erhu*, the Malay *kompang*, or the Indian *sitar*), and embodied cultural expressions (e.g., the Chinese lion dance, the Malay *Tarian Melayu*, or the Indian *Bharatanatyam*) (Chong 2010: 137).

As these material stereotypes circulate and consolidate themselves through repeated performances at multiple levels (e.g., celebration of cultural festivals in schools and community centers versus the National Day Parade), they become recognizable as "the approved expression of an instant Singapore multicultural identity" (Koh 1989: 716, cited in Chong 2010: 137). Multiculturalism in Singapore then becomes compressed into an instant identity template that can be readily retrieved and activated, entraining the public into recognizing the Chinese, Malay, Indian, Others (CMIO) order and, by extension, the quadrilingual schema, as naturally arising taxonomies. It is here that the arts and culture function as ideological sites for "the visual and symbolic disciplining of races" (Chong 2010: 137). Produced as "a convenient space" (or *place* in de Certeau's schema) where the public partakes of "the fantasies of a multicultural society," the arts and culture facilitate "the animation of a *multicultural utopia*" (Chong 2010: 138 [emphasis added]) through the reproduction of mythified imagery—the collectivity of images arrested by the imperatives of multicultural management and naturalized into default icons for individuated cultures.

Apart from cultural imagery, language and literature are key in the construction of statal narratives on multilingualism predicated on the CMIO. St. André (2006a) observes that Singapore literary collections, in English or English translation, are largely flattened into a monoglossic Standard English register, whereby

> only names of objects culturally specific to Southeast Asia are likely to be introduced into otherwise standard English texts (often with footnotes or glossaries); the few grammatical peculiarities seem to have "slipped through" rather than been introduced for local flavor. Almost all of the few occurrences of nonstandard English which seem purposeful occur in dialogue; in other words, it is only acceptable to use Singlish/Malay/dialect terms when trying to represent the spoken language. (778)

If the hegemonic vision of a multicultural utopia hinges on a multilingual grid sanitized of "grammatical peculiarities" and "occurrences of non-standard English," what are the implications of heteroglossic practices characterized by textual mobilities within and across language codes? In Bakhtin's (1981) original formulation, heteroglossia refers to

> [t]he internal stratification of any single national language into social dialects, characteristic group behavior, professional jargons, generic languages, languages of generations and age groups, tendentious languages, languages of the authorities, of various circles and of passing fashion, languages that serve the specific sociopolitical purposes of the day, even of the hour (each day has its own slogan, its own vocabulary, its own emphases)—this internal stratification present in every language at any given moment of its historical existence is the indispensable prerequisite for the novel as a genre. (262–63)

To put this in our context, we might tentatively read "national language" as "official language." Neat multilingualism, then, operates on the suppression of the internal stratification within each of the four official languages that constitute the quadrilingual schema. What I have called quadruple monolingualism therefore belies and embeds the state's multicultural utopia (per Chong 2010), which is a multilingual but monoglossic ideal.

Herein lies the ethicopolitical import of heteroglossia, which is to expose the immanent heterogeneity within each of the official languages, whose prima facie unity conceals interweaving strands of multiple tongues and registers—languages that "serve the specific sociopolitical purposes of the day, even of the hour." By reveling in the lived experience of language (Busch 2017), heteroglossia celebrates marginalized aspects of the Singaporean repertoire, creating rhizomatic connections into social dialects to counter the vertical striations of policy infrastructure. Heteroglossia thus moves us from a monological to a dialogical view of communication, offering a more egalitarian multicultural utopia than the one sustained in state discourses.

Heteroglossia as a writing practice is about more than just mixing languages; it transcends various boundaries of formal expression, including but not limited to language. This may involve, for instance, composing poetry under self-imposed constraints (e.g., avoiding an entire class of words) or using certain sound/shape patterns, effecting a gamification of literature. Ultimately, heteroglossia is as much about enacting multivoicedness (Busch 2017)—the intermingling of different modes of utterances that in turn represent different perspectives—as it is about linguistic diversity. Its ethical point lies in puncturing the façade of cultural homogeneity and unleashing a plenitude of creative energies from different voices and perspectives usually submerged by the institution of writing, hence symbolically disrupting the literary establishment from within.

Importantly, heteroglossia is a stylistic instantiation of what we might call Anglophone literature in Singapore. The term "Anglophone" with a capitalized "A" does not refer simply to the use of the English language in writing—we might call the latter "anglophone" with a lower case "a." The capitalized "Anglophone" entrenches the locale-specificity of writing by articulating the English language to a discursively constructed Singaporean sensibility. The typographical distinction here is inspired by Sinophone studies, where scholars have proposed using "sinophone" with a lower case "s" to refer to cultural productions in the Chinese language in general (on par with francophone, hispanophone, etc.), and "Sinophone" with a capitalized "S" to indicate rupture with a putatively authentic and universal "Chineseness" emanating from mainland China (Peng 2008).

According to this definition, the Anglophone is a counterpart of the Sinophone in cultural and literary studies. The Sinophone "locates its objects of attention at the conjuncture of China's internal colonialism and Sinophone communities everywhere immigrants from China have settled" (Shih 2011: 710). As opposed to "Chinese-speaking," the Sinophone

> disrupts the chain of equivalence established, since the rise of nation-states, among language, culture, ethnicity, and nationality and explores the protean, kaleidoscopic, creative, and overlapping margins of China and Chineseness, America and Americanness, Malaysia and Malaysianness, Taiwan and Taiwanness, and so on, by a consideration of specific, local Sinophone texts, cultures, and practices produced in and from these margins. (Shih 2011: 710–11)

The Sinophone thus unravels the critical potentiality of the space between the universal rubric of Chineseness and the contingent localities of Chinese-using regions outside China. Encompassing "Sinitic-language communities and their expressions (cultural, political, social, etc.) on the margins of nations and nationalness in the internal colonies and other minority communities in China as well as outside it" (Shih 2011: 716), the Sinophone, when applied to literature, refers to any writing that flaunts its geopolitical situatedness in resistance to "the hegemonic call of Chineseness" (Shih 2011: 717).[2]

According to the same logic, the Anglophone too can be theorized as a critical category to interrogate the political economy of Englishness in English-using territories.[3] It bases itself on English while differentiating itself with oral–aural inflections peculiar to the local tongue, hence disrupting "the chain of equivalence." Ontologically, the Anglophone overlaps substantively with Postcolonial English (Schneider 2007) or World Englishes (Kirkpatrick 2021), but it does more than describe systematic differences between global varieties of English and a perceived Standard English arising as a result of historical language contact. Instead, as a counterpart of the Sinophone, the Anglophone actively pursues its difference as a radical agenda, enunciating itself flagrantly from the periphery into the mainstream; it turns its aberrance into a resource to transform the "scriptural economy" (de Certeau 1984: 131) grounded in English into the power of the local tongue.

## HETEROGLOSSIC EXPERIMENTS IN ANGLOPHONE POETRY

With its postcolonial legacy, Singapore is a privileged zone for exploring the ideological implications of the Anglophone for literary writing. The ubiquitous first language in mainstream education, English as used in Singapore is inflected by a plethora of other tongues, in particular Malay and Hokkien, creating a liminal zone cut through by "protean, kaleidoscopic, creative, and overlapping margins" (Shih 2011: 710–11). Anglophone writing in Singapore—in the dual senses discussed above—took root after World War II in the wake of a regional wave of anticolonial sentiment and the rise of left-wing activism. Spawned by English-educated undergraduates from the University of Malaya,

2. Hence, Sinophone Singaporean literature would refer to the corpus of Sinitic-language literary works penned by Singaporean Chinese authors, thematically focused on issues specific to Singapore or linguistically shaped by local languages (or any combination thereof). A case in point is *Memorandum*, a collection of stories from Singapore originally written in Chinese, subtitled "A Sinophone Singaporean Short Story Reader" (Quah and Hee 2020).

3. My understanding of the Anglophone, as inspired by the Sinophone, is largely in accord with the concept's development within the field of Postcolonial English literature, although in my usage, the Anglophone is understood as a critical practice not pertaining exclusively to literary writing. In my reading of literary data, I also maintain a sociolinguistic angle, focusing more on the linguistic enunciation than the thematic content of a work.

it developed through the medium of literary magazines as part of efforts to articulate a Malayan identity consciousness.

The irony of writing against British colonial hegemony in English was not lost on the student writers. One writer was reported as lamenting that a Malayan student writing in English "is doing no more than echoing the English poets he has learnt at school," for there was no tradition of Anglophone Singapore literature to rely on (cited in Patke and Holden 2010: 50). As Koh (2018) observes, these early writers, apart from the burden of having to shape up a nascent cultural identity, "struggled additionally with a self-conscious awareness that they were writing not in their own 'mother-tongues,' but inevitably by dint of their education, in the non-Asian language of the colonial power, necessarily influenced by a familiar yet foreign literary tradition" (11).

Within this sociopolitical context, a handful of poets "stand out in historical significance for the lead they took in approaching the challenge and opportunity of injecting local elements into their verse" (Patke and Holden 2010: 51), creating a heteroglossic register that came to be called EngMalChin. A portmanteau combining "English," "Malay," and "Chinese" that floated in the literary scene of 1950s British Malaya (including Singapore), EngMalChin "alluded to the way in which the English of a poem made room for Malay and Chinese words and phrases," featuring "occasional scraps of multilingual usage" within the matrix of Anglophone poetry (Patke and Holden 2010: 51–52).

As an experimental Anglophone practice, EngMalChin did not quite make it into mainstream writing, for it tended to alienate English-language readers who had no Malay or Chinese vocabulary in their repertoire. Using a heteroglossic register like this therefore carries the risk of "needing a gloss that might impede the flow of the reading experience," and of leaving readers "discomfited or alienated" when eluded by language-specific allusions (Patke and Holden 2010: 38). Thus, for all its efforts to endear to a local aurality, critical reception of heteroglossic poetry has not always been enthusiastic. Platt and Singh (1984) comment, for instance, that such works were often "too artificial an attempt, too constrictive to allow for genuine creativity" (46). This view is echoed by Patke and Holden (2010), who maintain that "not all attempts at mixing words from one language with a literary discourse in another language feel either comfortable or apt," citing EngMalChin pioneer Wang Gungwu's "Ahmad" as one such attempt that "does not quite come off" (38).

Nevertheless, EngMalChin's signature technique of invoking "occasional scraps of multilingual usage" has persisted in Singapore's Anglophone poetry, "which remains indebted to the mimeticism that subsidized *Engmalchin* for a while" (Patke and Holden 2010: 52). Later developments have shown more nuance in using Singlish, for example, to express "a more complicated ambivalence in which amused self-deprecation is mixed with the recognition that, for better or worse, Singlish serves as a unique marker of local identity" (Patke and

Holden 2010: 40–41). Some of the more mature works, notably Arthur Yap's "2 mothers in a h d b playground," are staged as a tacit response to top-down language campaigns launched to institute a verbal-hygienic regime. In these cases, heteroglossia is choreographed into a "stylistic ventriloquism," to arrest "with an equivocal mix of satire and sympathy precisely those speech habits that such campaigns would like to eradicate" (Patke and Holden 2010: 40). We now consider in detail another example with a similar ideological thrust.

### "Speaking in tongues"

Goh Sin Tub's poem "Speaking in tongues" was first published in the 1993 volume *Moments in a Singapore Life*, and later in the state-supported anthology *Rhythms* (see my discussion in Chapter 3). Goh belonged to the generation of EngMalChin poets mentioned above, although much of his later literary works were of prose fiction. The poem is a high performance of street multilingualism in Singapore, choreographing a plethora of tongues into its narrative, with a metadiscursive title pointing to its linguistic constitution. It traces the vicissitudes of Singapore's language ecology within the city-state's eclectic demographic, taking us through major historical epochs and events (e.g., British colonial rule, regional migrations, Japanese occupation, and language campaigns) until the early or mid-1980s (the narrative ends with the Speak Mandarin Campaign [SMC], which commenced in 1979).

Stylistically, "Speaking in tongues" exemplifies the Anglophone: it is intensively worked through with transliterated words from Malay and Hokkien, topped with a casual sprinkling of Japanese and Mandarin and a heavy inflection of Singlish grammar. These stylistic undulations are meant to echo the oralities–auralities that map different registers of patois to corresponding moments in history. Code-mixing is thus a central device in this "English" poem, where non-Standard English intrusions stud the text extensively, and where what St. André (2006a: 778) calls "grammatical peculiarities" are not merely "slipped through" but figure in significant proportion.

**Speaking in Tongues—Singapore Style** (by Goh Sin Tub)
In days of yore Grandpa laid down the law,
Speak mother tongue he used to say:
"Hokkien lang kong Hokkien way."

Though Grandma from Java spoke only Bahasa,
She followed Grandpa's rule to kong Hokkien way,
And she saw to it we grew up kong-ing Hokkien way.

Then we moved from Chinatown to Emerald Hill
Our friends now Muthu, Dollah, Bongsu,

So (*boh pien lah!*) we also chakap Melayu.
At school, Sir insisted: "Speak English!"
So, apa lagi, we anyhow speak English too,
Chin-chye, chap-chye, choba kind also can do.

Then Japanese came and we benkyo Nippon-go;
Their ABC kata-kana: Ah, ee, oo, eh, oh,
No problem, we just champor: Kaki lu bengko.

And now (*kao peh!*) Speak Mandarin campaign!
Must jiang hua yu, Hokkien way no can do.
Kena again: t'ak ch'e, belajar, benkyo, study, du shu.

At first we may swear at those campaign mandarins:
"Dammit, sial only, so suay one!"
But being kiasu, soon it's Xian Sheng zao an!

(Goh, in Singh and Wong 2000: 201 [emphasis in the original])

Meandering through at least five discrete languages—counting Hokkien and Mandarin separately, although they are often subsumed under the "Chinese" umbrella—"Speaking in Tongues" is a translator's nightmare (more below). What interests me at this juncture, however, is not how the poem is translated, but how it is translational by way of embedding the motif of translation into its own textuality.

The poem starts off with archaic English ("In the days of yore . . ."), then transits to Hokkien, the historical mother tongue of the majority of the Singapore Chinese population, hence: *Hokkien lang kong Hokkien way* (Hokkien people speak the Hokkien language). Crucially, *way* is conceived as a double entendre, at once pointing to the English word meaning "method" and the Hokkien word meaning "talk" or "spoken language," thus converting the space between the two languages into a duplicitous sign.

Coming next is Malay (*Bahasa Melayu*), the language of the Malay population and of the immediate region in which Singapore is located. Here we see an acculturation theme at play, where Grandma, whose mother tongue is Malay, is said to *kong Hokkien way* (speak Hokkien) following Grandpa, making sure that her offspring follow suit. The situation changed with the family's resettlement from Chinatown to Emerald Hill (where the poet lived), where Malay was widely used among the Straits Chinese residing in the new neighborhood: "So (*boh pien lah!*) we also chakap Melayu" (So [*no choice!*] we also spoke Malay). Note how, in this utterance, the Hokkien phrase is set in italic and snuck in as a parenthetical exclamation, where the parentheses and italicization together function as a visual–spatial signal to indicate the layering of one tongue over another.

The scene then shuttles to English-medium schools (Goh studied at the prestigious Raffles Institution), where English was taught: "So, apa lagi, we anyhow speak English too,/Chin-chye, chap-chye, choba kind also can do" (So, what else can we do, we too speak English in a haphazard way/Including the kind [of English] that's nonstandard and mixed with other languages). Apparently, the English spoken in these schools is of a hybrid variety, as indicated by the trilingual code-mixing among English, Malay, and Hokkien, not to forget the obvious traces of Singlish grammar in, for instance, "we anyhow speak English" and "also can do," metalinguistically undermining the efficacy of the English-medium education being discussed.

The already complex language matrix is further complicated by the Japanese occupation of Singapore during World War II, which introduces a new imperative to *benkyo Nippon-go* (study the Japanese language). In the face of this imposition of a second imperial language (the first being English, which came with the British), the poet's persona puts up a discursive resistance from below: "No problem, we just champor." The *champor*, or "mixing," in question is effected through a distortion of rudimentary Japanese phonics: "Ah, ee, oo, eh, oh" turns the Japanese sound sequence *a-i-u-e-o* into a ludic series of interjections, just as "kaki lu bengko" plays on the sound sequence *ka-ki-ku-ke-ko*, playfully substituting *benko* for *ke-ko*. Orthographically and phonically, *benko* (a nonexistent string in Japanese) evokes *benkyo* (the Japanese word for "study"), but plausibly also hints at the Malay word *bengkok*, meaning "bent" or "crooked." The phonetic slippage in these lines offers an ironic, metalinguistic commentary on language education in a colonial context, where an imposed language is never learnt (*benkyo*) in some pristine form but always with adulteration from preexisting tongues. The language from above is surreptitiously undercut by the messy heteroglossia from below, which queers the colonial language, making it "crooked" (*bengkok*).

Finally, the onset of the SMC drastically overhauled the language environment of the Chinese-speaking populace of Singapore in the 1980s and beyond. Of this, the poet's persona is evidently critical: "And now (*kao peh!*) Speak Mandarin campaign! Must jiang hua yu, Hokkien way no can do" (And now [damn!] Speak Mandarin campaign! Must speak Mandarin, Hokkien language won't do). The parenthetical exclamation *kao peh!*, a vulgar word from Hokkien, encodes a suppressed (hence parenthetically contained) voice of the vernacular, here directed against the SMC, which aimed to eradicate Chinese dialects from the linguistic landscape. Yet this hegemonic imposition of Mandarin is at most a faint veil of homogeneity beneath which diverse tongues continue to irreparably twist together. The ironic representation of the Chinese phrase *jiang hua yu* (speak Mandarin) in romanized form within a Singlish grammatical frame ("Hokkien way no can do") demonstrates the persistent heterogeneity of street patois that the Campaign set out to regulate.

In a final expression of frustration, the poet's persona juxtaposes the word "study" in five tongues at one go: *t'ak ch'e, belajar, benkyo*, study, *du shu*. The iteration of the same word in Hokkien, Malay, Japanese, English, and Mandarin unravels a translational dynamic within the metrolingual, going against the SMC's objective to flatten an originally heteroglossic repertoire into a monoglossic "official" language. The poem ends with a tone of resignation, where the poet's persona succumbs to Mandarin, as instantiated in the transliterated Mandarin phatic communion *Xian Sheng zao an* (Good morning, sir/teacher) even as he "swears at those campaign mandarins." Here the poet does not miss his last opportunity to insinuate an ironic pun: "campaign mandarins" is both an inversion of the (Speak) Mandarin Campaign and a reference to an obsolete sense of the word "mandarin," meaning government official.

With its intense heteroglossia, "Speaking in tongues" certainly alludes to an EngMalChin ethos (and arguably goes beyond it by incorporating scraps of Japanese), although by the time this poem was written, EngMalChin had receded into history. But in the context of *Rhythms*, published in 2000, the poem presents something of an anomaly, its mildly critical stance on language policies and its Anglophone, not simply anglophone, texture out of sync within the quadrilingual straitjacket of institutionalized anthologies.

## Heteroglossia as a critical practice

If attempts at heteroglossia in Anglophone poetry by Goh and his contemporaries evince an authorial style "whose individuality is based on failing to achieve, or managing to be ignorant of, collective and consensual norms about what constitutes competence for a given community of language users" (Patke and Holden 2010: 40), then current and still-evolving developments have shored up such individuality to engage in a politics of intelligibility. Poets like Alfian Sa'at, Joshua Ip, and Ng Yi-sheng pursue a poetics that is much more provocative in stance, often polarizing an ethic of resistance, even asserting "a notion of nation that bypasses and challenges, because it is thwarted by, the idea of nation disseminated by the state" (Patke and Holden 2010: 184). In terms of form, these writers tend toward a register that is "casual-colloquial" and "cool-quirky," occasionally rising to a "pungent" rhetoric (Patke and Holden 2010: 185). As Patke and Holden (2010) put it succinctly:

> Perhaps, in such writing, the desire to startle and amuse produces a surplus that entertains more than it enlightens or enriches. . . . In neat and clean Singapore, the younger poets continue to show signs of a dishevelled energy that seems to thrive in inverse [pro]portion to how much their society is sanitized by a paternal nation-state. (186)

It is against this trajectory that Singlish gains an ethicopolitical edge in Anglophone Singapore literature. Consider, for instance, Joshua Ip's *sonnets from the singlish*, a volume of poems said to be "loosely translated from the english-based [sic] creole language colloquially spoken in singapore [sic], widely known as singlish [sic]" (Ip 2015: back cover). It is at first baffling that Ip's poems are said to be translated *from* Singlish. On the poet's own account, the title derives from Elizabeth Barrett Browning's *Sonnets from the Portuguese*, with Browning passing off her original English poems as translated Portuguese (Ip 2015: xx). Notwithstanding this, there is something more to Ip's curious title, which hinges on a translational logic that construes Singlish as a source language.[4] This has the effect of alienating a familiar tongue of the locale into a translated Other: "I too wanted to appropriate that idea of translating poems 'from' a foreign language—Singlish, playing on that odd, mystical, fortune-cookie quality of translations" (Ip 2015: xx).

The odd construal of Singlish as "a foreign language" is striking, as if the poet is deliberately trying to place the vernacular at a psychological distance. Speaking of Singlish as a foreign language also implies the existence of a "local" language.[5] What might that be? Since it exists only by implication, we can't be sure, but English would seem a likely candidate. According to this speculation, there is a sense that whatever appears in this volume of Anglophone poetry is *always already translated*, to use Holden's (2017) phrase; crucially, what is initially considered secondary, because nonsanctioned, is now Cinderella-ed into an Original. The tables are then turned on English (if I am right to say it is the implied "local language"), now relegated to the status of a derivative language prone to aberrations and deviations, with that "odd, mystical, fortune-cookie quality," hence reversing the asymmetrical power relation between Singlish and English.

*sonnets from the singlish* is an oddball book of poetry. Its quirkiness is manifest in the marked coupling of a local vernacular and a global, canonical literary form; the mischievous, hypercolored images on its cover;[6] and its idiosyncratic but consistent use of the lower case throughout, including in titles of the poems and the book as well as in the author's name on the inside cover.

4. Compare Holden (2017: n.p.), where it is suggested that the title implies "the absence of an original."
5. For Ip, Singlish refers not only to the language but also to "the nature of being Singaporean" or "Singapore-ish." More than that: "it means a person from Singapore. I am the Singlish! These sonnets are from me!" (Ip 2015: xx). This broadening of the Singlish rubric to cover a reified consciousness betrays an essentialist stance toward cultural distinctiveness. Yet its fetishizing of locale and locality, as evident in the poet's embodiment of the language's appellation as his very identity ("I am the Singlish!"), is precisely in line with the ethos the book conveys, perhaps with knowing irony on the part of the poet.
6. The book cover design is available at https://www.booksactuallyshop.com/produ cts/sonnets-from-the-singlish-upsize-edition.

Unsurprisingly, it contains an abundance of references to practices, institutions, social phenomena, and fragments of speech particular to Singapore. All of these aim at taking poetry down from the lofty pedestal of elite literature and pegging it at a more pedestrian and locale-specific register.

Exemplifying this register are the poet's Singlish interventions, which generate creative tension within the formal constraints of a sonnet and between the covers of a collection of English-language (or anglophone) poetry.[7] Take for instance the poem "conversaytion":

**conversaytion** (by Joshua Ip)
"not say i want to say, but then this one
who say one?" "i say one lor, arbuthen."
"this one you say one? liedat also can??
today you say ho say, later bueh gum

then you say I saw who confirm?" "you say
what what lor. anyway I say one thing
is one thing one. not like you everything
also say people like mm sam mm say."

"you say some more?" "you say first one ma." "wan
to come outside say? say louder?" "dun wan.
ok la, i say wrongly, ho say bo?
take it i never say la." "then say so!
your mouth damn suey. you dun wan me to say
then dun say me—not say I want to say."

(Ip 2015: 87)

The poem is presented as an excerpt of a trivial argument between two persons. The phonetic pun in the title, "conversaytion," offers metalinguistic humor, pointing to the poem's theme, namely, Singlish talk. The subject of the conversation remains enigmatic: we are completely clueless as to what is being said between the interlocutors, and it is precisely this relative paucity in the content of speech that foregrounds the saying itself.

The poem is worked through with a heavy Singlish syntax and replete with English words transcribed in eye-dialect spellings as well as transliterated expressions from Chinese dialects. Here is a sampling of relevant items:[8]

7. Not all the poems in *sonnets from the singlish* are heavily marked with Singlish. But insofar as Singlish, as both a linguistic and an identity register, represents a conceptual brand for the collection, my observations bear general relevance to the work as a whole.

8. The word glosses are adapted from *A Dictionary of Singlish and Singapore English*, http://www.mysmu.edu/faculty/jacklee/singlish_A.htm, and from a glossary included in *sonnets from the singlish* (Ip 2015: 103).

a. *arbuthen*: a conflation of "ah, but then," meaning something is manifestly self-evident or obvious

b. *liedat:* a conflation of "like that," which in Singlish expresses annoyance

c. *ho say*: a Hokkien phrase expressing affirmation, roughly "all right"; *ho say bo*: the interrogative form of *ho say*

d. *bueh gum*: "not suitable or desirable"

e. *you say I saw who confirm*: an expression meaning everyone has their own version of the facts

f. *you say what what*: a literal translation of a Chinese expression meaning "you can say whatever you want to say, and it will be so"

g. *I say one thing is one thing*: an approximate translation of a Chinese expression meaning "I mean what I say"

h. *mm sam mm say*: a Cantonese expression that reads "neither three nor four," meaning "to be ambivalent"

i. *you say first one ma*: "You said it first," where *one* and *ma* are sentence-final particles in Singlish.

j. *wan to come outside say*: the Singlish version of "want to come outside and talk?", but specifically meaning "want to fight it out?"'

k. *dun wan*: an eye-dialect spelling of 'don't want'

l. *suey*: "unlucky," "wretched"

Also interesting is how the poem smuggles an orthographic duplicity into the central sign "say," which represents the English word, as in "talk" (although in Singlish, *say* is intransitive) while also camouflaging several dialect words. Echoing the double entendre enacted by *way* in Goh Sin Tub's "Speaking in tongues," a translingual homophony is constructed: for example, in the phrases *ho* **say**, *ho* **say** *bo*, *mm sam mm* **say**, each of the bolded segments is an anglicized spelling of *say*, which is the Hokkien word for "disposition" in the first two phrases and the Cantonese word for "four" in the last.

As an English poem—crucially, Ip's book won a national literary prize in that category[9]— "conversaytion" flaunts a highly foreignized tone; here indeed the register is the message. In using Singlish not as an intermittent gesture to afford a dash of local flavor but as an entrenched identity register, the poem inscribes untranslatability unto itself, at once invoking and precluding the absent Other: Standard English. As a thought experiment along this line, let us attempt an English translation of "conversaytion":

> "it's not that i want to complain, but
> who said this?" "i did. who else?"

9. *sonnets from the singlish* was awarded the 2014 Singapore Literature Prize in the category of English poetry: https://bookcouncil.sg/awards/singapore-literature-prize#shortlist2014.

"you did? is that even proper??
now you say you agree, now you say you don't
then we each have our story, so who has the final say?"
"whatever you say. anyway, i mean
whatever i say. unlike you, always criticising people
for being ambivalent about everything."

"you say that again?" "you picked on me first." "want
to talk outside? i dare you to speak louder." "no, i don't.
okay, it's my fault, alright?
take it i never said that." "then say so!
your mouth is wretched. if you don't want me to give it to you
then don't start on me—it's not that i want to complain."

In translating Ip's poem, I have found it necessary at several points to find a precise formulation to render *say*, whose meaning potential in Singlish is more layered and ambivalent than in English, as noted above. I find myself impelled to interpret each instance of *say* differently according to its cotext, thus leveling the cross-lingual nuances of the iterative sign into English and compromising the lexical economy of the original poem. In doing so, I inadvertently—but also inevitably—tilt the poem's disposition from the Anglophone to the anglophone. For example, "not I want to *say*" is translated as "not that I want to *complain*," while "you *say* first one ma" and "then don't *say* me" become "you *picked on me* first" and "don't *start on me*," respectively. Dialect expressions, including those containing the Hokkien or Cantonese *say*, and Singlish grammar are flattened, or sanitized, into a grammatical English register. In taming the chaotic register of the poem, my translation evinces a different affect: it becomes much too straight-laced, too verbally hygienic (Cameron 2012).

Erasure of heteroglossia in translation has been well attested in the literature, most famously indicted by Berman (2004: 287) as a "deforming tendency" that effaces "the superimposition of languages." Goh Sin Tub's "Speaking in tongues" has been subject to similar treatment. In the anthology *Rhythms*, the poem is rendered into Chinese, Malay, and Tamil, raising the question of how the code-switched elements in the original should be treated. In the Chinese translation, for instance, most of the Hokkien (*lang, kong, boh pien, chin-chye, chap-chye, kao peh, suay*) and Malay (*chakap, apa lagi, choba, champor, kena*) words are semantically translated into Mandarin (Standard Chinese); Malay names are transliterated with Chinese characters; and Singlish grammar (e.g., "Hokkien way *no can do*") is recast in Mandarin grammar (St. André 2006a: 779).[10]

10. A contrastive case is Kuo Pao Kun's multilingual play *Mama Looking for Her Cat*, which features several mutually unintelligible Chinese dialects. Kuo reportedly refused to provide surtitles, "asking audiences to struggle with their own partial

In the context of the multilingual anthology in which the poem was published, such effacement of heterolingualism instances discursive violence in translation (Venuti 2008) by way of domesticating heterogeneous shards of language into a streamlined register in the standard language (here, Mandarin Chinese). Even more illustrative is Ming Cher's 1995 novel *Spider Boys*, which stood out for extensive use of nonstandard English in its narrative prose, representing "a world in which Chinese topolects such as Hokkien and Cantonese were widely spoken, and English was rarely used" (Holden 2017: n.p.). In its 2012 revised edition, the novel's heteroglossic prose was flattened via an intralingual translation; more specifically, it was "substantially edited to fit the default mode of much Singapore fiction in English, with standard English for narration, nonstandard structures associated with Singlish in dialogue, and with words from languages such as Malay and Hokkien italicized rather than being run seamlessly into the text," all this notwithstanding that the author gave his permission for such adaptations to be made (Holden 2017: n.p.).[11]

Such acts of effacing heteroglossia dovetail with a larger imperative to "participate in maintaining a hierarchy of Mandarins and Englishes," with the implication that "[a]s long as the [Singapore] government, media, and educated classes perceive 'standard' English and Mandarin to be more prestigious, there will be pressure on translators and interpreters to produce such language, *even in local contexts, when local usage would be perfectly intelligible*" (St. André 2006a: 784 [emphasis added]). Against this tension between heteroglossic performance and monoglossic standardization, the point of my hypothetical translation of "conversaytion" is to illustrate what Shapiro (2019) calls the "perils of intelligibility" (6). By defaulting to a Standard English register, my translation can be said to have made Ip's poem intelligible to a

comprehension of minoritised languages, and to focus on actors' expressions and gestures" (Holden 2017: n.p.). Untranslatability, then, is an integral part of the aesthetic of the work.

11. As an example, the original edition of *Spider Boys* carries the phrase "Don't talk prick words," exactly calquing a vulgar Hokkien expression that literally means "speak penis language." In the revised edition of the novel, this becomes "Don't talk cock," a stock Singlish phrase that means "don't utter nonsense." For Holden (2017: n.p.), whereas "talk cock" domesticates the Hokkien phrase into idiomatic Singlish, "talk prick words" recalls the vulgarity of the original Hokkien phrase much more vividly via literal translation. Interestingly, the author of *Spider Boys* seems to be in favor of the Standard English version. This points to different conceptions of authenticity, with the Singaporean author, Ming Cher, favoring standardization and the foreign academic, Holden (a native speaker of English), inclined toward heteroglossia. In a conversation with me, the poet Ng Yi-sheng referenced the same example, making the pertinent point that "there are many Singlishes, what sounds inauthentic to someone is actually authentic to someone else" (personal communication, July 2020).

hypothetical anglophone readership.[12] But in so doing I effectively nullify the poem's Anglophone disposition, which lies entirely in the corporeal contours of vernacular speech, betraying a presupposition—from the vantage point of Standard English—that Singlish instantiates the unintelligible.

The aesthetics of the vernacular must therefore be appreciated within a politics of intelligibility in Anglophone poetics: because instrumental communication is conditioned by the "reigning structures of intelligibility" (Shapiro 2019: 6), poets and artists have resorted to creating spaces of unintelligibility—Stéphane Mallarmé's interspersing of blank spaces in his poetry is a case in point—in order to disentangle themselves from "the forces of recognition" and "the facilitating paths . . . of dominant opinions" (Deleuze and Guattari 1994, cited in Shapiro 2019: 6). In this light, Ip's Singlish orientation in writing can be seen as performing a critical textuality (Shapiro 2019: 7) within Singapore's language ideological regime and the "verbal hygiene" (Cameron 2012) it institutes, offering a counterpoint to the state's multicultural fantasy by limning the borders of (un)intelligibility and (un)translatability.

## SINGPOWRIMO AND THE RISE OF CITIZEN POETRY

Ip's contribution to fostering an egalitarian literature goes well beyond his own work. In 2014, as part of a small group of kindred Singaporean poets, he cofounded the Facebook-based literary initiative Singapore Poetry Writing Month, affectionately known as SingPoWriMo and further abbreviated to SPWM when hashtagged. Originally meant as private forum—"a cosy gathering of fanatics who just needed that extra push to write, a closed group on Facebook where those sado-masochistic enough would egg each other on through con/destructive criticism and poetic blood-sport" (Ang 2014: vii)—the platform became a public group thanks to a serendipitous human error. Within a few years, SingPoWriMo gained tremendous traction, recording exponential growth in both membership and submissions from just hundreds in its early days to thousands in more recent years (at the time of this writing, the Facebook page has attracted more than 7,000 members).

SingPoWriMo heralds a participatory literary culture in Singapore, representing a less elitist modality of writing than that offered on institutional platforms. In the terms developed here, it speaks to the Anglophone, represented

12. My translation may be hypothetical, but if Goh's "Speaking in tongues" can be translated and anthologized in *Rhythms*, it is not implausible for "conversaytion" to follow suit at some point.

by a multiplicity of tongues spliced into a locally accented English, rather than simply the anglophone, represented by Standard English. Rolling out in April each year, it is an open forum where poet-moderators post a writing "prompt" on a daily basis during the month, encouraging participants to try their hand at composing poems tailored to certain formal or thematic cues. Upon completing their poems, contributors are asked to hashtag their work, share it on SingPoWriMo's Facebook site, and comment on or critique one another's works (with veteran poets often taking the lead in providing feedback to entries by emerging writers).

This creates an internet-based community of gamic practice in poetry, giving rise to an expanding pool of citizen poets. For the purpose of this chapter, citizen poets are the literary counterpart of citizen sociolinguists (Rymes 2020; see Ch. 4), mostly comprising young, amateur writers who have not formally published their writing.[13] Citizen poetry also relates to the rise of citizen media (Baker et al. 2020; Baker and Blaagaard 2016), in which ordinary people engage with sociopolitical contingencies through social media platforms.

Riding on the affordances of Facebook, SingPoWriMo galvanizes an imagined literary community, converging to write the locale on a casual, occasional, voluntary, and virtual basis without having to cross the high thresholds of literary publishing. They are a loose or "light" literary community as opposed to a regulated or "thick" one (Blommaert and Varis 2015), such as formerly registered literary associations.[14] Just as citizen sociolinguists participate in nonacademic debates over the role of the vernacular languages, so the citizen poets of SingPoWriMo can voice their mundane concerns and express subjective identities through poetry beyond the traditional constraints of meter, feet, and rhyme. In so doing, they create a conviviality around literature and locality.

Formulated as wacky challenges rather than grim-faced prescriptions, SingPoWriMo prompts provide a lighthearted, game-like momentum to the writing event. Not meant to be taken with absolute seriousness, the prompts are often written in a mischievous tone, encouraging participants to adopt countercultural standpoints in their writing. This is exemplified in one prompt inviting poets to "[challenge] a rule, a law, a habit, a form, a subject, a theme,

13. According to figures provided by Joshua Ip (personal communication, July 2020), 77% of SingPoWriMo contributors fall within the age range 18–34. The demographic distribution is as follows (numbers outside parentheses indicate ages): 25–34 (46.4%), 18–24 (30.7%), 35–44 (13.7%), 45–54 (4.7%), 65+ (2.0%), 55–64 (1.8%), 13–17 (0.7%).

14. Where light communities are defined as *"focused but diverse occasioned coagulations* of people . . . [who] converge or coagulate around a shared focus—an object, a shared interest, another person, an event"* (Blommaert and Varis 2015: 54 [emphasis in the original]).

a mind-set—or as many of these as possible" (#SPWM15day6). This playful character is furthered by multiple subcues, called bonus challenges, appended to each prompt, placing layers of constraints on citizen poets, which they are free to flout in part or in full. The following example shows the structure of a typical prompt:

> **THE PASSENGER PROMPT** (by Rodrigo Dela Peña Jr.)
> Write a poem that includes any road sign, safety warning, and other found text that you see while walking/driving/riding the bus/train/any moving vehicle.
>
> #GraphicDesignIsMyPassionBonus: Self-explanatory
> #IsItBecauseImBonus: Make it a poem about race.
> #GrabBonus: Mention any kind of food OR pet in your poem.
> #InterchangeBonus: Combine different languages.
> #spwm19day25 #passengerprompt

This "passenger prompt" invites writers to incorporate into their poetry ordinary pieces of language found on the road—precisely our subject matter in Chapter 2. The creatively hashtagged bonus challenges push the envelope by soliciting visual material, designated themes (race, food, pet), or multiple languages to be included in poems. The two hashtags at the bottom, unique to social media writing, mark the prompt responded to and the day of the event, where #spwm19day25 is the shorthand for Day 25 of SingPoWriMo 2019 (i.e., April 25, 2019). The affordance of hashtags adds the function of searchable talk (Zappavigna 2015) while aligning users around certain values (Zappavigna and Martin 2018), which, as we shall see, tend to nonconformity with normative values.

## A guerrilla poetics

SingPoWriMo's literary signature lies in its espousal of what can be called a guerrilla poetics, one that seeks out a niche within the writing establishment by appealing to a younger audience and riding on social media affordances. Just as, in de Certeau's (1984) conception, popular culture creates "a space for maneuvers of unequal forces and for utopian points of reference" (18) by making tactical use of overarching structures, SingPoWriMo creates playful ambiguities within the governing conventions of poetry as an institution, which represents a discursive "universe of technocratic transparency" (18) with all the baggage of the literary canon. By opening the space of writing to potentially all English-language users with a Facebook account—and, crucially, with a sense of humor—it uses, but does not reproduce, the normative framework of literature with a "combination of manipulation and enjoyment," relishing in spontaneous experimentations with no systematic goals and taking "no responsibility for the administration of a totality" (18).

SingPoWriMo's guerrilla tactics are manifest in the use of innovative, provocative prompts that challenge citizen poets to transgress the formal straitjackets of poetry.[15] Just like speech acts are particular enunciations effected by speakers through their reappropriation of elements from a linguistic system (de Certeau 1984: xiii), so SingPoWriMo comprises "innumerable practices by means of which users reappropriate the space organized by techniques of sociocultural [here, literary] production" (de Certeau 1984: xiv). It is a social media *space*, in the de Certeauean sense, that proliferates quotidian creativities through social networking—quotidian because they operate outside the purview of the literary establishment, do not aspire to canonization, and tap into a decidedly local rather than cosmopolitan sensibility.[16]

To choreograph a guerrilla poetics is to decenter the institution of writing, a minoritizing act that entails the transgression of normative forms. One of the major features of SingPoWriMo prompts is their high level of experimentation with poetic form. A plethora of recognizable forms, such as the haiku, the etheree, the ghazal, the lipogram, acrostic poetry, found poetry, blackout (erasure) poetry, and shape poetry have been used in prompts throughout the years. In consequence of its interest in form, SingPoWriMo has popularized emerging patterns of poetry and invented new ones, including:

15. Other examples include prompts inviting contributors to write poems in Q&A style (#SPWM16day13); without any nouns (#SPWM15day22, with a bonus challenge of not repeating any word except articles) or verbs (#SPWM14day25); in at least ten lines, where the last word of each line is the first word of the next line, and the last word of the poem is the first word of the poem (#SPWM14day 27), with an added challenge of having the last letter of every word as the first letter of the next word; in "snowball" format, with each line containing one more letter (or word) than the previous line (#SPWM15day13), with a #madnessbonus challenge to write the snowball poem as one coherent sentence; as a lipogram, where the poem avoids a particular letter of the alphabet (#SPWM14day18, #SPWM15day6); publishable as a Tweet (#SPWM15day4); in the first-person plural with a minimum word count of seventy in one stanza without line breaks (#SPWM16day14); inclusive of symbols (question mark, dollar sign, ampersand, asterisk, parenthesis, etc.), with a #madnessbonus challenge to include ten emoji (#SPWM15day8); and in intersemiotic response to a given photograph (#SPWM15day2) or video (#SPWM16day27).

16. While SingPoWriMo can be seen as developing away from the literary establishment, it is also important to note their connecting threads. Notably, SingPoWriMo is supported by the Arts Fund, and is now subsumed under Sing Lit Station (SLS), a registered charity and Institution of Public Character funded by the National Arts Council (more on the SLS in Chapter 6). Many of the active contributors to SingPoWriMo, including Joshua Ip himself, were also trained under the state-organized Creative Arts Programme in their formative years, some garnering state-sponsored literary awards such as the Golden Point Award and the Singapore Literature Prize (Joshua Ip, personal communication, July 2020).

a. *Asingbol*: a poetic form indigenous to Singapore, composed of exactly 140 characters including spaces. Written as a single clause, the words are not capitalized, with the sentence always end-stopping on a period to emphasize its statement of exposition and assertion.

b. *Twin cinema*: invented in Singapore and made popular by SingPoWriMo 2016, this poetic form consists of two discrete columns that can be read horizontally across the two columns as well as vertically down each column.

c. *Nucleus poem*: invented by a Bangladeshi poet based in Singapore, this form uses a concentric structure inspired by the number of electrons in the subshells of an atom—that is, two syllables in the first line, eight syllables in the second, eighteen syllables in the third, and one to thirty-two syllables in the fourth.

Also noteworthy is the featuring of ostensibly historical forms indigenous to the region, which had putatively fallen into obscurity and are now resuscitated through SingPoWriMo—or so we are made to believe. These include:

a. *Pantun*: a fifteenth-century Malay poetic form, made up of four lines of roughly equal length, with an ABAB rhyme scheme; the first two lines, or *pembayang* (shadow), set out a riddle, while the last two lines, or *maksud* (meaning), solve the riddle.

b. *Kural*: an ancient form of Tamil poetry consisting of two lines, the first with four words and the second with three words; it is usually written in series.

c. *Syair*: a seventeenth-century Malay narrative poetic form, consisting of a series of four-line stanzas (each line usually four or five beats long) with an AAAA rhyme scheme.

d. *Liwuli*: an ancient form of poetry originating from Southeast Asia. It consists of three stanzas, the first containing thirty-one syllables in the form of a prose poem, the second consisting of fourteen syllables divided into three lines, and the third comprising questions.

e. *Empat perkataan*: a fifteenth-century poetic form invented in Malacca, with each line consisting of four words (two syllables each, in the strictest version) fragmentarily juxtaposed.

f. *Udaiyaathathu*: an ancient Southeast Asian form of poetry also known as "the unbroken chain," where the first word of every line is repeated as the last word of the next line, and the first word of the last line is the last word of the first line.

g. *Peneira poroso*: a poetic form of Eurasian (Portuguese–Malay) origin, with fragments distributed across the page with uneven spacing.

The twist in this archaeology of Southeast Asian poetic forms is that it is, in large part, a farce. Of the forms listed above, the *pantun, kural,* and *syair* are historically attested though largely forgotten, and by virtue of appearing frequently on SingPoWriMo, they are being resuscitated out of obscurity. By contrast, the *liwuli, empat perkaatan, udaiyaathathu,* and *peneira poroso* are deceptions: they are in fact Joshua Ip's recent inventions masquerading as venerable forms of poetry—yet another instance of SingPoWriMo's playful gambits. In this regard, Ip describes himself as a "troll" who "invent[s] new forms but pass[es] them off as 'ancient,' 'long-lost' forms in the tradition of literary hoaxes" (Joshua Ip, personal communication, July 2020).

These franken-forms of literature are made to amuse and bemuse, with a creative-critical strain running through the make-believe names and rules.[17] The motivation behind their invention is more political than literary: "Part of this is anti/decolonial, part of it is anti-history/establishment," Ip says (personal communication, July 2020). For example, the four invented forms correspond, respectively, to the four ethnic categories encapsulated by the CMIO schema.[18] This makes it possible to read the fabrication involved in the nomenclature and syllabic/meter requirements as an ironic metacommentary on the arbitrariness of the racial divisions underlying the CMIO.

This proliferation of forms hailing from different cultural traditions, be they historically derived or recently invented, speaks to a keen interest in textual form, the upshot of which is a semiotic vibrancy unseen in any other literary

17. In a related vein, Joshua Ip invented at least two other forms of poetry. The *kōel* is said to be of Southeast Asian origin, comprising three lines, the constraint being that the first and third lines are to rhyme with an open vowel sound while the second line should be alliterative. Ip coined the term for a presentation at WrICE (Writers Intercultural Exchange), an international residency run by RMIT University, to demonstrate how SingPoWriMo worked. At the beginning of his hour-long presentation, Ip posted a "kōel prompt" on SingPoWriMo, and asked the community to help write kōels in the thread, which Ip then presented to the audience. By the end of an hour, more than a hundred kōels were contributed. More intriguing is the form called *vlle*, which Ip invented in critique of Art. 377a in Singapore, a notorious piece of legislation prohibiting homosexual acts in Singapore. The number 377 is insinuated into its structure of one three-syllable line followed by two seven-syllable lines. Crucially, the form is made to require a "masculine" rhyme (whatever that means), where a "feminine" rhyme is said to "[pervert] the natural order of the vlle" (http://formsofsea.blogspot.com/2018/09/vlle.html). The phrasing of the rule here ironically references Art. 377a, in which homosexuality is constructed as a perversion of the normative masculine/feminine order. The putative origin of the form, said to be invented by British ecclesiasticals in the sixteenth century, is part of this ironic setup, as Art. 377a is a legacy of British colonial rule in Singapore. According to Ip (personal communication), within the SingPoWriMo community the *vlle* "has become almost a form of in-joke by now."

18. The *liwuli* was jointly invented by Joshua Ip and fellow Singaporean poet Alvin Pang. The "Chinese" term has political undertones, derived by combining the first letters of the family names of three prime ministers of Singapore, namely, Lee Kuan Yew (where Lee is *Li* in hanyu pinyin romanization), Goh Chok Tong, (where Goh is *Wu* in hanyu pinyin romanization), and Lee Hsien Loong (*Li,* as above); hence "liwuli." And while the metric structure of the *empat perkataan* (meaning "four words" in Malay) is a preexisting one, its rules of composition and variations are invented by Ip. The word *udaiyaathathu* means "unbroken chain" in Tamil, while *peneira poroso* means "porous sieve" in Portuguese (Joshua Ip, personal communication, July 2020).

endeavor in Singapore. Such vibrancy is amply showcased in several contributions to #SPWM17day25, which invited participants to write a "faithless translation" based on any source text. Here we witness the free play of nonverbal and embodied resources, taking poetry beyond the interlingual into the intersemiotic. One contributor, for example, offered an emoticon translation of Shakespeare's Sonnet 18;[19] another used the concept of solfège to translate *Aerith's Theme*, the well-known musical theme for the video game Final Fantasy VII, into poetry by composing words whose first letters are based on musical alphabets derived from the theme song (e.g., doh→d, reh→r, and fah→f).[20]

These bold experimentations with form offer a ludic, hence egalitarian, touch to poetry, conventionally seen as a relatively inaccessible mode of writing. Beneath all this lightheartedness is a more serious intent: to demonstrate how the strictures of poetry as a venerable literary institution can be subverted by ordinary writers to cultivate their own sense of a locale-specific poetry. Compared to the institutional anthologies in Chapter 3, which represent a "collective mode" of administering various literatures using a stable and reusable semiotic structure, SingPoWriMo is more akin to a loose assemblage in which collective modes of writing are unpacked by "individual modes of reappropriation" (de Certeau 1984: 96). These latter modes are "ways of operating" poetry, exhibiting what de Certeau (1984) calls tactics: "victories of the 'weak' over the 'strong' . . . clever tricks, knowing how to get away with things, 'hunter's cunning,' maneuvers, polymorphic simulations, joyful discoveries" (xix). All of these point to a guerrilla approach to writing that renders it decentered, unpredictable, and fluid.

**Poetry on the Move**

One of the most interesting prompts in this regard is #SPWM16day24, moderated by Joshua Ip. Called "The Last Train Prompt," Ip challenged his fellow citizen poets to write a poem about a specific Mass Rapid Transit (MRT) station. The poems were then embedded, by way of hyperlinks, into an interactive MRT map, created on ThingLink, distributed with multicolored nodes (the colors representing major train lines) bearing the names of train stations on the island. The map initially appears like an ordinary train map, until one mouses over it to reveal the nodes populating the map; clicking on these nodes takes one to the poems written about particular train stations on the SingPoWriMo Facebook page. The figure of a public transportation map

19. https://www.facebook.com/photo?fbid=1374836389206163&set=gm.13233
47374447177.
20. https://www.facebook.com/photo?fbid=10155264230567156&set=gm.13242
73034354611.

is thus layered over with a virtual literary landscape to create a palimpsest, waiting to be activated by the reader.[21]

The invocation of the map as a visual trope gains theoretical interest in light of de Certeau's idea of "spatial stories." de Certeau (1984) argues that the map has emerged in contemporary culture as an institutional tool to delineate boundaries on a scientific basis rather than to indicate traversed itineraries on the ground. Maps are "a totalizing stage on which elements of diverse origin are brought together to form the tableau of a "state" of geographical knowledge"; they are collations "on the same plane [of] heterogeneous places" at the erasure of concrete and dynamic itineraries that condition the possibility of maps in the first place (121). The Text in the City mobile application discussed in Chapter 3 illustrates such a cartographic vision of literature from above. Referring to Figure 3.3 again, the application choreographs a spatial network out of a hundred poems (written and published independently of the application) by superimposing on them a structured geographical frame, complete with defined zones and trails. That frame, as we have seen, comprises many urban landmarks, symbolizing a fixity that is further reinforced by their association with poems invoking the imagery of the site in question.

In contrast to the literary cartography exhibited in Text in the City, the ThingLink map created out of #SPWM16day24 presents a different choreography. It is not a static and objectified representation of Singapore's terrain; on the contrary, based as it is on a public transport network, it foregrounds mobility. Here, the panoramic visuality of the Singapore map is hijacked by individual poets, giving rise to a dispersed literary itinerary, "a discursive series of operations" where lyrical sensibilities of ordinary writers are injected into a "plane projection [of] totalizing observations" (de Certeau 1984: 119). As each train station was supposed to take on one poem, citizen poets were asked to *chope* (reserve) their preferred station with the moderator, who would mark a reserved station in black; a station for which a poem had been submitted was marked in red. The ThingLink map was updated continually during the day on Facebook, with the train map first occupied all over with black nodes, which then gradually morphed into red nodes.[22]

There is a strong participatory, game-like element in all of this, contrasting with the highly planned distribution of poems across the map interface in Text in the City, whose poems are written by published and canonical poets. Methodologically, the ThingLink map instances a quasi-culture jamming, whereby a train map designed by transport authorities is appropriated and subverted into a poetry itinerary. It is as if citizen poets, the literary

---

21. https://www.thinglink.com/scene/780612664316395521?fbclid=IwAR1-aC5of-pZWYl95NiI8hxeo9orCWIeCCFmOhBBN4UFlgZKNtFFgkieQltg.
22. https://www.facebook.com/groups/singpowrimo/permalink/98347010 8434907/.

counterpart of de Certeau's pedestrians, have taken over discursive control of the island's terrain with their writing, leashing out the mobile energies inherent in the transportation theme and frozen in an inert cartographic representation.

The mobility theme of #SPWM16day24 was subsequently taken a notch further by Joshua Ip with an offshoot event called SingPoOnTheMRT or SPOTM.[23] On June 4, 2016, fans of SingPoWriMo physically boarded an MRT train along the East–West line, riding from one terminal station to the other and taking turns reading their own "MRT poems" (i.e., poems themed on MRT train stations, including those written for #SPWM16day24) aloud in the train car along the journey.[24]

A bold extension of SingPoWriMo's penchant for experimental forms, SPOTM pushes poetry out of the (web)page and reinserts it into the spatial settings that inspired it, thus transforming a transportation infrastructure into a temporary poetry platform. The stations on the MRT line, initially discrete *places* situated on the train map, are strung up into a continuous *space* for poetry by virtue of being traversed by citizen poets. Poetry becomes literally mobile, embodied in informal, party-like performances in a public facility, hence subverting stereotyped notions of poetry as that which is printed on the page, written and read in contemplative solitude, and appreciated for its somber quality.

## A locale-specific poetics

In line with its experimental stance on writing, SingPoWriMo has become a testing ground for developing a transgressive, locale-specific poetics. It serves as a literary platform to celebrate facets of so-called Singaporeaness (an essentialist notion) and to perform localized inflections of English. It is in this sense that SingPoWriMo represents an Anglophone practice: it deterritorializes English (the anglophone), together with its scriptural economy and discursive institutions (poetry in this case), by punctuating it with an ultraterritorial consciousness and heteroglossic textuality, even as it operates within the frame of that language.

SingPoWriMo's rootedness in locality is instanced in its many locale-based prompts. For example, the prompt for #SPWM20day4, titled "The Forgotten

23. https://www.facebook.com/events/pasir-ris-mrt/singpoonthemrt-spotm/8386 71252906196/.

24. A quick snapshot of the event can be viewed at https://www.youtube.com/ watch?v=Iwgn6w-CSUQ; video clips of citizen poets reading their works on the train also can be viewed at https://www.youtube.com/playlist?list=PLRQhQYk4yDAvK3 XS4QuA8Clnec36HEKJH.

City Prompt,"[25] challenges participants to write about a bygone place in Singapore. The place in question is delimited by a number of geographical parameters defined by landmarks, it should be

- no further north than the former NLB (now a tunnel).
- no further south than the former Yangtze Cinema/Pearls Centre (soon to be integrated into Outram MRT Thomson line).
- no further west than the former Zouk at Jiak Kim St (now a condo).
- no further east than the former Singapore Stone (roughly where the Merlion is).

Here we see abbreviations (NLB [National Library Board], condo), landmarks (Zouk, Merlion, Singapore Stone), public infrastructure (Outram MRT Thomson line), and entertainment venues (Yangtze Cinema, Pearls Centre). A nostalgic concept motivates the prompt, calling for a throwback to places of yesteryear, thus presupposing a familiarity with (or, alternatively, a willingness to conduct some research into) the shifting cultural landscape of Singapore. Some of these places are decidedly vernacular, tracing a memory trail that falls outside the purview of official narratives: Zouk (in its former location) was an iconic nightclub in Singapore, the Yangtze Cinema a now-demolished theater known for its shady repertoire of adult films, and Pearls Centre an old-school shopping mall built in the 1970s. Locale-specific signifiers and references like these are a staple feature of SingPoWriMo.

A recent and most trenchant demonstration of locality is Low Kian Seng's 2020 poem, "blessings, Uniquely Singapore" (#SPWM20day30).[26] Low's poem, whose title parodies Singapore Tourism Board's promotional tagline, is marked by an extremely high concentration of abbreviated proper nouns (Singapore Pools, ERP, BTO, HDB, CPF, Medisave, Medishield Life) as well as items, notions, practices, or sensibilities imbued with the identity value of Singaporeanness: the hope of getting "extra servings of meat" on one's *chap chye png* (rice with an assortment of dishes); the notion of the "ideal thickness" of *kopi* (coffee) or *teh* (tea); the act of *chope*-ing or reserving a seat in a public eatery with a packet of tissue paper, all of which invoke stereotyped mundanities of everyday life in Singapore.

Yet Anglophone Singapore poetry, defined contrapuntally with respect to "Singapore poetry in English," is more than a smattering of names of local streets, institutions, food, personages, and habits. In line with a fascination with things local is a performance of multiple tongues, including those Othered

25. https://www.facebook.com/notes/singpowrimo/singpowrimo-2020-all-prom pts-to-date/2882379515210614/.
26. https://www.facebook.com/groups/singpowrimo/permalink/294311838 9136726/.

by the institution, typifying a conscious departure from a linguistic primness and properness. A desire to go against the dictates of official language policy is palpable. One of the clearest examples is the prompt for #SPWM17day14, which exhorts poets to write in Singlish:

**The Good Prompt**[27]

Write a poem in Singlish.

#formbonus: Singlish is not just a pidginised version of your mother tongue! if you are Chinese, try to incorporate more root words from non-Chinese languages, if you are Malay, try to incorporate more root words from non-Malay languages, and so on and so forth. Please make your mother tongue a minority. If you are running out of words, Singlish is a rich and constantly evolving language, so feel free to evolve it any-howly! You can also refer to the amazing Singlish Dictionary here: http://www.mysmu.edu/faculty/jacklee/

#substancebonus: post your poem as a comment on the home page of the Speak Good English Movement! (screenshot or permalink or it didn't happen)

#spwm17 #spwm17day14 #speakgoodsinglish

This prompt seeks out an extreme heteroglossia that cross-fertilizes among Singlish and the mother tongues. Yet "mother tongue" here is not coextensive with the official term MTL (mother tongue language): the terms "non-Chinese languages" and "non-Malay languages" are notably in the plural, referencing Chinese dialects and varieties of spoken Malay not recognized by the authorities as MTLs. The fluidity of the language being promoted here speaks to a policy-defying stance. Participants are invited to experiment with Singlish itself, seen as "rich and constantly evolving," and are referred not to some well-established English dictionary but to an online Singlish dictionary.

More tellingly, a bonus challenge asks writers to post their Singlish poems on the Speak Good English Movement (SGEM) website and attach a screenshot or a link as evidence. The SGEM, as we recall, posits Singlish as the archenemy of Standard English, a position that has recently been attenuated but is nonetheless still palpable. As such, to post Singlish poems as comments in the SGEM website is to openly provoke the language establishment, illustrating the antagonistic edge of SingPoWriMo in promulgating a language ideology diametrically opposed to the state's.

27. https://www.facebook.com/hashtag/spwm17day14?source=feed_text&epa=HASHTAG.

Further examples along similar lines include #SPWM20day17, where a "mother tongue" prompt instructs readers to "Write a poem that contains words from a language that isn't the usual kosher options, i.e. English, Malay, Mandarin or Tamil." The explicit exclusion of the four official languages, cynically labeled "kosher options" (i.e., safe, conformist options), sidesteps the quadrilingual schema, opening up the discursive space to alternative language realms, with a bonus prompt asking for poems to be written in a Southeast Asian language. (The language ideological incorrectness is, however, undercut by the additional request for poets to supply an English translation to ease the language barrier.) The usual signifier for heteroglossia, namely, the Hokkien dialect, figures prominently in the poems grouped under this prompt,[28] although a host of unexpected languages also appear, including lesser-known heritage languages such as Kristang (a creole spoken by indigenous people of mixed Portuguese–Malay descent).

Other transgressive experiments abound, ensuing in extreme forms of heteroglossia that would have difficulty seeing the light of day in conventional print venues. In SingPoWriMo 2020, one contributor puts the phrase "oh fuck" through Google Translate, churning out dozens of renditions in various languages;[29] another "writes" a verse in Khalani, an imaginary language from science fiction game worlds;[30] and yet another comes up with a poem in sign language and then translates it into English (or so we are led to believe), thus reversing the usual source-target order in sign interpreting.[31]

It is also significant that vulgarity has come to be a characteristic ingredient in SingPoWriMo verse, adding that deliberate tinge of uncouthness to create tension with the lofty associations of poetry.[32] Together with the linguistic

28. For an example where Hokkien is used in extensive proportion, see Dustin Wong's contribution to #SPWM20day10, "my joss stick malboro make one," https://www.facebook.com/groups/singpowrimo/permalink/2895796113868954/.

29. https://www.facebook.com/photo?fbid=3182991531734765&set=gm.2910476455734253

30. https://www.facebook.com/photo?fbid=10157078402077747&set=pcb.2912165292232036.

31. https://www.facebook.com/photo?fbid=10217124613493803&set=gm.2910582122390353.

32. A few examples suffice to illustrate the kind of vulgarity in SingPoWriMo verse: "My stealth game is prime, but my scent will betray these fuckers got noses that find needles in hay" (Karisa Poedjirahardjo, https://www.facebook.com/groups/singpowrimo/permalink/2939653716149860/); "And if I see one more fucking smiley face/Preceding an exclamation mark" (Jared Ho, https://www.facebook.com/groups/singpowrimo/permalink/2907053752743190/); "cry mother cry father for what? what I talk cock? kanina you say I jiao wei?" (Wong Cheng Him, https://www.facebook.com/groups/singpowrimo/permalink/2887085498073349/); and "I think just extent to knnbccb" (Sven Tan, https://www.facebook.com/groups/singpowrimo/permalink/2933179870130578/). Kanina, jiao wei, and knnbccb are specimens of vulgar speech in Hokkien.

inflections and cultural allusions mentioned above, such vulgarity pivots anglophone writing in Singapore toward the Anglophone, with all the latter's resistance against orthodox orders of language and culture as represented by Standard English.

## Beyond code-mixing

SingPoWriMo has gone a long way toward maturing entrenched forms of heteroglossia, tactically exploiting the synergies between English and several languages spoken on the ground beyond the occasional code-switching.[33] Although SingPoWriMo poetry for the most part uses English as a matrix language, the boundary between English and Singlish discourses—the latter incorporating elements from Malay and the Chinese dialects—is not always clear. Some authors consciously problematize the Englishness of their work by crowding out English words with non-English ones as well as creating nonce Singlish items out of English morphology.

For example, June Loh's "Salahful" (#SPWM20day16) is a short poem of twenty-five words (including the title), seventeen of which are non-English. The latter include Malay and Hokkien words, some of which are inflected as if they were English, leading to playful lexical outcomes: *salahful* (*salah* [wrong] + *-ful* suffix); *aiyohed* (*aiyo* [exclamatory word] + *-ed* suffix); *paktorful* (*paktor* [to date] + *-ful* suffix); *cheemological* (*cheem* [profound] + *-ological* suffix); *kay kianged* (*kay kiang* [lit. to pretend being clever, meaning to do something superfluous] + *-ed* suffix).[34]

Similar morphological experiments are attested in Joshua Ip's piece, "An expression used to wish oneself prosperity." The poem works the Hokkien verb *huat* (to be prosperous) so extensively throughout the verse as to destabilize its identity as an English poem. Once again, contingent formations are created by meshing *huat* into an English morphological frame, an operation that I have elsewhere called translanguaging (Lee and Li 2021). A hybrid register emerges where *huat* as a dialect word comes to behave like an English word; hence cross-lingual inflections, such as *huats* (plural inflection: *huat* + *-s*); *huatting* (present progressive aspect: *huat* + *-ing*); *huatterly* (adjectival form: *huat* + *-ly*); as well as parodic imitations, such as *huatas* (an ambivalent construction that both mimics the Chinese word *fa da* [to get rich], as well

33. Here we should note that so-called Standard English itself is far from a homogeneous category in Singapore. Although British English is taught in schools and used in media and government communications, American English is increasingly prevalent at all levels, often leading to mixed usage.

34. https://www.facebook.com/groups/singpowrimo/permalink/290930798 2517767/.

as playing on the Singlish word *atas* [to act out a high-class disposition in a pretentious manner]); *huataboutists* (from whataboutism); *huatisan* (from partisan); *huatchitecture* (from architecture); *huatelier* (from hotelier); and *huaternal* (riffing off eternal).[35]

Crucially, what we are seeing here are conscious linguistic excursions into Singlish, not to be mistaken for representations of how the language is empirically spoken on the ground. The ensuing multilingualism bears signs of a curated artifact, and therefore is not completely coextensive with Pennycook and Otsuji's (2019a) "mundane multilingualism." Not unlike the verbal artifice of *Spiaking Singlish*, the Singlish of SingPoWriMo is a much more aggressive, though also more entertaining, rendition of everyday empirical Singlish. It cannibalizes English morphology and grammar, as if seeking to create a scandal of English as an institution. And in so doing, it evidences increased confidence in stylizing the vernacular into a poetic register, boasting a degree of verbal inventiveness not witnessed in street Singlish; it performs a rustic and variegated orality–aurality that rubs against the smooth homogeneity of Standard English. More than that, this is a multilingualism that attempts to "represent and codify spoken Singlish as an identity project," one that foregrounds "everyday translation in Singapore, the linguistic crossings that are often disavowed or forgotten" (Holden 2017: n.p.).

What makes Singlish a good basis for the making of this register is its apparent distance from power, giving it a perceived affective force. As Ng Yi-sheng, an award-winning poet and active contributor to SingPoWriMo, puts it, Singlish is "a language of emotion, home, a more private language," sometimes giving off the impression of nonseriousness: "people find that when you choose to write in Singlish rather than standard English . . . you're not taking this completely seriously, you're not thinking logically" (personal communication, July 2020). As gestures in communication, this kind of Singlish at once mocks the language establishment for its self-seriousness and demonstrates the capacity of the vernacular to write itself into a queer brand of English. Such queering of English precipitates an oral–aural theatricalization of a Singaporean identity conceived from the bottom up.

Overall, there is a semiotic unruliness in SingPoWriMo that stands it in contrast with the multicultural utopia envisioned by the state, presenting an alternative utopia that challenges the ideology of neat multilingualism. Heteroglossia, as an irregular, punctuative form of multilingualism, is a key feature of this pushback from below, constituting an entropic vernacular discourse that articulates against the tenets of neat multilingualism. This alternative utopia comes through most clearly in SingPoWriMo's metadiscursive

35. https://www.facebook.com/groups/singpowrimo/permalink/2943163765798855/.

poems, which, through their ironic subversion of the prevailing language ideological order, demonstrate the increasing maturity of Singlish writing.

Most exemplary in this regard is Tang ZX's "The Speak Good Singlish Movement" (#SPWM20day16),[36] a futuristic and fantastical counternarrative to the official discourse on Singlish. The poem imagines a future Singapore, branded as the "global Grammar Garden City" in parody of its reputation as a "garden city," facing a major crisis. Thanks to a bureaucratic initiative calling for "Cultural Retention" (a wry evocation of the sound-image of Cultural Revolution), the long-forgotten language of Singlish is rehabilitated overnight as a valuable heritage resource. The problem is that Singlish has been lost to most people who have "eradicated their roots": "the nation came to a/Stifling realization. No one really remembers/How to speak good Singlish." The government scrambles to promote the Speak Good Singlish Movement (SGSM), which "Seeped rapidly into every nook and cranny/Of our infrastructure." At this juncture, the poet invents specimens of "broken Singlish," making a metalinguistic note of the "jumble[d] up syntax" and random insertion of slang:

> but, sia some la wrong, you think got so?
> sinkies we seriously got leh try, but some ting not working. Eh?
> . . .
> hor we listen really hard, jumble up syntax insert
> slang randomly like, sia, we got taught. we got ask
> mor-Ang to listen to us, they say
> Biang! You wah-ing engrish beh-si bad!

In the above extract, Singlish errors are built in as part of the poem's narrative that people have forgotten how to speak "proper" Singlish: "*sia* some *la* wrong" (misplacing sentence-final particles in sentence-initial and sentence-medial positions), "you think *got* so?" (inappropriate use of "got"), "we seriously got *leh* try" (misplacing sentence-final particle in sentence-medial position), *Biang* (truncating *wah biang*), *mor-Ang* (morphologically inverting *ang-mo*, meaning "foreigner"), and *beh-si* (inverting the intensifier *si-beh*). Later in the poem, the education minister is quoted as saying "lah, every school is good eh school. because all/got . . . got zai speak singlish"; here *lah* and *eh* are misplaced and the insertion of the Chinese dialect adjective *zai* ('smart,' 'competent') messes up the otherwise well-formed (as far as this poem goes) "got speak singlish."

This construal of broken Singlish as something to be bemoaned exudes ironic fun, given that in the real world, Singlish is often labeled by language

36. https://www.facebook.com/groups/singpowrimo/permalink/2907940485987850/.

authorities as a form of broken English (Chng 2008: 62). The idea of broken Singlish is subversive because it presupposes a standard variety, described in the poem as "classical, quintessential SINGLISH" (capitalization in the original), implying that Singlish has obtained the exemplary status of an official language, if only in the poetic scenario. The alternative utopia thus evoked is one where "humiliating dialect and broken English" is a thing of a "long-forgotten era," superseded by the new language ideological imperative to resuscitate the lost tongue. This is encapsulated in the figure of "the oldest man alive in singapore [sic]" who holds the closely kept secrets of Singlish hushed up by years of English dominance, and who is now keenly consulted by the administration to impart his knowledge so that "we can construct anew/the armoury of our nation's merits,/the saccharine victory of numerical merits,/ we can triumph."

In a radical reversal of fates, the SGSM, which as we saw in the last chapter is an under-the-radar social media initiative in resistance to the SGEM, is elevated into a project of national importance and utmost urgency in the poem. (There is a palpable sense in which the imaginary trajectory of Singlish is inspired by the actual fate of Singapore's Chinese dialects, which have been systematically eradicated by another hegemonic language, namely, Mandarin and its corollary machinery, the SMC.) On the other hand, Standard English, with its "clockwork precision" and global aspirations, is relegated to the role of an outdated Other in the poet's fantasy, soon to be overshadowed by the inexorable rise of Singlish in the same way that Standard English marginalizes Singlish as a low-status, underground language in reality. By staging a return of the repressed with light-hearted irony, the poem makes a wry poke at the language establishment in Singapore, deconstructing the fundamentals of language education and policymaking and mocking the bureaucracy for its instrumental pragmatism in relation to language.

## ANTIPOETRY: HETEROGLOSSIA AND THE LITERARY CARNIVALESQUE

From the pre-1965 EngMalChin poets through the overtly pro-Singlish contemporary writers of the younger generation to the citizen poets of SingPoWriMo, heteroglossic poetry in Singapore has grown from a short-lived movement based on print magazines and involving just a handful of kindred writers into an annual social media event espousing a radical poetics and attracting thousands of participants. Throughout this trajectory, the tactical use of local vernaculars in writing is embroiled in the identity politics of the day. While the EngMalChin movement attempted to imagine a Malayan identity against the then-colonial status of Singapore, SingPoWriMo citizen poets seek to articulate a vernacular Singaporean identity by pursuing Anglophone expressions and transgressing instituted boundaries, including those surrounding the multilingual order.

The linguistic practices of SingPoWriMo point to the maturation of Singlish as an assemblage of features, acquiring the status of a stable register that performs identity work. These practices reiterate and reinforce the positive valuation of Singlish within the digital-literary community as the instantiation of a heartlander Singaporean persona.[37] Following Schneider's (2003) Dynamic Model of World Englishes, Singlish can be said to have attained endonormative stabilization (Phase Four in Schneider's model), at which point the "psychological independence and the acceptance of a new, indigenous identity result in the acceptance of local forms of English as a means of expression of that new identity" (250). According to this view, the proliferation of creative expressions in SingPoWriMo, in which elements from colloquial speech are incorporated and transformed, indicates a high degree of linguistic autonomy and self-confidence (Schneider 2003: 252, 2007: 289) among younger Singaporean authors.

SingPoWriMo, then, is not just a frivolous playground for Singlish experiments, which are only a means to an end. What its heteroglossic composition signals is a recalcitrant Anglophone identity articulated within a guerrilla poetics. A guerrilla poetics is also an *antipoetics*, one that pushes against the discursive orthodoxies issued from the institution of poetry. Discussing the work of Nicanor Parra, Edith Grossman (1971) notes "the prosaic quality of speech for its very impurity, its profound expressive and ironic possibilities" and "the uncommon use of common language, with its attendant complex ironic organization and direct involvement of the reader" (72) as defining features of Parra's antipoetry.

The poetics of SingPoWriMo shares these characteristics, in particular prosaicness, impurity, and irony. It exhibits a strong propensity to a political incorrectness (from the perspective of the authorities); it critiques all forms of regimentation, vaunting a Singlish-based intelligibility poised not against foreign readers but vis-à-vis a bureaucracy based around English.[38] To be intelligible from a Singlish vantage point is also

37. This formulation is based on Johnstone (2009) with respect to Pittsburghese, to which Singlish has close parallels: "By virtue of a variety of discursive and metadiscursive activities, a set of features associated with an accent can come to be represented collectively in the public imagination as a stable register . . . and maintained across time via practices that reiterate and reinforce the evaluation of the register and its link to the social identity associated with a particular type of persona (the authentic Pittsburgher, in this case)" (160).

38. With its at times politically oriented humor, SingPoWriMo aligns with recent developments in the use of internet memes as a tacit form of political resistance in Singapore (Soh 2020).

to be (at least partially) unintelligible as English. Since the bureaucracy values a homogeneous standard of English, as enshrined in the objectives of the SGEM, heteroglossia would seem the most natural tactic to inscribe resistance.

Not all poems from SingPoWriMo are in Singlish, but many feature latent sociopolitical allusions without annotation, and the most exemplary works, including some of those discussed above, address locally situated themes through the local vernaculars, such as to be virtually impenetrable to "outsiders," and perhaps even to some "insiders." To my mind, this is the niche that SingPoWriMo creates for itself in performing the Anglophone in Singapore, specifically a Singlish-based, locally grounded Anglophone that rhizomatically departs from the top-down, English-based, and globally oriented anglophone.

It is perhaps unsurprising, then, that SingPoWriMo has also become a site for voicing antiestablishment sentiments. On this note, I want to end this discussion with one such antipoem, Ng Yi-sheng's BTBS, written for #SPWM16day14, which flaunts the rhetorical connection between heteroglossia and heterodoxy.

| BTBS (by Ng Yi-sheng, boldface added) | [Translation of bolded items:] |
|---|---|
| Watch out, little fucks, what your father-mother say; | |
| We're the dangerous ones, **boh tua boh suay**; | [Hokkien: "no big, no small," behaving without |
| Don't say don't like, don't like don't care, | propriety] |
| We are north south east west everywhere; | |
| Catch us in the schools, see us in the streets, | |
| In the park when we're rallying for parliament seats; | |
| Call the **mata** also we won't go away, | [Malay: "police"] |
| We're the dangerous ones, **boh tua boh suay**; | [Hokkien: "no big, no small," as above] |
| So you built this land, so you pioneer, | |
| So you **haolian** there, then you **wayang** here; | [Teochew: "show-off"/Malay: "put on a show," to |
| So you wash our brain, with your moral ed, | laze around while pretending to work] |
| So we **majulah** under white and red; | [Malay: "onward," alluding to national anthem] |
| So you **blur like cock**, so you **sotong king**, | [Singlish: confused/clueless like a chicken/squid] |
| When we run amok, when we will not sing; | |
| Let the **cikgu** cry, let the **cher kaobei**, | [Malay: "teacher"/Singlish: shorthand for |
| We're the dangerous ones, **boh tua boh suay**; | "teacher"+ Hokkien: "cry father," to complain] |
| Yah we contradict, yah we no respect, Yah we | [Hokkien: "no big, no small," as above] |
| **hantam** you on the internet; | [Malay: "beat-up," to find fault with someone] |
| Yah we do campaign, yah we stir the shit, | |
| Yah we say out loud what you won't admit; | |
| You can vomit blood, call us **yau siu kia**; | [Hokkien: "die-early kid," expletive] |
| Tell us **anak ini kurang ajar**; | [Malay: "rude/brash kid"] |

| | |
|---|---|
| But we won't **chitoh-chitoh** how you want to play, | [Hokkien: "play-play," to be unserious] |
| We're the dangerous ones, **boh tua boh suay**; | [Hokkien: "no big, no small," as above] |
| And you also know, time is on our side, | |
| You all better **siam**, better run and hide; | [Hokkien/Teochew: "get out of the way"] |
| Then one day you go, then we **ownself rule**, | [Singlish: "self-rule"] |
| Then we build this land, then we run this school; | |
| Then we **merdeka**, then we own the street, | [Malay: "independent"] |
| Then we **gerek-gerek** with our stamping feet; | [Malay: "cool," "groovy"] |
| Then our own **see geenas** turn around and say: | [Hokkien: "damn kid"] |
| We're the dangerous ones, **boh tua boh suay**. | [Hokkien: "no big, no small," as above] |

The poem has the feel of a boisterous school cheer (Ng Yi-sheng, personal communication, July 2020), its title abbreviated from the Hokkien phrase *boh tua boh suay* (behaving without propriety). It can also be read like the manifesto of a young anarchic tribe, self-identified as "the dangerous ones." The cynical references to the state (the referent of "you") convey a repulsion for complacent politicians and distaste for conformity with statal ideologies (So you built this land, so you pioneer/So you *haolian* [Hokkien, to show off] there, then you *wayang* [Malay, to laze around] here), as well as for the local education system ("So you wash our brain, with your moral ed [abbreviated from Moral Education, a local education curriculum that inculcates values]/So we *majulah* [Malay, move forward], under white and red [the two colours of Singapore's national flag]"). At certain junctures there is almost a call to action in resistance to the powers-that-be, threatening to "contradict," "hantam ['beat up"] you on the internet," "stir the shit," and expose underlying agendas ("say out loud what you won't admit"), but with an ironic twist at the end: these young rebels would eventually become the establishment, only to be resisted again by the next generation of rebellious youngsters.

The unmitigated heteroglossia of the poem is a hyperbolic display of the language on the streets, with the end rhymes betraying its rhetorical design. What this kind of heteroglossia resonates is an ambiance whose turbulent frequency discomfits those attuned to an erudite, pristine English. This ludic and deliberately low-handed writing in the vernacular is what the poet calls "fun Singlish" (personal communication, July 2020). Fun Singlish is a variety of grassroots English. But fun Singlish is not the outcome of a substandard proficiency in English, nor is it a liability for its users. Whereas grassroots English reveals "a struggle with norms [of Standard English], a series of orientations to stylistic conventions in local lingua franca varieties, and a lack of exposure to the normative codes of their addressees" (Blommaert 2010: 128–29), fun Singlish is a tactically concocted register reorienting precisely these traits used to discriminate against itself to index the noncosmopolitan and nonelite as a recalcitrant stance.

This brings me to my final point on the politics of humor. Gesturing toward the local and the incidental, fun Singlish represents the linguistic carnivalesque in Singapore. Writing on Bakhtin's idea of the carnival, Eagleton (2019) explains that carnivalesque laughter signals "a distinctive form of knowledge," "an entire world view" (31) at odds with the realm of humorless bureaucratic orders. It is "an extravaganza," "a privileged form of cognition" that "grasps the world as it actually is, in its ceaseless growth, decay, fertility, mutability, rebirth and renewal, and in doing so undercuts the spuriously eternal schemas of official ideology" (33). Bakhtinian laughter can therefore be a form of resistance. It represents the Rabelaisian spirit, so esteemed by Bakhtin, which "punctuate[s] urban life, introducing moments of anarchy into structures of institutionalized seriousness and chaos into practices of identity recognition" (Shapiro 2019: 73).

In my view, there is a Rabelaisian edge to fun Singlish with all its raucous exuberance and satirical, wicked humor. It partakes of a multilingual choreography set against a hegemonic regime symptomized by Standard English. In Milan Kundera's scheme, espoused in *The Book of Laughter and Forgetting*, this latter world would represent the "angelic": "drearily legible and intelligible"; "orderly, harmonious and stuffed to the seams with meaning"; and cleansed of all negativity, deficiency, awryness, or dysfunctionality (Eagleton 2019: 25). Fun Singlish, by contrast, would be symptomatic of the "demonic," "the perverse, refractory factor in any social order": it "deflates the pretensions of the angelic, puncturing its portentousness," "figuring as the grit in its oyster, the glitch in its mechanism" (Eagleton 2019: 26).

"Fun Singlish" may be a new coinage, but it is worth keeping in mind that heteroglossia as a practice harks back to preindependence writing in Singapore and has always had a minor presence in the development of the local literature. SingPoWriMo is a culmination of this tradition, at a juncture where an emerging local consciousness is fueled by social media technologies to shape the literary dynamic along a critical, ludic, and self-reflexive trajectory.

In the terms related above, SingPoWriMo's intervention lies in how it self-consciously embodies a "demonic" disposition, tactically riding on the stigma of the heartlands to carve out an iconoclastic positionality. By mobilizing citizen poets to write outside the box of institutional apparatuses and invoking vernacular oralities–auralities, it eludes the literary canon and language establishment. If Standard English, representing the anglophone, emblematizes the "mandated, regulated and standardised visions" and "the sanctioned, top-down, hegemonic world of normative action and beliefs"

(Pennycook and Otsuji 2019a: 177) in Singapore, then SingPoWriMo represents the Anglophone (and not merely anglophone, or English-speaking) within the cracks of a neatly delineated multilingualism. It articulates a multilingual *space*, in de Certeau's sense, a time-space of the carnivalesque in which the strictures and structures of top-down language policies are temporarily undone, thus offering its users an alternative multicultural fantasy from below.

One should point out, however, that although SingPoWriMo represents writing practices through a bottom-up modality, it has the potential to accrue into another kind of center. As a convivial discursive community, the platform has, over the course of several years since its inception, developed its own "ideal-types of norms or appropriateness criteria" (Blommaert 2010: 40), predisposed against what "proper" literary writing is deemed to be. The antiestablishment ideologies of SingPoWriMo underlie its "indexical direction of communication" (Blommaert 2010: 40), determining the kind of semiotic features that would be perceived as felicitous to this scale of discourse. Ludicity, as my discussion has shown, constitutes a sustained characteristic (i.e., norm) of SingPoWriMo poetry, such that a highly lyrical poem devoid of a sense of humor would come across as marked within this community of practice.

What this means is that, in performing a subversive stance as part of its espousal of a nonelitist ethos, SingPoWriMo has also constructed its own insider/outsider divide. As a platform promoting an idiosyncratic poetics partially rooted in the local vernacular, it embodies "small peer-group identity dynamics in which group-specific, exclusive, enregistered phonological, morphosyntactic, lexical and genre features are made emblematic of membership and eligibility" (Blommaert 2018: 33). This point is corroborated in an observation by Ng Yi-sheng: "when you look at SingPoWriMo you notice people respond to one another's poems, people start making inside jokes and so you're in [this] community . . . this is great but if you're not inside you say this is a clique, [you] feel excluded" (personal communication, July 2020).

Hence, while there are far fewer barriers to publishing in SingPoWriMo than in a conventional poetry journal, the perceived egalitarianism in the former can produce its own form of power and differentiation. Even though the vernacular poetry we have explored in this chapter is arguably democratic in positioning itself apart from the canon, it should not be romanticized as a premium site of resistance against linguistic hegemony. These writing practices from below, too, may garner enough momentum and resources to become yet another source of authority within a polycentric (Blommaert 2010: 39–41) literary system, recursively scaling its own center-periphery relations on a fractal level. Adapting Blommaert's

(2018: 56–60) terms, they can potentially accrue into a particular "chrono-topic environment" based on social media, develop their own "behavioral script" and "interaction rituals" to choreograph a nonconformist stance, and constitute a "microhegemony" of sorts in their own right. Such latent potential of vernacular practices to evolve into a new source of power desta-bilizes any perceived opposition between institutional and grassroots cho-reographies, a point to which we now turn.

# CHAPTER 6

# Beyond the divide

## *Toward a postmultilingual Singapore*

In lieu of a formal conclusion, this chapter throws critical light on the basic setup of the preceding chapters, with a view to understanding multilingual choreographies in Singapore beyond a top-down versus bottom-up divide. The cases presented thus far are structured along Michel de Certeau's spatial theory, as outlined in the introduction. According to this theory, the rhetoric of walking as an everyday practice both operates within and pushes against the urban spatial framework in which it is embedded. In respect to our Singapore data, this latter framework is represented by institutional discourses that circulate a fixed constellation of official languages in the form of an iterative, multiply entextualizable signifier: the quadrilingual schema.

The quadrilingual schema is a pervasive visual–spatial heuristic that encapsulates the contours of language policy in Singapore, instantiating a verbally hygienic affect grounded in neat multilingualism. It specifically enacts a complementary distribution model under which English, Chinese, Malay, and Tamil are streamlined into bounded entities of (more or less) equal standing. At the same time, these languages consolidate into a fetish (Kelly-Holmes 2014, 2020), signaling an impression of multicultural conviviality by means of a stable visual matrix. The schema's invocation on various scales and in diverse genres of official writing (including the representation of writing), such as public sign-making (Chapter 2) and literary anthologization (Chapter 3), activates a macroinstitutional frame for thinking multilingualism. That frame, I have suggested, may be captured using de Certeau's notion of *place*, constituted by all the paths and sites in a city that are

*Choreographies of Multilingualism.* Tong King Lee, Oxford University Press. © Oxford University Press 2022.
DOI: 10.1093/oso/9780197644645.003.0006

delineated, designated, named, and mapped as part of the strategic governance of urban geographies.

Against this multilingual *place*, a different modality of writing is engendered by heteroglossic linguistic energies working against the affect of balance instituted by official discourses. Drawing heavily on vernacular resources, particularly Singlish, colloquial Malay, and the Chinese dialects, this emergent body of writing often adopts a ludic character in parody of straight-faced official discourses. We have seen that the controversies surrounding Singlish have generated transgressive registers and vernacular movements from below that question the language establishment in its eradication of local language varieties. This culminates in the staging of florid textual performances of Singlish, in both lexicographical genres such as *Spiaking Singlish* (Chapter 4) and social media poetry evincing resistant sensibilities (Chapter 5). In transcending the quadrilingual schema and transgressing the verbal hygiene entailed therein, this discursive trajectory articulates a queering of the regime of neat multilingualism. It is tactical, as opposed to strategic: it intermittently punctures the multilingual infrastructure conceived under prevailing language policies, producing its own *space* through microscale interventions while subsisting within the establishment framework, not unlike the shortcuts and detours undertaken by de Certeau's pedestrian.

By reimagining multilingualism through a recalcitrant praxis, such writing from below is a prefigurative performance, where prefiguration, as Baker (2020), explains, is a political strategy "often associated with anarchism and defined as 'a political practice in which social movements attempt to bring about a desired goal or vision for society by enacting and embodying that vision themselves in their own daily organizing'" (4, quoting Maeckelbergh 2020). More pertinent for us are the textual and semiotic manifestations of prefiguration, which can be seen in acts of translation in activist contexts (e.g., the Arab Spring), entailing a "willingness to explore alternatives, to create anew, to depart from and subvert conventions" (Baker 2016: 6). Prefigurative writing, then, is a kind of tactical discourse that, like more embodied modes of prefiguration, aims at creatively intervening in the present to "make things better by acting now in particular ways," in such a way that ensues in "greater justice and equality for all" (Baker 2020: 6).

The critical interventions of Singlish proponents and of citizen poetry initiatives like SingPoWriMo can be said to perform a prefigurative politics of multilingual writing. They challenge prevailing assumptions about linguistic hierarchies in Singapore and explore alternative means of expressing affect by playfully experimenting with vernaculars. In so doing, they unravel a reimagination of Singapore's linguistic landscape, whereby "making the future present becomes a question of creating affectively imbued representations [images, symbols, narratives] that move and mobilize" (Anderson 2010: 784, cited in Baker 2020: 4). Returning to de Certeauean lingo, they transform a *place*, whose multilingualism is worked through by delineated borders and scaffolded structures, into a *space*, whose multilingualism is dynamic rather than static, "light" (with social rather than traditional media as a key platform) rather than "heavy" (think metal signage and print anthologies), and spontaneous (undertaken by individuals at their whim) rather than institutionalized (executed by bureaucrats as part of systemic planning).

The two modalities of writing represent different choreographies of multilingualism instantiating different spatiotemporal scales: the one articulating a technocratic neatness aspiring to a global, future-oriented cosmopolitanism, and the other, a carnivalesque messiness associated with the earthy and nostalgic heartlands. In line with our choreography metaphor, it is perhaps apt to put this dichotomy in the dramaturgical terms of Peter Brook (1996). Hence, like refined theatre, institutional signage and anthologies are undergirded by a "conscious, articulate design" (65) whose object is to preserve the integrity of the quadrilingual schema, thereby rationalizing multilingualism in terms of a geometric order and dovetailing with public narratives on multilingualism.

In contradistinction, Singlish writing and citizen poetry map onto what Brook terms "rough theater," which foregrounds fun and laughter with all its "bearbaiting, ferocious satire and grotesque caricature," whereby "the spectacle takes on its socially liberating role, for by nature the popular theatre is anti-authoritarian, anti-traditional, anti-pomp, anti-pretence" (68). These choreographies represent competing narratives on how multilingual Singapore is to be imagined, and together they offer a well-rounded glimpse into the city's sociolinguistic dynamic.

## ESCHEWING THE DICHOTOMY

The above characterization runs the risk of reifying the dichotomy between the top down and the bottom up in relation to how multilingual Singapore is imagined and performed. Like all dichotomies, this one, if articulated to the extreme, suffers from an essentialist tendency to polarize the two modalities of writing as diametrical opposites. And almost invariably, it is the perceived "weaker" pole—the bottom-up, from-below, and noninstitutionalized—that attracts critical sympathy. Thus, it is "rough theater" *sans* intricate designs and clinical measurements that prevails among theater critics. "It is always the popular theater that saves the day," Brook (1996: 65) proclaims; and that is because it is released from one thing that constrains refined theater, namely, "unity of style" (67). Similarly, in de Certeau's theory it is the messiness of *space*, grounded in the spontaneous tactical maneuvers of empirical users, that is deemed to have more ethical, because egalitarian, value than the neatness of *place*, as produced by the strategic scientific plans of faceless bureaucracies.

Yet this type of argumentation can slip into a romanticization of resistance and a concomitant demonization of the establishment. Univocally privileging resistance may result in "an automatic theory generating an automatic politics" (Bennett 1998: 168), a politics of nonconformity for its own sake, thereby blunting the critical edge of our analysis. In this regard, reflecting on de Certeau's framework helps us revisit our thinking with an eye to identifying subtle connections between the top down and the bottom up, as well as exploring alternative routes to choreographing multilingualism beyond the two planes.

Morris (2004: 679) maintains that de Certeau's theory of walking reduces "the operation of a more complicated order of power that is articulated through practices that are neither strictly compliant nor resistant." The limits of de Certeau's conception lies in his

> opposition between "the official" and "the everyday," and his subsequently rigid differentiation between strategies and tactics. Social practices of walking rarely conform to this either/or model. It is never simply a case of "us" and "them," or individual walkers versus the city authorities who seek to organize the movement and dispositions of bodies in urban space, as Certeau's model implies. (Morris 2004: 679)

The dichotomization of official and everyday culture and strategies and tactics pits "the oppressed 'man in the street' . . . against the powers-that-be" (Morris 2004: 681), eliding complex negotiations of power in the space between. The so-called powers-that-be may exploit vernacular resources from below and masquerade as the "man in the street" in furtherance of their hegemony. By the same token, the so-called man in the street is not always recalcitrant but may draw upon resources from the establishment in pursuit of their aesthetic or ideological agendas, or even occasionally take on a persona associated with the establishment.

We must therefore question whether the act of walking the streets (or in our case, writing from below) necessarily registers, by default, a resistance against an institutional architecture governing urban (or in our case, discursive-semiotic) space. Citing Bennett (1998: 181), Morris (2004) reminds us that "the creative walker championed by Certeau may 'merely be following another order or, indeed, instituting such an order'" (680). What this means, in the context of writing and language ideology, is that in resisting the verbal hygiene (Cameron 2012) imposed by writings from above, writings from below could also institute a verbal hygiene of their own.

This brings us to a Gramscian conception of hegemony, which is not simply about the implementation of formal rules and the fostering of top-down regimes. It is "not simply a dominant ideology that shuts out all alternative visions and political projects. One of the important aspects of a hegemonic project is the way that it absorbs counter-hegemonic ideas through at least partially addressing some of the concerns and demands of the subaltern classes" (Wills 2017: 25). According to this view, hegemony is not simply one way or top down; it is not just about manipulation or propaganda. Rather, it is "a process of (asymmetric) dialogue between the ruling group and the subaltern classes" (Wills 2017: 25). This means that counterhegemony is also necessarily part of a dialogical relation; it resists hegemony while remaining within the power grid, all the while susceptible to cooptation, to "pressures and temptations to relapse into pursuit of incremental gains" (Cox 1993: 53, cited in Wills 2017: 25).

This does not mean the institutional versus grassroots framework guiding the foregoing chapters is wrong as such. The four case studies, it is hoped, have demonstrated the empirical grounds for establishing the dichotomy as a heuristic to outline the basic tensions in writing Singapore. Without first setting out the two endpoints of the spectrum, there would be no dialogical relations, or so-called third spaces, to speak of. Now that the from-above and from-below poles are in view, we are ready to give some analytical premium to the entanglements in between. Doing so helps us avoid zero-sum thinking between a languagized fixity (regulated, institutionalized usage of language) and a languaging fluidity (flexible mobilization of linguistic and nonlinguistic resources to fulfill contingent communicative needs) (Pennycook and Otsuji 2019b: 88–90), with a view to arriving at "a fuller and richer cartography of the spaces between total compliance and resistance" (Bennett 1998: 169).

## CONTRAPUNTAL MULTILINGUALISM

In view of this, I propose looking at choreographies of multilingualism in Singapore contrapuntally. I have in mind here Edward Said's (1993) contrapuntal reading of colonial-era fiction, with its "simultaneous awareness both of the metropolitan history that is narrated and of those other histories against which (and together with which) the dominating discourse acts" (51). A contrapuntal perspective thus enables us to "think through and interpret together experiences that are discrepant, each with its particular agenda and pace of development, its own internal formations, its internal coherence and system of external relationships, all of them coexisting and interacting with others" (Said 1993: 32). As in counterpoint music, in which different melodic lines play off each other yet retain their autonomous development, the different modalities of multilingual writing in Singapore can be conceived as contrapuntal pathways that are individually viable but also engage each other in polyphonic tension. In other words, these modalities play out the dialectic between iterativity, the use of "already existing genre templates," and creativity, the "deviation from such templates in unique instances of genre performance" (Blommaert 2018: 52).

On the one hand, there is the technocratic management of languages, as underpinned by the quadrilingual schema and worked through various scales of public discourse, which aims at representing a convivial multilingualism in which all four official languages are visible and audible. As I have mentioned at several points in Chapters 2 and 3, the affect of balance evinced by such representations is based on the preclusion of languages and language varieties precluded from the quadrilingual schema by language policy. These outlier languages are therefore the counterpoint of official multilingualism: they are suppressed through an enforced absence from public writing, but at the same time, they retain a phantom presence by being the perennial other against which the quadrilingual schema obtains legitimacy.

On the other hand, the marginalized status of these languages in relation to the establishment puts them at the center of the bottom-up praxis of Singlish proponents and citizen poets. By articulating a heteroglossic and not simply multilingual discourse, these latter writers capitalize on that which is sidelined by language authorities (i.e., Singlish and Chinese dialects), performing a discursive resistance and reversing the state's utopian multilingual imaginary. As we have seen in Chapters 4 and 5, top-down language initiatives, in particular the Speak Good English Movement (SGSM), can become an object of ridicule and parody in vernacular writing; in contrapuntal terms, these initiatives are played off as a counterpoint of fluid bottom-up practices.

A contrapuntal reading of multilingualism in Singapore sees the two modalities as mutually constitutive, each holding a line of their own while sustaining a tension between them, that is, between strategy and tactic, *place* and *space*. Such a reading extends our understanding of dominant language formations, of which the quadrilingual schema is exemplary, to include that which has been forcibly excluded (see Said 1993: 67), namely, vernacular writing as a burgeoning practice riding on social media affordances. At the same time, it recuperates the institutional within minoritizing narratives (e.g., the SGSM), connecting them back to the ideas, concepts, and experiences that create the conditions of marginalization in the first place (e.g., the SGEM).

Perhaps this tension is always already immanent to the concept of conviviality, a term that has recurred throughout this book. Conviviality is generally defined as "the attitude that enables people to accept different trajectories of life and different ways of going about things within the same space, and creates a level of sharedness that can generate solidarity and sympathy with others" (Blommaert 2013: 89). Yet for all its positive overtones, conviviality should not be romanticized, as it also embeds power and conflict (Valentine 2008; Rampton 2015).

In the case at hand, the neat multilingualism of public signage and institutional anthologies conjures up a cosy image of conviviality in which English, Chinese, Malay, and Tamil (and their presumed speech communities) enjoy a peaceful, polite coexistence. But underlying this coexistence are the power asymmetries between English and the mother tongue languages (MTLs) as well as the proscription of unofficial vernaculars. Vernacular exponents, for their part, may be transgressive in deploying resources from these vernaculars to undermine the multicultural fantasies constructed by the establishment. Yet like stand-up comedy and hip-hop shows, their performative practices can also be considered convivial in fostering a "linguistic citizenship" and "politics of civility" through a heteroglossic discourse (Jaworski and Lou 2021: 128, citing Stroud and Jegels 2014).

## ARTICULATIONS BETWEEN STRATEGY AND TACTIC

A contrapuntal reading of multilingual practices in Singapore requires us to attend to how semiotic resources are articulated in complex ways between strategic management and tactical manipulation. Articulation has been developed as a methodological notion by post-Gramscian scholars to provide a nuanced account of the power consequences of practices. As Morris (2004) maintains, "there is no such thing as an intrinsically oppressive practice or a resistant act: it is the nature of these acts' articulation to social formations and sites that finally determines their social effects" (681–82). For example, the act of marching on the streets and blockading motor traffic is not inherently resistant but can have resistant effects when articulated to specific anti-establishment struggles. As Grossberg (1992) argues, articulation enables us to describe "the process of forging connections between practices and effects, as well as of enabling practices to have different, often unpredicted effects" (54). Articulation therefore helps us understand how particular multilingual choreographies become attached to notions like power and resistance in contrapuntal tension with each other.

This leads us to complicate the issue of indexicality, or what languages and language varieties point to, in the Singapore context. The examples presented in the preceding chapters seem to suggest that the quadrilingual schema comprised of the official languages indexes establishment power, whereas the stylized invocation of Singlish, together with other languages excluded by the schema, indexes a resistance to such power. But resistance as an ethical value is not intrinsic to Singlish in particular or to nonofficial or nonstandard languages in general. These languages should therefore not be seen as the basis of an oppositional vocabulary codifying a fixed, bottom-up ideological disposition but, rather, as distributed resources that can be articulated to different ends.

Evidence for this view can be found in cases where the vernacular languages are used by the state and articulated for the pragmatic purpose of transmitting critical information in a manner accessible to certain sectors of the population. In 2015, a promotion campaign was launched by the Ministry of Communications and Information for a medical subsidies package. In a move that departed from normative language practices, the Ministry produced videos in Chinese dialects such as Hokkien, Teochew, and Cantonese to explain details of the package to elderly Chinese citizens who may not have been conversant in English or Mandarin. Given that Chinese dialects have been systematically disenfranchised since the inception of the Speak Mandarin Campaign in the late 1970s, these videos point to a planned and temporary deviation from the usual prohibitive stance on nonofficial languages as a way to resolve the contingencies of health communication.

More illuminating is the oft-cited example of a music video choreographed by the Ministry of Health in 2003 during the SARS pandemic to communicate health advice to citizens. Performed by the popular sitcom character Phua Chu Kang, whose tensions with the establishment were noted in earlier chapters, the video took the form of a rap, replete with linguistic features associated with Singlish. The *SARS-Vivor Rap*, as it is called, beseeches citizens to "*kiasu* ['be overly cautious'] a bit—be safe, not SAR-ry"; to "[s]pread *kaya* [a type of jam], but don't spread SARS!"; to refrain from going to work "[e]ven if your boss is a jerk!," and not "be a hero and continue working" in case, "[l]ater the whole company *kena* [passive marker] quarantine!"[1] After the SARS music video, the Phua Chu Kang rap became a regular method for official bodies to disseminate civic values in a ludic manner. For example, the Land Transport Authority put out a "graciousness rap" in 2009, in which Phua Chu Kang exhorted passengers on public transport not to rush into trains (with the Singlish turn of phrase "wait your turn to board the train"), hoard seats, or stand by the doorway.[2]

Phua Chu Kang as a prototype of the heartlander Singaporean was invoked again during the COVID-19 pandemic. As for SARS, the health ministry came up with another rap in in 2020, titled "PCK—Singapore Be Steady!," in which Phua Chu Kang made a comeback in translating health advice into the local idiom, in particular using his famous line: "don't play play." The rap, which is posted on the government's official YouTube channel *govsg*, starts as follows:

1. The full lyrics of the rap are available at https://eresources.nlb.gov.sg/music/music/track/dacdae94-2863-4c82-bde1-5e184d235927. A recording of the music video can be found at https://www.facebook.com/wakeupSG/videos/2534782523457597.
2. https://www.youtube.com/watch?v=y1yO-ejQrCs.

First, don't *kan cheong* ["be anxious"], don't be confused.
Check the source then share the news.
Shop at the market, don't be *kiasu* [i.e., overbuy].
Just buy what you need, don't jam the queue.
Our frontline workers don't *play play* ["mess around"].
They give their all every day.
If you meet them, say thank you.
*Belanja* ["treat"] them to *mee rebus* [Malay noodles in thick spicy soup].

The song ends with Phua Chu Kang entreating Singaporeans to practice good hygiene based on common sense: "Not say I want to say but I say *la hor*/Don't *play play*, please use your brain."[3] The phrase "not say I want to say" recalls Joshua Ip's poem "conversaytion," discussed in Chapter 5, which uses a similar jingle: "not say i want to say, but then this one who say one?," "i say one lor, arbuthen." The ministry-commissioned COVID rap, together with a related video titled "Gurmit Singh (Phua Chu Kang) Get Serious on COVID-19" (note: "get" is not inflected here, per Singlish grammar),[4] therefore draws on the same linguistic resources as Ip's overtly Singlish poem.

This series of Phua Chu Kang videos is of interest not for their comic quality but because, as we saw in Chapter 4, Phua Chu Kang was once the target of the government's critique in the context of the SGEM. The invocation of this sitcom character, together with his signature colloquialisms, demonstrates that

> when push comes to shove, and a governing body needs to communicate with its people on matters of utmost urgency, with enough confidence that the message is conveyed and taken to heart, it is the real mother tongue of the people that it must call on—which in the case of (English-speaking) Singaporeans would appear to be Singlish. (Lim 2015: 62)

Arguing along with Lim, I would push further to say that Singlish is simultaneously marginalized by the state as a mundane variety of English and fetishized as a spectacular medium of public communication—the latter precisely because the language is deemed substandard and hence of appeal to the grassroots. Underlying the state's appropriation of Singlish, therefore, is still a fundamentally elitist conception that reifies rather than problematizes the hierarchy between English and Singlish.

It is this linguistic elitism that underpins the state's mobilization of Singlish in the performance of an egalitarian institutional identity, whereby

3. https://www.youtube.com/watch?v=7ccjPJUROzA. Parenthetical glosses and explanations are mine.
4. https://www.youtube.com/watch?v=LFjZbDPc0tE.

the indexical potentiality of Singlish as an assemblage of enregistered vernacular resources is articulated toward enhancing the establishment's image. As noted in the introduction, the year 2015 witnessed unprecedented experiments with Singlish by government or government-affiliated bodies in the lead-up to the celebrations of SG50 (the year of the golden jubilee). The celebration parade featured props depicting the Singlish particles *lah* and *leh*, and expressions such as *blur like sotong* (to be clueless, lit. clueless like a squid). These Singlish props received positive commentary from Prime Minister Lee Hsien Loong in a Facebook post: "These props were crowd favorites at the National Day Parade./I'm glad that at 50, we are less 'blur like sotong,' and more confident and comfortable with everything that makes us Singaporean" (cited in Lim 2015: 267).

This represents a curious endorsement of Singlish by the authorities, considering that Singlish had hitherto always been excluded from official discourse. It is "unexpected and authentic," to use Sweetland's (2002) terms, a *spectacular* usage in which the vernacular is "begged, borrowed, or stolen by speakers who don't normally claim it" (515). The state's anxieties around Singlish become transformed and rechoreographed into a performance of an egalitarian ethos. Prima facie, this act could symbolically exonerate Singlish as an aberrant variety of English and vindicate its value as a solidarity marker. It coheres with observations that official discourses surrounding Singlish have shifted, if only subtly, over the years.

As noted in Chapter 1, the SGEM has attenuated its previously more antagonistic stance toward Singlish. Its earlier mission statement, which read "to help Singaporeans *move away from* the use of Singlish" (cited in Lim 2015: 264 [emphasis added]), has since been replaced by a new one, which acknowledges "the existence of Singlish as a cultural marker for many Singaporeans," while seeking to help Singaporeans "to speak and write in Standard English."[5] Although the new statement falls short of an express endorsement of Singlish, its rhetoric in respect of the vernacular is more measured and less authoritarian.

In this light, the National Day Parade (NDP) Singlish floats can be read as a tactical, opportunistic appropriation of Singlish from above to soften the state's image in relation to the street vernacular, thereby signaling an egalitarian, people-oriented stance on the all-important occasion of SG50. The formulation "tactics from above" would be a contradiction in de Certeauean terms. Yet the NDP floats are indeed contingent—aligning with tactic—rather than strategic; as we have seen in the Singlish controversy in Chapter 4, the government's proscriptive view on the widespread use of Singlish has not fundamentally shifted. According to this view, the

5. https://www.languagecouncils.sg/goodenglish/.

government's approach to Singlish overlaps with that of the Singlish advocates: both operate on the third order of indexicality (see Table 4.1) in relation to Singlish, tapping into its meaning potential to index mundaneness but articulating it to different ends. The difference is that the state concurrently marginalizes Singlish on a policy level while fetishizing its form to cash in on its indexical potential. Looking at this contrapuntally allows us to understand the two routes of multilingual choreographies—one taken by the institution and the other by individual writers—as developing at once in opposition and in intersection.

Notwithstanding the contradictions inherent in the state's double take on Singlish, NDP 2015 seems to have heralded a subtle shift in institutional choreographies of writing, in which Singlish has since gained more visibility than before in top-down communications. On the face of it, this should be seen as a positive development from the regimented picture of multilingualism painted in Chapters 2 and 3. It promotes opening the bureaucratic discursive space to a range of rhetorically interesting registers. Here the boundary between the instrumental imperative to communicate effectively with the masses and the ideological imperative to construct an egalitarian statal image is often blurred and shifts with contingencies.

Hence, in 2018, the statutory board Workforce Singapore launched a job-matching campaign on mycareersfuture.sg. One of its posters reads: "For a 'Zai' way to One-up the Job Competition," using the slang Hokkien word *zai* (impressive) together with "one-up" to add a ludic touch to the relatively somber matter of employment (Hiramoto 2019: 458). As part of the celebrations for Singapore's fifty-fourth National Day celebrations in August 2019, the national healthy lifestyle campaign GetActive! Singapore displayed poster boards at their roadshows in heartland neighborhoods, infused with a strong dose of colloquialisms. Figure 6.1 shows two of these posters, where *Better chope first* (on the left) means "it's better to reserve [a place] first" and *Shiok! Makan also can* (on the right) means "Satisfying! Can eat [meals] too."

Singlish has also occasionally appeared on the government's Twitter account, @govsingapore (Hiramoto 2019: 457). Three Twitter posts introducing the Central Provident Fund (CPF, Singapore's retirement fund) read as follows: "#CPF too cheem to understand? #Factually keeps it simple on sg.sg/CPFnYou" (January 7, 2015); "They say gahmen use our CPF money to invest overseas. Real or not? Find out what the gahmen has to say on sg.sg/CPFnU" (January 14, 2015); "Who says you can't #paktor in your golden years: sg.sg/1Nu1mYM #WhatsYourPlan" (January 29, 2016). Here the words *cheem*, *gahmen* (both mentioned earlier), and *paktor* (to go dating), along with the expression *real or not*, are often recognized as Singlish vocabulary. It is especially interesting to see a government agency invoking *gahmen* for self-reference, considering the word frequently occurs in grassroots discourse as part of a performative use of eye-spelling to subvert standard English.

**Figure 6.1.** Two posters at GetActive! Singapore roadshow, Ang Mo Kio Central, Singapore, 2019. *Left*: "Better Chope First"; *right*: "Shiok! Makan Also Can."

"Real or not" is also the title of an animated video put out by Singapore's CPF Board in 2019 to explain how the CPF works.[6] The video starts with a Chinese woman speaking in a distinctively Singlish intonation accentuated by particles: "*Eh*, my friend say *ah*, my CPF savings will automatically go to my son's CPF when I die." A bewildered Malay lady replies, "Huh, real or not?," with a hyper-rhotacized "r" mimicking how the word "real" is perceived to be pronounced by Malay persons in Singapore. An executive-attired man then enters to debunk the myth around CPF inheritance, this time using a learned Standard English register associated with administrative genres (e.g., "by default," "monies in cash," "make a CPF nomination," "according to intestacy or inheritance law," and "not part of your estate").

The generous use of Singlish in the video appears to indicate a positive recognition of its widespread use in society. But it is important to realize that the script is premised on an interplay between Singlish-based utterances ("*Then* they will not get *lor*," "So if I don't nominate, *also* never mind *lah*," "But I *already* made a will. Same thing right?") associated with a gullible ignorance of administrative procedures, and Standard English utterances associated with rational knowledge.[7] The same logic is at work in another video in the same

6. https://www.youtube.com/watch?v=jtlsavoa8x4.
7. There is another "real or not" video using the same character setup, but with different dialogue; see https://www.youtube.com/watch?v=ME95ZFDsIac.
This time, the Singlish speakers are a Malay woman and an Indian man who are uncertain about how the CPF works, and an executive-looking Chinese man pops

series, titled "Ah Bengs explain CPF,"[8] in which Singlish, with a small sprinkling of Mandarin, becomes associated with the *ah bengs*, or gangsters: "I *never connect* my Bluetooth speaker to my e-scooter eh" (I didn't connect . . .), "I straight away come here" (I came here straight away), "everything I can settle" (I can settle everything), and so forth.[9]

These CPF videos give us yet another glimpse of the state's bifurcated approach to the vernaculars. They tap into the meaning potential of Singlish (incorporating the Chinese dialects and colloquial Malay) as an enregistered variety in public education discourses, while still overtly marginalizing it on the level of language policy and language planning. Singlish, in other words, is at once an instrument reinforcing prevailing linguistic hierarchies and a fetish exploited for its orality–aurality in more pointed communications. This two-pronged approach exemplifies how resources from the vernacular can be articulated to different choreographies in tandem, without the two canceling each other out.

National elections are particularly illuminating, when political candidates of different persuasions draw on Chinese dialects in their campaigning speeches. This exceptional use of dialects in public discourse aims at seeking rapport with elderly Chinese Singaporeans, many of whom speak next to no English and have only partial proficiency in Mandarin. This linguistic ground was first broken in 1991, when opposition party leader Low Thia Khiang gained immense popularity after speaking to his supporters entirely in Teochew (Kuo and Chan 2016: 50). Thereafter, establishment politicians followed suit, including in the most recent 2020 general election. Among them was People's Action Party (proestablishment) candidate and then-Second Minister for Trade and Industry Dr. Tan See Leng, who made a video targeted at elderly citizens in which he explained voting procedures in Cantonese with a dash of Teochew and Hokkien.[10] This points to the ambivalent status of Chinese dialects, which, on the one hand, have been subject to structural erasure by the state, and, on the other, are resuscitated by proestablishment figures as living languages (Kuo and Chan 2016: 93) in exigent circumstances.

in to answer their queries. Here the representation of the three major ethnic communities within the Chinese, Malay, Indian, Others formula is a sign of institutional choreography.

8. https://www.youtube.com/watch?v=wtr-Ki9PyGw.

9. Other relevant expressions in the video include "Why got bandage one" (Why is [your head] bandaged?), "Means everything settled *already lah*" (That means everything has been settled), *You call me down for what* (Why did you ask me to come down to the void deck of the building?), and "My life is now in a series of *jialat* events" (where *jialat* is a Hokkien word meaning "terrible").

10. Tan's speech can be viewed at https://www.facebook.com/DrTanSeeLeng/videos/571915776780341/.

Granting that these examples are intermittent attempts at invoking Singlish, they are, in my view, sociolinguistic moments that offer a window into the tension between fixity and fluidity. They demonstrate that Singlish, enregistered as a streetwise tongue, is not the reserve of multilingual performativity from below. It can also be coopted as a styling resource by state-affiliated bodies to trigger locale-specific resonances, to enhance the efficacy of top-down communications, and to project an egalitarian institutional outlook. This means that Singlish, precisely because it enregisters a heartland authenticity, can be articulated to the "professional design and institutional management of words, as well as their ideologically-structured commodification and regulation," or what Thurlow (2020: 3) calls the "working life" of language.

Singlish can therefore be choreographed to work outside a resistant politics, and to serve the state's discursive strategy of performing a "post-class" ideology (Thurlow 2016) entailing the "politics of (dis)avowed privilege" (Thurlow 2020: 3). The momentum of such institutional uptake of Singlish (and Chinese dialects) has been increasing since 2015, extending beyond the usual contexts of health crises and political campaigns. This indicates the rise of a vernacular praxis in official discourse in competition with a similar trajectory burgeoning among individual, neoliberal-minded writers.

## Institutionalizing resistance

By the same token, one should not romanticize the resistant values seemingly espoused by vernacular writers, for although these writers generally define their heteroglossic niches against monoglossic language policies, it is not the case that they are always at odds with the establishment. We have seen in Chapter 5 how SingPoWriMo exhibits a strong grassroots character through its celebration of antipoetic language. Yet between 2014 and 2018, SingPoWriMo also published five print anthologies based on a fraction of the voluminous contributions on its Facebook page.[11] In other words, the open virtual space on the SingPoWriMo Facebook page is eventually funneled into the structured discursive space of anthologies. Anthologization, as noted in Chapter 3, always involves selection based on a set of editorial criteria, even if, as in the case of SingPoWriMo, the criteria are nonnormative. And such nonnormative criteria can in turn become hegemonic within their own realm of discursive governance. Hence, for instance, a lyrical English poem that is "prim and proper" by canonical standards may or may not win the favor of SingPoWriMo editors.

11. Due to poor sales of these print volumes, since 2019 SingPoWriMo has taken its anthologies online in the form of journal issues; see https://www.singpowrimo.com

Although the five SingPoWriMo anthologies published between 2014 and 2018 were crowdfunded, since 2016, SingPoWriMo has been subsumed into a larger entity called Sing Lit Station (SLS).[12] SLS is a registered charity and Institution of Public Character set up with the support of a seed grant from the National Arts Council (NAC),[13] whose mission is to nurture the local literary community by serving as a nexus for local writers, readers, and critics. While SingPoWriMo started out as, and still very much is, a free-standing Facebook initiative managed by individual poets, it now also operates under the umbrella framework of SLS. The latter has much more structure to its organization, featuring a sprawling constellation of regular programs and projects, sometimes in collaboration with overseas partners.[14] If SingPoWriMo advocates vernacular and other nonnormative modes of poetry, then these are, in a manner of speaking, now enfolded into a larger, arguably more institutionalized structure represented by the NAC-funded SLS. The "light" community of SingPoWriMo is embedded into a somewhat "thicker" community (Blommaert and Varis 2015: 54–57), so to speak, although SingPoWriMo still retains its autonomy by keeping SLS at "arms' length" (Joshua Ip, personal communication, July 2020).

This explains why the copyright page in SingPoWriMo's 2017 anthology states that "SingPoWriMo and its itinerant activities were supported by the National Arts Council and the Arts Fund" (Chan et al. 2017: n.p.), and in its 2018 anthology, SLS and the NAC-managed Arts Fund were listed as patrons. While SingPoWriMo may speak to *space* in the de Certeauean sense, with its anticanonical and highly experimental stance, SLS evinces more of a *place*. The latter has a clear mission statement, complex itineraries involving logistical planning and collaboration with external partners, an online shop, a hierarchy of patrons, and a lineup of institutional supporters including, among

12. http://www.singlitstation.com.

13. Institutions of Public Character are defined as "exempt or registered charities which are able to issue tax deduction receipts to donors for qualifying donations made." https://www.mccy.gov.sg/sector/policies/charities-and-institutions-of-a-public-character.

14. These include a Translation Retreat in collaboration with Literature Across Frontiers (SLS's counterpart in Europe); Singapore Poetry on the Sidewalks (SPOTS, where excerpts of local poetry are inscribed in downtown areas using rain-activated technology); Writing in the City (an initiative for emerging prose writers to meet and share their work); poetry.sg (an online database of Singapore poets complete with biographies, writing samples, video recordings, and critical commentaries); the Manuscript Bootcamp (a writing camp where budding writers submit a literary manuscript for critique by academics, writers, and publishers); the Manuscript Assessment Scheme (similar to the Bootcamp, except manuscripts are sent to the UK-based The Literary Consultancy for professional feedback); and Book A Writer (an outreach program providing creative writing workshops and classes to secondary and preuniversity students). In addition, SLS hosts literary art exhibitions, writing residencies, literary prizes and workshops, and, of course, SingPoWriMo.

others, the NAC (and its Arts Fund), The Arts House, the National Library Board (NLB), and the Malay Heritage Centre. As an initiative under SLS, SingPoWriMo thus arguably functions as a nodal point that articulates vernacular poetry to a more sophisticated institutional network. This demonstrates the contrapuntal tensions within which different modalities of literary expression are choreographed in relation to each other.

The notion of a bottom-up discourse is also problematized by the fluid personae of professional writers. Gwee Li Sui, as we have seen in Chapters 3 and 4, is both the editor of *Singathology* and the author of *Spiaking Singlish*: the former a state-sponsored anthology encapsulating the literary canon within the framework of the quadrilingual schema,[15] and the latter an experimental book that expressly undermines the quadrilingual schema by celebrating a stylized, heteroglossic Singlish. What this suggests is that there is little purchase in pigeonholing specific individuals to prefixed ideological positions, because highly multilingual individuals are able to straddle different identities simultaneously. Likewise, the work of Joshua Ip and the citizen poets of SingPoWriMo may be considered radical insofar as it is critical of the state's language policies. But this does not prevent the most talented among them, including Joshua Ip and Ng Yi-sheng, from being awarded national-level honors such as the Singapore Literature Prize, which, in a manner of speaking, absorbs them into the canon. (In this connection, it is perhaps significant that Ip won the national-level prize with his *sonnets from the singlish*.)

None of this is at all wrong from an ethical standpoint, nor is there necessarily any contradiction. What these double identities suggest is that nominal labels such as "Singlish advocate/proponent" (used several times in this book) are necessarily partial. They obfuscate the capacity of multilingual individuals to articulate themselves flexibly in relation to the language establishment and to engage with different modalities of multilingual choreography. There is no contradiction as such if we consider that writers are professional users of language—or "wordsmiths," as Thurlow (2020) might call them—but are not Duchêne's (2020) *parole d'oeuvre*, or underprivileged, often exploited, language workers. And as with all professionals, language practitioners can strategically scale and rescale themselves, articulating resources at their disposal (e.g., Singlish or the quadrilingual schema) to differential identity registers.

## COMMODIFYING THE VERNACULARS

Finally, turning to commercial articulations of language in Singapore allows us to appreciate how linguistic registers or modes of discourse are creatively

15. We should recall that in 2015, the year *Singathology* was published, Gwee delivered a TED talk celebrating Singlish as a global language (see Chapter 1).

appropriated to ends that go beyond the dyadic tension between regulation and recalcitrance.

Language has been conceived as a commodity in different ways, for instance, as an acquirable resource with exchange value and part of one's embodied capital in the Bourdieusian sense (see Heller 2010), or, following the Marxist notion of commodity, as a marketable object external to individuals, one that is intimately tied to notions of cultural identity and native speakership (Wee 2018: 123). My interest, however, lies with a narrower definition of commodification, which looks at how language is marketed as part of text-based commodities. These commodities perform a ludic multilingual discourse framed by consumerist profit-seeking, representing a choreographic modality that cannot be simply described as top down or bottom up.

Singlish, for example, has appeared extensively in marketing campaigns in recent years. This usage is neither conformist nor resistant in nature but, rather, falls in line with observations that minority languages or stigmatized varieties can be fetishized in advertising contexts for their symbolic value to index cultural authenticity (Kelly-Holmes 2014: 146–48; see also Kelly-Holmes 2020) and "fabricate synthetic membership" with a local audience (Hiramoto 2011: 247). The word *shiok* comes up yet again in Figure 6.2, this time in an advertising poster by DBS Bank for its mobile-pay app *PayLah!*—a term that creatively blends the Singlish particle *lah* into the product name.

Figure 6.3 shows the packaging of Nestle's popular beverage Milo, on which is printed *gao kosong* (concentrated and without sugar); the latter is a Chinese-dialect expression invoking a vernacular lingo as used in Singapore's ubiquitous *kopitiam* (local coffee shops). In Figure 6.4 we have a different kind of coffee shop: Starbucks, whose poster advertises a new Frappuccino concoction that goes by the name *shiok-ah-ccino*. This Singlish portmanteau morphologically combines the exclamatory phrase *shiok ah* (Satisfying!) with the *-ccino* suffix. At the bottom-right corner of the advertisement are two other translingual portmanteaus, "SWEE-TREAT" and "SWEE-T DEAL," playing on the Hokkien word *swee* (beautiful) to pun with the English "sweet."

Recent years have also seen the commodification of Singlish in the form of text-based collectibles, whereby Singlish is appropriated to articulate a locale-specific identity. Figure 6.5 shows a series of bookmarks from The Super Blessed, a Singapore-based online Christian gift shop.[16] These belong to a range of products (pouches, notebooks, pin buttons, keychains) that creatively combine faith, language identity, and marketing by entextualizing Singlish epithets in the context of an ecclesiastical discourse.

To give an idea of how such entextualization works, I briefly unpack the texts on the bookmarks as follows:

16. https://www.thesuperblessed.com/.

**Figure 6.2.** Poster for DBS *PayLah!*

a. "HUAT AH!/GOD WILL SUPPLY All your needs according to His Riches (Philippians 4:19)": *Huat* is a Hokkien verb meaning to get rich, often coupled with the interjection *ah!* to create an auspicious expression to invoke wealth luck. Here it coheres with the idea of "riches" in the Philippians quote, exalting God's power to take care of our material needs in the vernacular.

b. "Tio Sabo? NO FEAR! No weapon formed against you shall prosper (Isaiah 54:17)": *Tio sabo* means to be sabotaged or sneak-attacked in Singlish (where *sabo* is truncated from "sabotage"). This sets out a problem that is dialogically resolved by the Isaiah quote, which assures one protection against attacking "weapons."

**Figure 6.3.** Packaging for Nestle's Milo beverage.

c. "CHIO BU/You are altogether beautiful, my darling; there is no flaw in you. (Song of Solomon 4:7)": *Chio bu* is a Hokkien expression meaning "pretty girl"; the quote from Song of Solomon, which has a resonant theme, can be seen as a poetic elaboration of the vernacular *chio bu* while transcending registers.

d. "MAI KAN CHEONG/Be Anxious for Nothing (Philippians 4:6)": *Mai kan cheong* means "do not be anxious" in Hokkien; the quote from the Philippians is thus a translation of said expression, enacting a double crossing of languages and registers.

e. "JIAK BUEY LIAO/Jesus Feeds the Five Thousand. (Matthew 14:13–21)": *Jiak buey liao* means "too much to eat," indicating an abundance of food. This provides a vernacular commentary on the Matthew quote.

**Figure 6.4.** Poster for Starbuck's Shiok-ah-ccino.

Because Singlish is not commonly associated with the elevated biblical register, this kind of creative juxtaposition gives rise to a reverse bathos, sliding us abruptly from the vernacular end to the venerable end of the language spectrum. As shown in my exposition above, there is also a dialogical, quasitranslational relationship between the Singlish epithets and ecclesiastical quotes. This unlikely juxtaposition of registers generates linguistic humor, commoditized through the medium of an ordinary stationary product, possibly appealing to a more egalitarian relationship to God.

E-commerce stores like The Super Blessed are proliferating. This marketing phenomenon signals the emergence of a different articulation to multilingual choreography, one based on the design of text-based memorabilia.

**Figure 6.5.** Singlish-based stationery. Courtesy of The Super Blessed.

A cursory search on the internet yields: The Little Drome Store,[17] LoveSG,[18] PewPewPatches,[19] SingapuLAH,[20] Temasek Clothings,[21] Statement,[22] Superwhite,[23] Roadside Stall,[24] Wet Tee Shirt,[25] Say What?,[26] and Sibey Nostalgic Publishing.[27] At the risk of sounding anecdotal, below are a few vernacular commodities in my modest collection purchased from some of the above-mentioned stores.

a. Card game decks designed around Singlish, Mandarin, Hokkien, and Cantonese, complete with online audio resources on pronunciation. These games, targeting people who have marginal or no proficiency in the respective languages or varieties, require players to split into two groups and read/act out the words on randomly picked cards for team members who would guess the meanings of those words. There is a humorous metalinguistic

17. https://thelittledromstore.com/.
18. https://www.lovesg.sg.
19. https://pewpewpatches.com.
20. https://www.singapulah.com.
21. https://www.temasekclothings.com.
22. https://statement.sg.
23. https://www.facebook.com/WeAreSuperWhite/.
24. https://www.facebook.com/roadsidestall/.
25. https://www.wetteeshirt.co.
26. https://www.saywhatwithfriends.com/shop.
27. https://www.sibeynostalgic.com.

twist to these cards: their instructions, although written in English, are littered with the language or variety in question. Hence, the Singlish deck asks players to shuffle the cards *kau kau* (thoroughly) and to act out the words expediently and expressively without regard to their image: "the more powderful your acting the better hor. Do until how obiang also can. Chop chop curry pop!" The Hokkien deck has two transliterated phrases printed on its box, one on the lid on top of the deck, which reads *kwee zi dao* (open here), and the other on the lid at the bottom, which reads *mm si zi dao* (not here).

b. A trilogy of classic children's tales, rewritten in Singlish by Casey Chen as a *Lah Book* series, playing on the iconic sentence-final particle. Titles include *The Red Riding Hood Lah*, *The Goldilocks Lah*, and *The Three Little Pigs Lah*. Retelling familiar stories in Singlish, these texts are replete with italicized words associated with Singlish; thus, *The Three Little Pigs Lah* begins:

> Very long time *already*, *got* three little pigs stay with their *ma*. The three pigs grew big so fast, that mother *buay tahan* and tell them: "*You all* so big *liao*, this house your father built got *no enough* space *lah*. You go build houses for yourselves *k*. But then *hor*, please remember to be careful don't let the wolf catch you and *makan* you." (Chen 2015: n.p. [emphasis in the original])

The texts are accompanied by illustrations conjuring familiar icons in the Singapore landscape, such as the Marina Bay Sands towers and the ubiquitous Housing Development Board flats, as if the stories unfolded in contemporary Singapore. On every other page, a glossary is provided for the Singlish terms, giving the books an infotainment touch. There is a great deal of parodic play, not just in respect of the tales but also within the paratexts. For example, at the bottom of the book covers is a mock statement: "Must read with a Singlish accent. This book contains broken English. NOW suitable for children (Parental guidance)," mimicking but also subverting the register of disclaimers.

c. A mock textbook series that parodies the format of school textbooks while presenting its content multilingually—not only in English and Mandarin, but notably in the five major Chinese dialects spoken in Singapore (Hokkien, Teochew, Cantonese, Hakka, and Hainanese). The texts are of the most rudimentary level; their titles (*Going to the Zoo*; *Going to the Swimming Pool*; *Going to the Clinic*; *Going to Second Uncle's House*), together with their design and composition, are reminiscent of Mandarin textbooks issued by the Ministry of Education and used in government primary schools. This reinforces the notion of linguistic fetish: the texts are not meant to be read—they are far too boring for this purpose. For example, the text of *Going to the Zoo* begins: "This is Gopal. These are his parents. They are at the zoo." They are, rather, fetishized for their form, namely, the dialectal translations and transliterations (complete with tone markers) of simple sentences in English and Mandarin. Note that even the name "Gopal" recalls textbook discourse, it being a familiar name used in simple dialogues in textbooks. The subversive potential of this product thus lies in its nostalgic invocation of an iconic semiotic form associated with official language (and in particular MTL) education, while introducing non-official languages in transgression of the setup. As it is impossible for Chinese dialects to appear in a real-world textbook context in Singapore, this exemplar of culture jamming creates a ludic, surreal artifact that is at once nostalgic and critical of the orthodox multilingual order.

d. A wide range of text-based collectibles, including a series marketed under the tagline "Strangely Singaporean and Proud of It," including crockery, collar pins, and keychains embossed with colloquial expressions. Other artifacts include bottle openers crafted in the letter shapes of slang terms (e.g., *Yum Seng* "cheers" in Cantonese); a "punny" (pun+funny) collectible series (canvas bags, face masks, pouches, coasters, magnets) that insinuate colloquial words phonetically into well-known formulations (e.g., *Lor Mee-O & Juliet*, punning Romeo & Juliet, where *lor mee* is a local noodle delicacy in thick soup; or "You are in-*kueh*-dible," punning "incredible," where *kueh* is a Hokkien/Teochew word meaning "rice cakes"); embroidered collectibles such as iron-on patches featuring words evocative of Singapore's cultural landscape; and a series of notebooks defining local slang terms in different domains (e.g., military service, *kopitiam*), complete with phonetic notation and sample sentences.

Such commodification of the languages of the heartlands—the "real mother tongue languages" (Lim 2009a) in Singapore, including Singlish, Chinese dialects, and colloquial Malay—can be attributed to an "explosion of sentimentality, a harking back to heritage" (Lim 2015: 266) following the death of Singapore's founder Lee Kuan Yew coinciding with SG50.

A notable phenomenon in this regard is the rise of vernacular T-shirts that invoke familiar expressions from the local repertoire with origins in colloquial Malay, Mandarin, and Hokkien. Figure 6.6 shows a T-shirt with the text, *no lah where got*. This expression conflates two colloquial clauses in Singlish to indicate disagreement with the truth conditions of a proposition in some prior utterance (e.g., A: I heard you're a rich man./B: No lah where got). *Lah* is a ubiquitous sentence-final particle in Singlish, serving an emphatic function here; *got* is an existential marker; and the interrogative *where got(?)* is derived under substrate influence from the Mandarin *nali you(?)*, lit. "where have." And although *no lah where got* is attested in naturally occurring speech, its emplacement on T-shirts turns it into a symbolic value-adding resource, giving it a different materiality and mobility as well as a playful quality it does not possess in speech.

**Figure 6.6.** "No lah where got." Courtesy of Statement.

Other examples include the T-shirt in Figure 6.7, texted with *blur sotong*, a phrase we encountered in relation to NDP 2015 (though without the comparative word "like" here). A different kind of personality trait is featured in Figure 6.8 with the expression *kan cheong spider*, referring to someone who is prone to anxiety (*kan cheong* in Hokkien) and does things in a haste. The word "professional" on the two T-shirts marks them out as a series, and gives rise to humorous readings, namely, "professional blur sotong" and "professional kan cheong spider."

It is no surprise that particles, often seen as a trademark of Singlish, are entextualized on these T-shirts.[28] *Wa lao eh*, seen in Figure 6.9, is a colloquial interjection that is not exclusive to Singlish but can nonetheless be considered part of its repertoire. *Wa lao* (sometimes romanized as *walau*) originates in a vulgar Hokkien phrase that means "my penis," coupled with the sentence-final particle *eh*, it expresses the speaker's frustration, functionally equivalent to "Oh my goodness." *Uh uh siol* in Figure 6.10, which comprises the two particles *uh* (reduplicated) and *siol*, originates in a subterranean register initially associated with Malay gangsters (*Matreps*), but is now used more widely by youngsters to express agreement with what someone has said.

Sexual vulgarity (albeit euphemized) is a common theme among vernacular T-shirts, striking at the heart of a taboo language. Such language can

---

28. Images below are reproduced from the websites of Statement (statement.sg) and Temasek Clothings (temasekclothings.com) with permission from the proprietors.

**Figure 6.7.** "Blur sotong." Courtesy of Statement.

**Figure 6.8.** "Kan cheong spider." Courtesy of Statement.

**Figure 6.9.** "Wa lao eh." Courtesy of Statement.

**Figure 6.10.** "Uh uh siol." Courtesy of Statement.

**Figure 6.11.** "Lazy man's nap lover." Courtesy of Statement.

never be attested in institutional communications, and its extreme forms are evaded even in grassroots writing.[29] Often, the vulgar intent is euphemistically couched in seemingly innocuous expressions, waiting to be deciphered by persons-in-the-culture, people "in the know." The Chinese (Mandarin) phrase in Figure 6.11 literally means "I love lazy naps," as indicated in the caption taken from the original catalogue. But the Mandarin word for "lazy nap," *lan jiao*, is duplicitous: it slyly invokes the Hokkien word with the same pronunciation that means "penis," such that the Mandarin phrase on the T-shirt belies the Hokkien phrase "I love penis."

A similar but even more intriguing example are the three Chinese characters in Figure 6.12, which read "super white." On one level, this evokes the detergent brand Super White, which coheres with a T-shirt context. Below the three characters are their romanized forms, following a Mandarin reading, complete with tone markers. This unusual, mock-pedagogical representation already tells us that there is something more here than meets the eye. And indeed, like the "lazy nap" phrase, this one is also a phonetic

29. Possibly it is the materiality that makes the difference. Writing as a literacy institution is generally loaded with expectations of propriety, especially when accessible to the general public. In contrast, as a type of discourse, inscriptions on T-shirts sit "somewhere between the private and the public," assuming "a close relationship to their human wearers" (Jaworski and Lou 2021: 109). If these T-shirts are actually worn, their inscriptions would constitute a fleeting communication, traveling as they do with moving bodies; if bought as collectibles, they would be totally private.

**Figure 6.12.** "Chao Ji Bai." Courtesy of Statement.

pun on a Hokkien expletive, pronounced *chao ji bai* as indicated in the Mandarin romanization (but with different tones), which means "smelly pussy."

Although this piece of communication is an expletive at its base, there is almost an artfulness to the phonetic slippage between Mandarin and Hokkien, as well as to the tension between the quotidian, surface-level meaning of the written phrase and its intense sexual innuendo when spoken. In fact, English is involved as well. The T-shirt originated from an e-commerce store called Superwhite. The Facebook page of the store relates the backstory of the brand's name—taken from a detergent label of the same name that was banned from the market in 1960s Singapore due to its sexual implications.[30] On the basis of this backstory, the store purports to celebrate the "ironic humor" behind the phrase "super white," now a phrase with a triple embedment in English, Mandarin, and Hokkien, thereby expressing a cynical stance toward the censorship regime in Singapore.

The vulgarity theme reaches an extreme in Figure 6.13, where *knnbccb*, euphemistically presented as a mock English abbreviation, is in fact an extended and more intense version of the Hokkien expletive underlying "super white" in the last example; it is literally "f*ck your mother's smelly pussy." The expletive is never used in this condensed and euphemized form in daily

30. https://www.facebook.com/WeAreSuperWhite/.

**Figure 6.13.** "Knnbccb." Courtesy of Statement.

conversation;[31] its abbreviation and emplacement on T-shirts resemiotizes it into an uncanny piece of humorous text for public display, rendering an unutterable expletive representable.

Abbreviations such as knnbccb epitomize the boundary-marking nature (Heller et al. 2014: 449) of Singlish epithets, beneath which there is often a subtext retrievable only by people in the know. Another example along this line is PCK in Figure 6.14, abbreviating the name of the popular sitcom character Phua Chu Kang. Based on our earlier discussion of Phua Chu Kang's uneasy relationship with the authorities, we know that the character (both his name and image) has been iconized into a championing figure of Singlish. The invocation of PCK on T-shirts is thus an expression of solidarity with bottom-up multilingualism, evincing an ethic of resistance against the state's elitist suppression of vernacular tongues.

As multimodal artifacts, vernacular T-shirts are not entirely discursive; visuality can be central, as my final set of examples show. The caption for Figure 6.15 reads "gay lapis"; the immediate intersemiotic references are the rainbow colors signifying LGBTQ identities. But it takes someone familiar with street food in Singapore to know that "gay lapis" is intended to pun *kueh lapis*, a multilayered, often multicolored traditional dessert cake. *Kueh lapis* is made of sticky glutinous rice, giving rise to the punning call-out statement "I'm

31. In local speech, the full form of the expletive would be uttered; see https://www.urbandictionary.com/define.php?term=knnbccb for a transliteration of the word.

TEMASEKCLOTHINGS.COM

**Figure 6.14.** "PCK." Courtesy of Temasek Clothings.

**Figure 6.15.** "Gay lapis." Courtesy of Temasek Clothings.

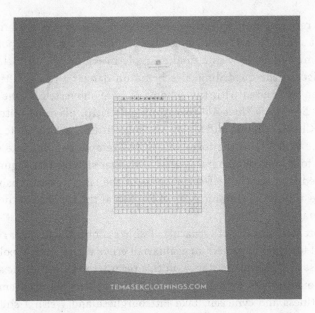

**Figure 6.16.** "Xiao Ming." Courtesy of Temasek Clothings.

sticking with you" beside the image, with romantic connotations in an LGBTQ context. Here we see intersections between different languages (Hokkien and Malay) as well as different discourses (food, sexuality), creatively encapsulated in one verbal–visual frame.

"Xiao Ming" in Figure 6.16 shows a multimodal invocation of linguistic nostalgia. It comprises a grid of small squares framed by four blank spaces on top (name, class, date, [student] number), invoking the visual frame of the standard foolscap paper used for Chinese-language composition exercises in Singapore schools. "Xiao Ming" is the protoname of male figures used in Chinese-language composition (the female counterpart being "Xiao Li"), popular among students because of the relative simplicity of its orthography.

In a variation of this design, "Xiao Ming goes to ACS,"[32] the term Anglo Chinese School (ACS) appears at the top center of the image, together with its logo. ACS (a real school in Singapore) is stereotypically associated with an anglophone educational system in which the Chinese language is relatively marginalized (note that this is a stereotype, as all government schools in Singapore are in fact English-medium schools). The juxtaposition of ACS with an iconic image of Chinese language pedagogy generates tension, as wittily encapsulated in the caption "Xiao Ming goes to ACS," as if the familiar character from Chinese compositions has leapt into reality and enrolled in an anglophone school. The verbal–visual intertextuality here is not merely a

32. https://www.temasekclothings.com/products/xiao-ming-goes-to-acs.

nostalgic reminiscence of Chinese composition classes; it recalls an ambivalent affect associated with the bilingual education system in Singapore.

We come full circle with a final example in Figure 6.17, which is a parodic twist on the quadrilingual schema on danger signage. The solemn tone often associated with the schema is here subverted by the spirited message, *Everybody Huat Ah!* (everyone gets rich), playfully reiterated in Singlish, Chinese, Tamil, and Malay. The substitution of Singlish for English within the visuality of the formulaic ECMT template—complete with the standard font and color characteristic of danger signage (see Figure 2.1)—is intended to mock the self-seriousness of the language establishment in Singapore and the hegemonic sway of English at the expense of the vernacular languages.

The potential mobility of vernacular T-shirts connects with their rhetorical and social function to project an egalitarian ethos with a dose of political incorrectness and playful resistance. In this regard, the heteroglossic and multimodal constitution of the language on these T-shirts affords them a sense of naughtiness and cynicism. Like Pittsburghese and Welsh T-shirts, they evince "a youthful sense of urban hipness" (Johnstone 2010: 399), representing a "laconic metacultural celebration" (Coupland 2012: 17) of an imagined Singaporean identity.

Yet being essentially commercial in nature, vernacular commodities such as T-shirts do not thrive on an ethic of resistance with respect to an imposed institutional order from above, even if the quirkiness of their language affords

**Figure 6.17.** "Everybody huat ah!" Courtesy of Statement.

them with a cynical stance toward normative orders. They belong to a different modality of practice than the vernacular writing discussed in Chapters 4 and 5, in which the state's discourse on language often constitutes a pointed target of critique. Instead, they are a different development that resonates with grassroots writing in terms of its ludic style but is primarily motivated by the desires of commercial profit-seeking.

## NEW SINGLISH: TOWARD POSTMULTILINGUALISM

All of this suggests that the boundaries between top-down language management, which tends to impose policy lines on spontaneous language behavior, and bottom-up writing practices, which seek to transgress those policy lines, are continually shifting. On the one hand, language authorities are keenly aware of the relevance of vernacular tongues in the daily lives of ordinary Singaporeans, and tactically appropriate these vernaculars for instrumental purposes in apparent breach of their own policies. On the other hand, advocates of local vernaculars, while adopting an idiosyncratic and prefigurative stance in their practices, draw on resources from state-affiliated institutions and can potentially scale up their activities into systemic structures. Finally, the commercial manipulation of vernacular registers stands outside both of these choreographies, remixing the indexical qualities of Singapore's languages for play and profit.

In the final analysis, there is no absolute regimentation or absolute resistance. Instead, there is seepage and slippage between *place* and *space*, which exist as two autonomous but contrapuntal planes in relation to how multilingualism is practised in Singapore. And herein lies the dynamic of multilingual Singapore, in which different paradigms of writing and the language ideologies they instantiate face off with each other in both competition and symbiosis. Here, I venture to suggest postmultilingualism as a potential route to steer us out of the competing narratives on multilingualism in Singapore and hypothesize a transition from a multilingual Singapore to a postmultilingual Singapore. Li Wei (2018b) defines a postmultilingual era as one where

> simply having many different languages is no longer sufficient either for the individual or for society as a whole, but where multiple ownerships and more complex interweaving of languages and language varieties, and where boundaries between languages, between languages and other communicative means and the relationship between language and the nation-state are being constantly reassessed, broken or adjusted. (22; see also Li 2021: 217)

Theoretically and methodologically, postmultilingualism responds to a practice-based approach to language, throwing light on the "emerging nature of linguistic diversity and the role of everyday social interaction in creating, maintaining and resolving differences between different groups of language users" (Li 2018b: 18). Examples of postmultilingual practice include New Chinglish and Kongish, emergent registers comprising new "English" expressions based on transliterations or translations of Chinese (Mandarin or Cantonese) words or phrases. Circulating on social media platforms in mainland China, New Chinglish and Kongish expressions are not the outcome of innocuous lexical creativity but ludic translingual experiments predicated on critical stances toward the normative and the mainstream. Some examples include (see also Lee and Li 2021):

a. *How old are you* (New Chinglish): A word-to-word translation from the Chinese *zenme laoshi ni* 怎麼老是你 (how + old + BE + you), meaning "Why always you?!" This plays on the bifurcation of the word *lao* (old), which in the Chinese expression functions as an adverb meaning "always," but takes on the literal sense of "old in age" in the literal English version.

b. *How senior are you?* (Kongish): Literally translating the Chinese expression *nei syun lou gei* 你算老幾, this expression is not used to inquire about someone's seniority in age or rank but instead conveys the meaning, "Who do you think you are?"

c. *I will give you some color to see see* (New Chinglish): This means "I will teach you a lesson," a literal translation of *wo yao gei ni dian yanse kankan* 我要給你點顏色看看.

d. *Zebra chops people* (Kongish): Translated from *baan ma pek yau* 班馬劈友, this means to call for back-up to fight others. Here "zebra" arises as the dictionary equivalent of 班馬—a farcical equivalence, because despite its appearance, the Cantonese word means "to call for back-up" in this stock expression, not the striped animal.

e. *You can you up, no can no BB* (New Chinglish): This means "If you have the ability then you do it. If you don't have the ability, then say nothing," a literal translation of *ni xing ni shang a, buxing bie bibi* 你行你上啊，不行別逼逼, where BB is the abbreviation of 逼逼 *bibi*, a colloquial reduplicative verb meaning "say unnecessary words."

f. *Do you old dot me?* (Kongish): A nonsensical expression in English, this translates the Cantonese expression *nei lou dim ngo a* 你老點我啊 meaning, "Are you fooling me?"

Applying this to our case at hand, a postmultilingual sensibility enables us to look beyond the quadrilingual schema and its vernacular alternatives. Like New Chinglish and Kongish practices, vernacular practices in Singapore exemplify a "more complex interweaving of languages and language varieties"

(Li 2018b: 22) by means of testing out a heteroglossic register, based around Singlish and incorporating doses of colloquial Malay and Chinese dialects. A New Singlish may indeed be in the making, as attested in the examples from grassroots writing seen in Chapters 4 and 5.

But for me, postmultilingualism does not simply reference a "messy" multilingualism in which boundaries between named languages, as well as between linguistic and nonlinguistic cognitive systems, are renegotiated and transgressed. Nor is it solely about the enactment of discursive resistance against a perceived hegemony. Postmultilingualism transcends structural practices articulated around multilingualism, be they institutional or grassroots. It points to a more general orientation to the ludic in ordinary communications, with a premium on creative moments rather than systematic choreographies.

The creative moment as a unit of sociolinguistic analysis takes us into "multilingual creativity in everyday social interactions," reorienting us from "frequent and regular patterns in linguistic behaviour to spur-of-the-moment creative actions that have both immediate and long-term consequences" (Li 2018b: 26). A focus on momentarity in a sociolinguistic context (Lee and Li 2020) orients to the mobility turn (or perspective/paradigm) in the social sciences (Sheller and Urry 2006; Urry 2007), which foregrounds the mediated circulations of people and data, languages and cultures, in an age of "liquid modernity." The liquid modern age is one in which stability and predictability give way to fluidity and change—in respect of occupation, place of residence, values, political affiliation, sexual orientation, and so forth (Bauman 2013).

But instead of mundane moments of creativity in real-time conversation (Li 2018b), a different kind of moment has arisen in respect of multilingual writing—that of "high-performance events" (Coupland 2007: 148), such as those captured in text-based commodities. Calling up a nostalgic affect of locality, these vernacular T-shirts herald the emergence of a postmultilingual sensibility in Singapore, under which "boundaries between languages, between languages and other communicative means and the relationship between language and the nation-state are being constantly reassessed, broken or adjusted" (Li 2018b: 22). Through their proclivities toward a playful multilingualism, these T-shirts signal the "ludification of culture" in Singapore and promote a ludoliteracy: a consciousness that involves "playing by the rules, bending and adjusting the rules in order to move easily through the system, or where necessary and possible, adjusting the system or playing the system" (Raessens 2014: 109). The system in question here is that of language.

All said, writing is a complex business, engaging multiple domains and articulating myriad desires simultaneously. The institutional versus grassroots divide helps us map out two broad categories of writing choreography, though we must remain cognizant of the tension and interactivities that transpire both within and beyond this divide. The key to investigating writing in the city, or, better still, how the city writes, is to focus on writing moments while not losing sight of sustained patterns that have emerged over time, and which continue to transform the semiotic landscape. This is the case in Singapore, where remarkable instances of language use are often contingent and transitory in nature, intermittently punctuating the shadow of relatively stable language practices. It is yet unclear what a postmultilingual Singapore might eventually look like, but its trajectory is surely toward a creative proliferation and cross-pollination of multilingual practices across different scales of communication.

# REFERENCES

Agha, A. 2003. The Social Life of Cultural Value. *Language and Communication* 23: 231–73.

Agha, A. 2007. *Language and Social Relations*. Cambridge: Cambridge University Press.

Agha, A. 2011. Meet Mediatization. *Language and Communication* 31: 163–70.

Alsagoff, L. 2010. English in Singapore: Culture, Capital and Identity in Linguistic Variation. *World Englishes* 29, no. 3: 336–48.

Anderson, B. 2010. Preemption, Precaution, Preparedness: Anticipatory Action and Future Geographies. *Progress in Human Geography* 34, no. 6: 777–98.

Ang, A. 2014. An Intro to SingPoWriMo. In *SingPoWriMo: The Anthology*. Edited by A. Ang, J. Ip, and P. Nansi, vii–viii. Singapore: Math Paper Press.

Anttila, A., V. Fong, Š. Beňuš, and J. Nycz. 2008. Variation and Opacity in Singapore English Consonant Clusters. *Phonology* 25, no. 2: 181–216.

Augé, M. 1995. *Non-Places: Introduction to an Anthropology of Supermodernity*. London: Verso.

Backhaus, P. 2006. Multilingualism in Tokyo: A Look into the Linguistic Landscape. *International Journal of Multilingualism* 3, no. 1: 52–66.

Backhaus, P. 2007. *Linguistic Landscapes: A Comparative Study of Urban Multilingualism in Tokyo*. Bristol, UK: Multilingual Matters.

Baker, M. 2016. The Prefigurative Politics of Translation in Place-Based Movements of Protest: Subtitling in the Egyptian Revolution. *Translator* 22, no. 1: 1–21.

Baker, M. 2019. *Translation and Conflict: A Narrative Account*. 2nd ed. Abingdon, UK: Routledge.

Baker, M. 2020. Translation and Solidarity in the Century with No Future: Prefiguration vs. Aspirational Translation. *Palgrave Communications* 6, no. 23, https://doi.org/10.1057/s41599-020-0400-0.

Baker, M., and B. Blaagaard. 2016. *Citizen Media and Public Spaces*. Abingdon, UK: Routledge.

Baker, M., B. Blaagaard, H. Jones, and L. Pérez-González, eds. 2020. *The Routledge Encyclopedia of Citizen Media*. Abingdon, UK: Routledge.

Bakhtin, M. 1981. *The Dialogic Imagination: Four Essays*. Translated by C. Emerson and M. Holquist. Austin: University of Texas Press.

Bao, Z. 2010. *Must* in Singapore English. *Lingua* 120, no. 7: 1727–37.

Bao, Z. 2015. *The Making of Vernacular Singapore English: System, Transfer and Filter*. Cambridge: Cambridge University Press.

Bao, Z., and L. Wee. 1998. *Until* in Singapore English. *World Englishes* 17, no. 1: 31–41.

Bao, Z., and L. Wee. 1999. The Passive in Singapore English. *World Englishes* 18, no. 1: 1–11.

Barthes, R. 2012. *Mythologies*. New York: Hill and Wang.

Batchelor, K. 2018. *Translation and Paratexts*. Abingdon, UK: Routledge.

Bauman, R., and C. L. Briggs. 1990. Poetics and Performance as Critical Perspectives on Language and Social Life. *Annual Review of Anthropology* 19: 59–88.

Bauman, Z. 2013. *Liquid Modernity*. Boston, MA: Wiley.

Ben-Rafael, E., E. Shohamy, M. H. Amara, and N. Trumper-Hecht. 2006. Linguistic Landscape as Symbolic Construction of the Public Space: The Case of Israel. *International Journal of Multilingualism* 3, no. 1: 7–30.

Bennett, T. 1998. *Culture: A Reformer's Science*. St. Leonards, NSW: Allen and Unwin.

Berman, A. 2004. Translation and the Trials of the Foreign. Translated by L. Venuti. In *The Translation Studies Reader*. 2nd ed. Edited by L. Venuti, 276–89. London: Routledge.

Bezemer, J., and G. Kress. 2008. Writing in Multimodal Texts: A Social Semiotic Account of Designs for Learning. *Written Communication* 25, no. 2: 166–95.

Bezemer, J., and G. Kress. 2010. Changing Text: A Social Semiotic Analysis of Textbooks. *Designs for Learning* 3, no. 1–2: 10–29.

Blommaert, J. 2008. *Grassroots Literacy: Writing, Identity and Voice in Central Africa*. Abingdon, UK: Routledge.

Blommaert, J. 2010. *The Sociolinguistics of Globalization*. Cambridge: Cambridge University Press.

Blommaert, J. 2013. *Ethnography, Superdiversity and Linguistic Landscapes*. Bristol, UK: Multilingual Matters.

Blommaert, J. 2015. Chronotopes, Scales, and Complexity in the Study of Language in Society. *Annual Review of Anthropology* 44, no. 1: 105–16.

Blommaert, J. 2018. *Durkheim and the Internet: Sociolinguistics and the Sociological Imagination*. London: Bloomsbury.

Blommaert, J., and P. Varis. 2015. Enoughness, Accent and Light Communities: Essays on Contemporary Identities. Working paper. Babylon Center, Tilburg University. Tilburg, The Netherlands. https://research.tilburguniversity.edu/en/publicati ons/enoughness-accent-and-light-communities-essays-on-contemporary-id.

Bokhorst-Heng, W. 1999a. *Language Is More Than a Language*. Singapore: Centre for Advanced Studies, National University of Singapore.

Bokhorst-Heng, W. 1999b. Singapore's *Speak Mandarin Campaign*: Language Ideological Debates and the Imagining of the Nation. In *Language Ideological Debates*. Edited by J. Blommaert, 235–65. Berlin: Mouton de Gryuter.

Bokhorst-Heng, W. 2005. Debating Singlish. *Multilingua* 24: 185–209.

Brook, P. 1996. *The Empty Space*. New York: Touchstone.

Bruthiaux, P. 2010. The Speak Good English Movement: A Web-User's Perspective. In *English in Singapore: Modernity and Management*. Edited by L. Lim, A. Pakir, and L. Wee, 91–108. Hong Kong: Hong Kong University Press.

Busch, B. 2017. Expanding the Notion of the Linguistic Repertoire: On the Concept of *Spracherleben*—The Lived Experience of Language. *Applied Linguistics* 38, no. 3: 340–58.

Calvet, L-.J. 1998. *Language Wars and Linguistic Politics*. Translated by Michel Petheram. Oxford: Oxford University Press.

Cameron, D. 2012. *Verbal Hygiene*. Abingdon, UK: Routledge.

Casanova, P. 2010. Consecration and Accumulation of Literary Capital: Translation as Unequal Exchange. Translated by S. Brownlie. In *Translation Studies: Critical Concepts in Linguistics*, Vol. II. Edited by M. Baker, 85–107. Abingdon, UK: Routledge.

Chan, S., R. Rang, and D. Q. Yam. 2017. *SingPoWriMo 2017: The Anthology*. Singapore: Math Paper Press.

Chang, L. L. 2016. The Reality behind Singlish. *The New York Times* (Op-ed), May 23, 2016. https://www.nytimes.com/2016/05/23/opinion/the-reality-behind-singlish.html.

Chen, C. 2015. *The Red Riding Hood Lah*. Self-published.

Chng, H. H. 2003. "You see me no up": Is Singlish a Problem? *Language Problems and Language Planning* 27, no. 1: 45–62.

Chng, H. H. 2008. Beyond Linguistic Instrumentalism: The Place of Singlish in Singapore. In *Language as Commodity: Global Structures, Local Marketplaces*. Edited by P. K. W. Tan and R. Rubdy, 57–69. London: Continuum.

Chong, T. 2010. The State and the New Society: The Role of the Arts in Singapore Nation-Building. *Asian Studies Review* 34, no. 2: 131–49.

Cook, V. 2013. The Language of the Street. *Applied Linguistics Review* 4, no. 1: 43–81.

Coupland, N. 2007. *Style: Language Variation and Identity*. Cambridge: Cambridge University Press.

Coupland, N. 2010. Welsh Linguistic Landscapes "From Above" and "From Below." In *Semiotic Landscapes: Language, Image, Space*. Edited by A. Jaworski and C. Thurlow, 77–101. London: Continuum.

Coupland, N. 2012. Bilingualism on Display: The Framing of Welsh and English in Welsh Public Spaces. *Language in Society* 41: 1–27.

Coupland, N., and P. Garrett. 2010. Linguistic Landscapes, Discursive Frames and Metacultural Performance: The Case of Welsh Patagonia. *International Journal of the Sociology of Language* 205: 7–36.

Cox, R. W. 1993. Gramsci, Hegemony and International Relations: An Essay in Method. In *Gramsci, Historical Materialism and International Relations*. Edited by S. Gill, 49–66. Cambridge: Cambridge University Press..

Cresswell, T. 2015. *Place: An Introduction*. 2nd ed. Chichester, UK: Wiley-Blackwell.

de Certeau, M. 1984. *The Practice of Everyday Life*. Translated by Steven Rendall. Berkeley: University of California Press.

Debord, G. 1995. *The Society of the Spectacle*. Translated by D. Nicholson-Smith. New York: Zone Books.

Del Percio, A., M. Flubacher, and A. Duchêne. 2017. *Language and Political Economy*. In *The Oxford Handbook of Language and Society*. Edited by O. Garcia, N. Flores N., and M. Spotti, 55–75. Oxford: Oxford University Press.

Deleuze, G., and F. Guattari. 1994. *What Is Philosophy?* Translated by H. Tomlinson and G. Burchell. New York: Columbia University Press.

Department of Statistics, Singapore. 2016. *General Household Survey 2015*. Singapore: Ministry of Trade and Industry. https://www.singstat.gov.sg/-/media/files/publications/ghs/ghs2015/ghs2015.pdf.

Department of Statistics, Singapore. 2020. *Population Trends, 2020*. Singapore: Ministry of Trade and Industry. https://www.singstat.gov.sg/-/media/files/publications/population/population2020.pdf.

Deterding, D. 2001. The Measurement of Rhythm: A Comparison of Singapore and British English. *Journal of Phonetics* 29, no. 2: 217–30.

Deterding, D. 2003. An Instrumental Study of the Monophthong Vowels of Singapore English. *English World-Wide* 24, no. 1: 1–16.

Dixon, L. Q. 2005. Bilingual Education Policy in Singapore: An analysis of Its Sociohistorical Roots and Current Academic Outcomes. *International Journal of Bilingual Education and Bilingualism* 8, no. 1: 25–47.

Dixon, L. Q. 2009. Assumptions behind Singapore's Language-in-Education Policy: Implications for Language Planning and Second Language Acquisition. *Language Policy* 8: 117–37.

Duchêne, A. 2020. Unequal Language Work(ers) in the Business of Words. In *The Business of Words: Wordsmiths, Linguists, and Other Language Workers*. Edited by C. Thurlow, 23–35. Abingdon, UK: Routledge.

Eagleton, T. 2019. *Humour*. New Haven, CT: Yale University Press.

Eckert, P. 2008. Variation and the Indexical Field. *Journal of Sociolinguistics* 12, no. 4: 453–76.

Essmann, H., and A. P. Frank. 1991. Translation Anthologies: An Invitation to the Curious and a Case Study. *Target* 3, no. 1: 65–90.

Frank, A. P. 1998. Anthologies of Literature. In *Routledge Encyclopedia of Translation Studies*. Edited by M. Baker, 13–16. London: Routledge.

Gee, J. P. 2001. Educational Linguistics. In *The Handbook of Linguistics*. Edited by M. Aronoff and J. Rees-Miller, 647–63. Oxford: Blackwell.

Goffman, E. 1974. *Frame Analysis: An Essay on the Organization of Experience*. New York: Harper and Row.

Goh, C., and Y. Y. Woo. 2009. *The Coxford Singlish Dictionary*. 2nd ed. Singapore: Angsana Books.

Goh, R. B. H., ed. 1998. *Memories and Desires: A Poetic History of Singapore*. Singapore: UniPress.

Goh, S. T. 2000. Speaking in Tongues—Singapore Style. In *Rhythms: A Singaporean Millenial Anthology of Poetry*. Edited by K. Singh and Y. W. Wong, 201. Singapore: National Arts Council.

Grossberg, L. 1992. *We Gotta Get Out of This Place: Popular Conservatism and Postmodern Culture*. New York: Routledge.

Grossman, E. 1971. The Technique of Antipoetry. *Review: Literature and Arts of the Americas* 4, no. 4/5: 72–83.

Gupta, A. F. 1994. *The Step-Tongue: Children's English in Singapore*. Clevedon, UK: Multilingual Matters.

Gupta, A. F. 2010. Singapore Standard English Revisited. In *English in Singapore: Modernity and Management*. Edited by L. Lim, A. Pakir, and L. Wee, 57–89. Hong Kong: Hong Kong University Press.

Gwee, L. S. 2015a. Introduction: The Age of a Number. In *Singathology: 50 New Works by Celebrated Singaporean Writers*. Edited by L. S. Gwee, 9–15. Singapore: Marshall Cavendish and National Arts Council.

Gwee, L. S. 2015b. *Who Wants to Buy an Expanded Edition of a Book of Poems?* Singapore: Landmark Books.

Gwee, L. S. 2015c. *The Other Merlion and Friends*. Singapore: Landmark Books.

Gwee, L. S. 2016. Do You Speak Singlish?. *The New York Times* (Op-ed), May 13, 2016. https://www.nytimes.com/2016/05/14/opinion/do-you-speak-singlish.html/.

Gwee, L. S. 2017. *Haikuku*. Singapore: Landmark Books.

Gwee, L. S. 2018. *Spiaking Singlish: A Companion to How Singaporeans Speak*. Singapore: Marshall Cavendish.

Gwee, L. S., C. L. Tan, S. B. Buang, and A. Pandiyan, eds. 2015. *Singathology: 50 New Works by Celebrated Singaporean Writers*. Singapore: Marshall Cavendish and National Arts Council.

Hall, S. 1997. The Work of Representation. In *Representations: Cultural Representations and Signifying Practices*. Edited by S. Hall, 13–74. London: Sage.

Heinrich, P. 2021. Urban Translation and the 2020 Tokyo Games. *The Routledge Handbook of Translation and the City*. Edited by T. K. Lee, 131–45. Abingdon, UK: Routledge.

Heller, M. 2002. Globalization and Commodification of Bilingualism in Canada. In *Globalization and Language Teaching*. Edited by D. Block and D. Cameron, 47–64. London: Routledge.

Heller, M. 2003. Globalization, the New Economy, and the Commodification of Language and Identity. *Journal of Sociolinguistics* 7, no. 4: 473–92.

Heller, M. 2010. The Commodification of Language. *Annual Review of Anthropology* 39: 101–14.

Heller, M., A. Jaworski, and C. Thurlow. 2014. Introduction: Sociolinguistics and Tourism: Mobilities, Markets, Multilingualism. *Journal of Sociolinguistics* 18, no. 4: 425–58.

Hiramoto, M. 2011. Consuming the Consumers: Semiotics of Hawai'i Creole in Advertisements. *Journal of Pidgin and Creole Languages* 26, no. 2: 247–75.

Hiramoto, M. 2019. *Blur like sotong* No More: Colloquial Singapore English in Advertisements. *World Englishes* 38: 450–62.

Hoa, K. T. 2020. Linguistic Landscaping in Singapore: Multilingualism or the Dominance of English and Its Dual Identity in the Local Linguistic Ecology? *International Journal of Multilingualism* 17, no. 2: 152–73.

Holden, P. 2017. Always Already Translated: Questions of Language in Singapore Literature. *Asymptote*. https://www.asymptotejournal.com/special-feature/phi lip-holden-singaporean-writers/.

Iedema, R. 2003. Multimodality, Resemiotization: Extending the Analysis of Discourse as Multi-Semiotic Practice. *Visual Communication* 2, no. 1: 29–57.

Inoue, M. 2016. Where Has "Japanese Women's Language" Gone? Notes on Language and Political Economy in the Age of Control Societies. *Hau: Journal of Ethnographic Theory* 6, no. 3: 151–77.

Ip, J. 2015. *sonnets from the singlish*. Upsize ed. Singapore: Math Paper Press.

Irvine, J. T., and S. Gal. 2000. Language Ideology and Linguistic Differentiation. In *Regimes of Language: Ideologies, Polities, and Identities*. Edited by P. V. Kroskrity, 35–84. Santa Fe, NM: School of American Research Press.

Jain, R., and L. Wee. 2019. Diversity Management and the Presumptive Universality of Categories: The Case of the Indians in Singapore. *Current Issues in Language Planning* 20, no. 1: 16–32.

Järlehed, J., H. L. Nielsen, and T. Rosendal. 2018. Language, Food and Gentrification: Signs of Socioeconomic Mobility in two Gothenburg Neighbourhoods. *Multilingual Margins* 5, no. 1: 40–65.

Jaworski, A. 2018. Writing as Spectacle: Between Aesthetics and Politics. Paper presented at the Sociolinguistics Symposium 22, University of Auckland, March 29.

Jaworski, A., and T. K. Lee. 2019. Sculptural Place Names: Tourist Self-Emplacement and the Ethos of Democratization in Unequal Urban Spaces. Plenary speech delivered at Linguistic Landscape Workshop XI, Chulalongkorn University, Bangkok, June 4.

Jaworski, A., and W. Li. 2021. Introducing Writing (in) the City. *Social Semiotics* 31, no. 1: 1–13.

Jaworski, A., and J. J. Lou. 2021. #wordswewear: Mobile Texts, Expressive Persons, and Conviviality in Urban Spaces. *Social Semiotics* 31, no. 1: 108–35.

Jaworski, A., and C. Thurlow. 2010. Introducing semiotic landscapes. In *Semiotic Landscapes: Language, Image, Space*. Edited by A. Jaworski and C. Thurlow, 1–40. London: Continuum.

Johnstone, B. 2009. Pittsburghese Shirts: Commodification and the Enregisterment of an Urban Dialect. *American Speech* 84, no. 2: 157–75.

Johnstone, B. 2010. Indexing the Local. In *The Handbook of Language and Globalization*. Edited by N. Coupland, 386–405. Oxford: Wiley-Blackwell.

Johnstone, B., A. Jennifer, and E. D. Andrew. 2006. Mobility, Indexicality, and the Enregisterment of "Pittsburghese." *Journal of English Linguistics* 34: 77–101.

Kallen, J. L. 2010. Changing Landscapes: Language, Space and policy in the Dublin Linguistic Landscape. In *Semiotic Landscapes: Language, Image, Space*. Edited by A. Jaworski and C. Thurlow, 41–58. London: Continuum.

Karlander, D. 2019. A Semiotics of Nonexistence?: Erasure and Erased Writing under Anti-Graffiti Regimes. *Linguistic Landscape* 5, no. 2: 198–216.

Kelly-Holmes, H. 2014. Linguistic Fetish: The Sociolinguistics of Visual Multilingualism. In *Handbook of Communication Science: Visual Communication* (Vol. 4). Edited by D. Machin, 135–51. Berlin: Mouton de Gruyter.

Kelly-Holmes, H. 2020. The Linguistic Business of Marketing. In *The Business of Words: Wordsmiths, Linguists, and Other Language Workers*. Edited by C. Thurlow, 36–50. Abingdon, UK: Routledge.

Khiun L. K., and B. Chan. 2013. Vestigial Pop: Hokkien Popular Music and the Cultural Fossilization of Subalternity in Singapore. *SOJOURN: Journal of Social Issues in Southeast Asia* 28, no. 2: 272–98.

Kiesling, S. F. 2009. Style as Stance: Stance as the Explanation for Patterns of Sociolinguistic Variation. In *Stance: Sociolinguistic Perspectives*. Edited by A. Jaffe, 171–94. Oxford: Oxford University Press.

Kirkpatrick, A., ed. 2021. *The Routledge Handbook of World Englishes*. 2nd ed. Abingdon, UK: Routledge.

Klein, N. 2000. *No Logo*. London: Flamingo.

Koh, T. A. 1989. Culture and the Arts. In *Management of Success: The Moulding of Modern Singapore*. Edited by K. Sandhu and P. Wheatley, 710–48. Singapore: Institute of Southeast Asian Studies.

Koh, T. A. 2018. Introduction. In *Singapore Chronicles: Literature*. Edited by T. A. Koh, C. L. Tan, R. Hadijah, and M. Arun, 7–17. Singapore: Straits Times Press and Institute of Policy Studies.

Krauss, R. 2006. Two Moments from the Post-Medium Condition. *October* 116: 55–62.

Kress, G. 2020. Transposing Meaning: Translation in a Multimodal Semiotic Landscape. In *Translation and Multimodality: Beyond Words*. Edited by M. Boria, Á. Carreres, M. Noriega-Sánchez, and M. Tomalin, 24–48. Abingdon, UK: Routledge.

Kress, G., and T. van Leeuwen. 2021. *Reading Images: The Grammar of Visual Design*, 3rd ed. Abingdon, UK: Routledge.

Kuo, E. C. Y., and B. Chan. 2016. *Singapore Chronicles: Language*. Singapore: Straits Times Press and Institute of Policy Studies.

Labov, W. 1971. The Study of Language in Its Social Context. In *Advances in the Sociology of Language* (Vol. 1). Edited by J. A. Fishman, 152–216. The Hague, The Netherlands: Mouton.

Lakoff, G., and M. Johnson. 2003. *Metaphors We Live By*. 2nd ed. Chicago, IL: Chicago University Press.

Landry, R., and R. Y. Bourhis. 1997. Linguistic Landscape and Ethnolinguistic Vitality: An Empirical Study. *Journal of Language and Social Psychology* 16, no. 1: 23–49.

Law, K. H. 2016. Singlish vs Standard English: I say, RELAK, lah! Blog. https://2econdsi ght.wordpress.com/2016/05/25/singlish-vs-standard-english-i-say-relak-lah/.

Lee, K. Y. 2000. *From Third World to First—The Singapore Story: 1965–2000: Memoirs of Lee Kuan Yew*. Singapore: Straits Times Press.

Lee, T. K. 2013. *Translating the Multilingual City: Translation and Language Ideology in Singapore*. Oxford: Peter Lang.

Lee, T. K. 2022. Translation and Translanguaging in (Post)Multilingual' Societies. In *The Cambridge Handbook of Translation*. Edited by K. Malmkjaer, 119–38. Cambridge: Cambridge University Press.

Lee, T. K., and W. Li. 2020. Translanguaging and Momentarity in Social Interaction. In *The Cambridge Handbook of Discourse Studies*. Edited by A. de Fina and A. Georgakopoulou, 394–416. Cambridge: Cambridge University Press.

Lee, T. K., and W. Li. 2021. Translanguaging and Multilingual Creativity with English in the Sinophone World. In *The Routledge Handbook of World Englishes*. 2nd ed. Edited by A. Kirkpatrick, 558–75. Abingdon, UK: Routledge..

Leeman, J., and G. Modan. 2009. Commodified Language in Chinatown: A Contextualized Approach to Linguistic Landscape. *Journal of Sociolinguistics* 13, no. 3: 332–62.

Lefebvre, H. 1991. *The Production of Space*. Oxford: Blackwell.

Lefevere, A. 1992. *Translation, Rewriting, and the Manipulation of Literary Fame*. Abingdon, UK: Routledge.

Leimgruber, J. R. E. 2013. *Singapore English: Structure, Variation, and Usage*. Cambridge: Cambridge University Press.

Li, W. 1994. *Three Generations, Two Languages, One Family: Language Choice and Language Shift in a Chinese Community in Britain*. Clevedon, UK: Multilingual Matters.

Li, W. 2018a. Translanguaging as a Practical Theory of Language. *Applied Linguistics* 39, no. 1: 9–30.

Li, W. 2018b. Linguistic (Super)Diversity, Post-Multilingualism and Translanguaging Moments. In *The Routledge Handbook of Language and Superdiversity: An Interdisciplinary Perspective*. Edited by A. Cresse and A. Blackledge, 16–29. Abingdon, UK: Routledge.

Li, W. 2021. Towards a Liquid-Multilingual Singapore: An Outsider's Perspective. In *Multilingual Singapore: Language Policies and Linguistic Realities*. Edited by R. Jain, 213–19. Abingdon, UK: Routledge.

Lillis, T. 2013. *The Sociolinguistics of Writing*. Edinburgh, Scotland: Edinburgh University Press.

Lim, L., ed. 2004. *Singapore English: A Grammatical Description*. Amsterdam: John Benjamins.

Lim, L. 2009a. Beyond Fear and Loathing: The Real Mother Tongues and Language Policies in Multilingual Singapore. *AILA Review* 22: 52–71.

Lim, L. 2009b. Revisiting English Prosody: (Some) New Englishes as Tone Languages? *English World-Wide* 30, no. 2: 218–39.

Lim, L. 2015. Coming of Age, Coming Full Circle: The (Re)positioning of (Singapore) English and Multilingualism in Singapore at 50. *Asian Englishes* 17, no. 3: 261–70.

Lim, L., A. Pakir, and L. Wee, eds. 2010. *English in Singapore: Modernity and Management*. Hong Kong: Hong Kong University Press.

Lou, J. 2016. *The Linguistic Landscape of Chinatown: A Sociolinguistic Ethnography*. Clevedon, UK: Multilingual Matters.

Maeckelbergh, M. 2020. Prefiguration. In *Routledge Encyclopedia of Citizen Media*. Edited by M. Baker, B. Blaagaard, H. Jones, and L. Pérez-González, 324–30. Abingdon, UK: Routledge.

Makoni, S., and A. Pennycook. 2007. Disinventing and Reconstituting Languages. In *Disinventing and Reconstituting Languages*. Edited by S. Makoni and A. Pennycook, 1–41. Clevedon, UK: Multilingual Matters.

Malinowski, D. 2018. Afterword. In *Making Sense of People and Place in Linguistic Landscapes*. Edited by A. Peck, C. Stroud, and Q. Williams, 223–29. London: Bloomsbury.

Massey, D. 2005. *For Space*. London: Sage.

Møller, J. S., and J. N. Jørgensen. 2011. Enregisterment among Adolescents in Superdiverse Copenhagen. In *Language Enregisterment and Attitudes*. Edited by J. S. Møller and J. N. Jørgensen, 99–121. Copenhagen, Denmark: University of Copenhagen.

Moriarty, M. 2014. Contesting Language Ideologies in the Linguistic Landscape of an Irish Tourist Town. *International Journal of Bilingualism* 18, no. 5: 464–77.

Morris, B. 2004. What We Talk about When We Talk about "Walking in the City." *Cultural Studies* 18, no. 5: 675–97.

Ms Demeanour Singapore. 2011. Hey you—speak good Singlish!, http://msdemeanoursingapore.blogspot.com/2011/10/hey-you-speak-good-singlish.html.

Mullany, L., and P. Stockwell. 2015. *Introducing English Language: A Resource for Students*. 2nd ed. Abingdon, UK: Routledge.

Myers-Scotton, C. 1997. *Duelling Languages: Grammatical Structure in Codeswitching*, 2nd ed. Oxford: Oxford University Press.

National Library Board. 2006. *Looking In, Looking Out*. Singapore: National Library Board.

National Library Board. 2007. *Ties That Bind*. Singapore: National Library Board.

National Library Board. 2008. *Home and Away*. Singapore: National Library Board.

National Library Board. 2009. *Dreams and Choices*. Singapore: National Library Board.

National Library Board. 2010. *Roads Less Travelled*. Singapore: National Library Board.

National Library Board. 2011. *Transitions*. Singapore: National Library Board.

National Library Board. 2012. *Bridges*. Singapore: National Library Board.

National Library Board. 2013. *Under One Sky*. Singapore: National Library Board.

National Library Board. 2014. *Tenacity: Stories Built to Last*. Singapore: National Library Board.

National Library Board. 2015. *SingaPoetry: An Anthology of Singapore Poems*. Singapore: National Library Board.

Ng, L., A. Ibrahim, T. S. Chow, K. Kanagalatha, and C. L. Tan, eds. 2019. *Contour: A Lyric Cartography of Singapore*. Singapore: Poetry Festival Singapore.

Ng, L., C. L. Tan, T. S. Chow, A. Zakaria, A. Ibrahim, and K. Kanagalatha, eds. 2018. *SG Poems 2017–2018*. Singapore: Ethos Books.

Pakir, A. 1991. The Range and Depth of English-Knowing Bilinguals in Singapore. *World Englishes* 10, no. 2: 167–79.

Patke, R. S., and P. Holden. 2010. *The Routledge Concise History of Southeast Asian Writing in English*. Abingdon, UK: Routledge.

Peng, H. 2008. The Writing of Literary History and the Position of Hong Kong Literature in Sinophone Literature. *Journal of Modern Literature in Chinese* 8, no. 2/9, no. 1: 40–50.

Pennycook, A., and E. Otsuji. 2015. *Metrolingualism: Language in the City*. Abingdon, UK: Routledge.

Pennycook, A., and E. Otsuji. 2019a. Mundane Metrolingualism. *International Journal of Multilingualism* 16, no. 2: 175–86.

Pennycook, A., and E. Otsuji. 2019b. Lingoing and Everyday Metrolingual Metalanguage. In *Critical Perspectives on Linguistic Fixity and Fluidity: Languagised Lives*. Edited by J. Jaspers and L. M. Madsen, 76–96. Abingdon, UK: Routledge.

Platt, J. 1975. The Singapore English Speech Continuum and Its Basilect "Singlish" as a Creoloid. *Anthropological Linguistics* 17, no. 7: 363–74.

Platt, J. 1977. The Sub-Varieties of Singapore English: Their Sociolectal and Functional Status. In *The English Language in Singapore*. Edited by W. J. Crewe, 83–95. Singapore: Eastern Universities Press.

Platt, J., and K. Singh. 1984. The Use of Localized English in Singapore Poetry. *English World-Wide* 5, no. 1: 43–54.

Quah, S. R., and W. S. Hee, eds. 2020. *Memorandum: A Sinophone Singaporean Short Story Reader*. Translated by D. F. Tan. Singapore: Ethos Books.

Raessens, J. 2014. The ludification of culture. In *Rethinking Gamification*. Edited by M. Fuchs, S. Fizek, P. Ruffino, and N. Schrape, 91–114. Lüneburg, Germany: Meson Press.

Rampton, B. 2015. Conviviality and Phatic Communication? *Multilingual Margins: A Journal of Multilingualism from the Periphery* 2, no. 1: 83–91.

Reh, M. 2004. Multilingual Writing: A Reader-Oriented Typology–With Examples from Lira Municipality (Uganda). *International Journal of the Sociology of Language* 170: 1–41.

Rubdy, R. 2001. Creative Destruction: Singapore's Speak Good English Movement. *World Englishes* 20, no. 3: 341–55.

Rymes, B. 2020. *How We Talk about Language: Exploring Citizen Sociolinguistics*. Cambridge: Cambridge University Press.

Rymes, B., and G. Smail. 2021. Citizen Sociolinguists Scaling Back. *Applied Linguistics Review* 12, no. 3: 419–44.

Said, E. 1993. *Culture and Imperialism*. New York: Vintage Books.

Schneider, E. W. 2003. The Dynamics of New Englishes: From Identity Construction to Dialect Birth. *Language* 79, no. 2: 233–81.

Schneider, E. W. 2007. *Postcolonial English: Varieties around the World*. Cambridge: Cambridge University Press.

Scollon, R. 2001. *Mediated Discourse: The Nexus of Practice*. London: Routledge.

Scollon, R., and S. W. Scollon. 2003. *Discourses in Place: Language in a Material World*. London: Routledge.

Scollon, R., and S. W. Scollon. 2004. *Nexus Analysis: Discourse and the Emerging Internet*. New York: Routledge.

Sebba, M. 2012. Multilingualism in Written Discourse: An Approach to the Analysis of Multilingual Texts. *International Journal of Bilingualism* 17, no. 1: 97–118.

Seruya, T., L. D'hulst, A. A. Rossa, and M. L. Moniz, eds. 2013. *Translation in Anthologies and Collections (19th and 20th Centuries)*. Amsterdam: John Benjamins.

Shapiro, M. 2019. *Punctuations: How the Arts Think the Political*. Durham, NC: Duke University Press.

Sheller, M., and J. Urry. 2006. The New Mobilities Paradigm. *Environment and Planning A* 38, no. 2: 207–26.

Shih, S. 2011. The Concept of the Sinophone. *PMLA* 126, no. 3: 709–18.

Shohamy, E. 2006. *Language Policy: Hidden Agendas and New Approaches*. New York: Routledge.

Shohamy, E. 2015. LL Research as Expanding Language and Language Policy. *Linguistic Landscape* 1, no. 1–2: 152–171.

Silverstein, M. 2003. Indexical Order and the Dialectics of Sociolinguistic Life. *Language and Communication* 23: 193–229.

Sim, C. 2015. Speak Good English Movement. *Singapore Infopedia*. https://eresources. nlb.gov.sg/infopedia/articles/SIP_575_2004-12-23.html.

Simpson, A. 2007. Singapore. In *Language and National Identity in Asia*. Edited by A. Simpson, 374–90. Oxford: Oxford University Press.

Singh, K., and Y. W. Wong, eds. 2000. *Rhythms: A Singaporean Millennial Anthology of Poetry* Singapore: National Arts Council.

Soh, W. Y. 2020. Digital Protest in Singapore: The Pragmatics of Political Internet Memes. *Media, Culture & Society* 42, no. 7/8: 1115–32.

Somers, M. 1992. Narrativity, Narrative Identity, and Social Action: Rethinking English Working-Class Formation. *Social Science History* 16, no. 4: 591–630.

Somers, M. 1997. Deconstructing and Reconstructing Class Formation Theory: Narrativity, Relational Analysis, and Social Theory. In *Reworking Class*. Edited by J. Hall, 73–105. Ithaca, NY: Cornell University Press..

Somers, M., and G. D. Gibson. 1994. Reclaiming the Epistemological "Other": Narrative and the Social Constitution of Identity. In *Social Theory and the Politics of Identity*. Edited by C. Calhoun, 37–99.Oxford: Blackwell.

Sontag, S. 1969. *Styles of Radical Will*. New York: Farrar, Straus and Giroux.

St. André, J. 2006a. "He 'catch no ball' leh!" Globalization versus Localization in the Singaporean translation market. *Meta* 51, no. 4: 771–86.

St. André, J. 2006b. Revealing the Invisible: Heterolingualism in Three Generations of Singaporean Playwrights. *Target* 18, no. 1: 139–61.

Starr, R. L. 2019. Attitudes and Exposure as Predictors of -t/d Deletion among Local and Expatriate Children in Singapore. *Language Variation and Change* 31, no. 3: 251–74.

Stroud, C., and D. Jegels. 2014. Semiotic Landscapes and Mobile Narrations of Place: Performing the Local. *International Journal of the Sociology of Language* 238: 179–99.

Sturge, K. 2007. *Representing Others: Translation, Ethnography and Museum*. Manchester, UK: St. Jerome.

Sweetland J. 2002. Unexpected but Authentic Use of an Ethnically-Marked Dialect. *Journal of Sociolinguistics* 6: 514–38.

Tagg, C. 2012. *Discourse of Text Messaging: Analysis of SMS Communication*. London: Continuum.

Tan, D. F., ed. 2017. *Living in Babel: Singapore Literature in Translation*. Singapore: Canopy.

Tan, E. K. B. 2003. Re-Engaging Chineseness: Political, Economic and Cultural Imperatives of Nation-Building in Singapore. *The China Quarterly* 175: 751–74.

Tan, E. K. B. 2021. Translation in global city Singapore: A holistic embrace in a multilingual milieu? In *The Routledge Handbook of Translation and the City*. Edited by T. K. Lee, 159–75. Abingdon, UK: Routledge.

Tan, P. K. W. 2014. Singapore's Balancing Act, from the Perspective of the Linguistic Landscape. *SOJOURN* 29, no. 2: 438–66.

Teo, P. 2005. Mandarinising Singapore: A Critical Analysis of Slogans in Singapore's "Speak Mandarin" Campaign. *Critical Discourse Studies* 2, no. 2: 121–42.

The Online Citizen. 2010. "Please stop hum-tumming Singlish! Just leebit alone!" Accessed July 30, 2020 https://www.theonlinecitizen.com/2010/09/17/"please-stop-hum-tumming-singlish-just-leebit-alone"/.

Thumboo, E., ed. 2010. & Words: Poems Singapore and Beyond. Singapore: Ethos Books and National Arts Council.

Thumboo, E., I. Kamari, H. P. Chia, and K. T. M. Iqbal, eds. 2009. Fifty on 50. Singapore: National Arts Council.

Thumboo, E., Y. W. Wong, K. C. Ban, N. Govindasamy, S. Maaruf, R. Goh, and P. Chan, eds. 1995. Journeys: Words, Home and Nation. Anthology of Singapore Poetry (1984–1995). Singapore: UniPress.

Thumboo, E., Y. W. Wong. T. P. Lee, M. Salikun, and V. T. Arasu, eds. 1985. Anthology of ASEAN Literatures: The Poetry of Singapore. Singapore: ASEAN Committee on Culture and Information.

Thumboo, E., Y. W. Wong, S. Maaruf, Elangovan, A. Yap, N. Govindasamy, M. V. Wong, M. Salikun, and D. de Souza, eds. 1990. Anthology of ASEAN Literatures: The Fiction of Singapore (Vols. II, IIa, III). Singapore: ASEAN Committee on Culture and Information. Repr, 1993 by UniPress (Singapore).

Thumboo, E., K. C. Yeo, E. Ng, I. Kamari, and S. Lakshimi, eds. 2009. Reflecting on the Merlion: An Anthology of Poems. Singapore: National Arts Council.

Thurlow, C. 2016. Queering Critical Discourse Studies or/and Performing Post-Class Ideologies. Critical Discourse Studies 13, no. 5: 485–514.

Thurlow, C. 2019. Semiotic Creativities in and with Space: Binaries and Boundaries, Beware! International Journal of Multilingualism 16, no. 1: 94–104.

Thurlow, C. 2020. The (Grubby) Business of Words: What George Clooney Tells Us. In The Business of Words: Wordsmiths, Linguists, and Other Language Workers. Edited by C. Thurlow, 1–19. Abingdon, UK: Routledge.

Toh, S. P. C. 2011. The Complete Eh, Goondu! Singapore: Marshall Cavendish.

Urry, J. 2007. Mobilities. Oxford: Polity.

Valentine, G. 2008. Living with Difference: Reflections on Geographies of Encounter. Progress in Human Geography 32, no. 3: 323–37.

Valles, E. T., I. Chung, C. L. Tan, W. K. Ow Yeong, T. S. Chow, A. Ibrahim, and K. Kanagalatha, eds. 2016. SG Poems 2015–2016. Singapore: Ethos Books.

Venuti, L. 2008. The Translator's Invisibility: A History of Translation. 2nd ed. Abingdon, UK: Routledge.

Wee, L. 2002. Lor in Colloquial Singapore English. Journal of Pragmatics 34, no. 6: 711–25.

Wee, L. 2003a. Linguistic Instrumentalism in Singapore. Journal of Multilingual and Multicultural Development 24, no. 3: 211–24.

Wee, L. 2003b. The Birth of a Particle: Know in Colloquial Singapore English. World Englishes 22, no. 1: 5–13.

Wee, L. 2005. Intra-Language Discrimination and Linguistic Hum n rights: The Case of Singlish. Applied Linguistics 26, no.1: 48–69.

Wee, L. 2006. The Semiotics of Language Ideologies in Singapore. Journal of Sociolinguistics 10, no. 3: 344–61.

Wee, L. 2007. Singapore English X-self and Ownself. World Englishes 26, no. 3: 360–72.

Wee, L. 2009. Resolving the Paradox of Singapore English hor. English World-Wide 30, no. 3: 241–61.

Wee, L. 2010. The Particle ya in Colloquial Singapore English. World Englishes 29, no. 1: 45–58.

Wee, L. 2016a. Situating Affect in Linguistic Landscapes. *Linguistic Landscape* 2, no. 2: 105–26.

Wee, L. 2016b. Singlish as Style: Implications for Language Policy. In *Managing Diversity in Singapore: Policies and Prospects*. Edited by M. Mathews and C. W. Fong, 41–63. London: Imperial College Press.

Wee, L. 2018. *The Singlish Controversy*. Cambridge: Cambridge University Press.

Wee, L. 2021a. The State of/and Language Planning in Singapore. In *Multilingual Global Cities: Singapore, Hong Kong, Dubai*. Edited by P. Siemund and J. R. E. Leimgruber, 83–98. Abingdon, UK: Routledge.

Wee, L. 2021b. The Fetishization of Official Languages. In *Multilingual Singapore: Language Policies and Linguistic Realities*. Edited by R. Jain, 12–27. Abingdon, UK: Routledge.

Wee, L., and W. Bokhorst-Heng. 2005. Language Policy and Nationalist Ideology: Statal Narratives in Singapore. *Multilingua* 24, no. 3: 159–83.

Wee, L., and R. B. H. Goh. 2020. *Language, Space, and Cultural Play: Theorizing Affect in the Semiotic Landscape*. Cambridge: Cambridge University Press.

Wills, J. J. 2017. *Contesting World Order? Socioeconomic Rights and Global Justice Movements*. Cambridge: Cambridge University Press.

Wong, J. 2004. The Reduplication of Nominal Modifiers in Singapore English: A Semantic and Cultural Interpretation. *World Englishes* 23, no. 3: 339–54.

Wong, J. 2005. Why you so Singlish *one*? A Semantic and Cultural Interpretation of the Singapore English Particle *one*. *Language in Society* 34, no. 2: 239–75.

Zappavigna, M. 2015. Searchable Talk: The Linguistic Functions of Hashtags. *Social Semiotics* 25, no. 3: 274–91.

Zappavigna, M., and J. R. Martin. 2018. #Communing Affiliation: Social Tagging as a Resource for Aligning around Values in Social Media. *Discourse, Context and Media* 22: 4–12.

# INDEX

*For the benefit of digital users, indexed terms that span two pages (e.g., 52–53) may, on occasion, appear on only one of those pages.*

Note: Tables and figures are indicated by *t* and *f* following the page number

canon, literary, 62–63, 92–94,
100, 139–40
and the nation, 62, 67, 75, 84, 85–87
and playful multilingualism, 150–51,
157–58, 174–76, 192
Cantonese, 7, 10–11, 12, 154
and Kongish, 210
in multilingual poetry, 152, 153
in state communications, 184, 189
in text-based memorabilia, 198–99
*See also* Chinese dialects
Casanova, Pascale, 70–71
Central Provident Fund (CPF), 187–89
Champion, Jennifer Anne, 94
Chang, Li Lin, 119–22, 123–24, 125,
126, 135n.33, 137
Cher, Ming, 154
China, 143–44, 210
Chinese dialects, 14, 33, 56
commodification of, 198–99
and resistant politics, 12–13, 16,
178, 182
in Singlish, 106, 108, 117, 151, 165,
167, 169
and the Speak Mandarin Campaign,
10–11, 12, 148
in state communications, 184,
189, 190
Chinese (ethnicity), 6–7, 143, 147
and language, 10–11, 12–13, 14,
58n.29, 143–44 (*see also* Speak
Mandarin Campaign [SMC])
*See also* CMIO (Chinese, Malay, Indian,
Others) framework
Chinese (language). *See* Cantonese;
Chinese dialects; Mandarin
Chong, Terence, 141, 142
choreographies of multilingualism, 5, 15,
17, 20, 179, 192, 211–12
commoditized, 193, 196–97, 209
as contrapuntal, 181–82, 183, 186–87,
189, 191–92
in cultural literacy programs, 95–
96, 98
grassroots, 101, 108, 136–37,
139, 162
institutional, 24–25, 59–60, 66, 99,
188–89n.7, 190
in literary anthologies, 62, 65–66, 69,
71, 78–79, 83–85, 89, 90

resistant, 115–16, 127, 145–46, 158,
174, 175–76
visual-spatial, 25–26, 31, 34, 57, 80
*See also* technologies of choreography
citizen poetry, 140, 155–70, 179, 182
politics of, 162–63, 170–71, 174–75,
178–79, 192
citizen sociolinguistics, 22, 135–38
CMIO (Chinese, Malay, Indian, Others)
framework, 6, 7, 21, 35, 141, 160
and language policy, 9, 25, 32
and literature and literacy programs,
81, 96, 99, 142
*See also* multiculturalism
code-mixing, 101, 140, 146, 148
code-switching, 106, 119–21, 123–24,
130–31, 133t, 153
and elitism, 120, 124, 137
Colloquial Singapore English. *See* Singlish
colonialism, British, 6, 73, 89, 145, 146,
160, 170–71
commodification, 95
of vernacular languages, 5, 12–13, 16–
17, 23, 111, 190, 192–209
commodities, text-based, 192–209
community clubs (CCs), 29, 31–32, 33
complementary distribution, 7–8, 27–
28, 177–78
in literary anthologies, 67, 70, 84,
95–96, 100
and neat multilingualism, 26, 58–59,
61, 177–78
complementary texts, 29n.9
consecration, 70–71
*Contour* (Ng et al.), 83
contrapuntal multilingualism, 181–83,
186–87, 191–92, 209
"conversaytion" (Ip), 151, 152–53, 154–
55, 185
conviviality, 182
linguistic, 59, 97, 183
racial-ethnic, 77, 178
Cook, Vivian, 55–56, 58
cosmopolitanism, 14–15, 31, 179
of English, 7, 33, 112t, 125
of Singlish, 3, 124, 137
Coupland, Nikolas, 25–26, 28
cultural literacy programs, 61–62, 63,
66, 91, 92–94, 95–99, 100. *See also*
Read! Singapore

Gwee Li Sui, 102, 109, 123–24, 125, 126, 192
   government critique of, 119–22
   ludic poetry of, 104n.4
   metacommentary in *Spiaking Singlish*, 103, 104–5, 107–8, 114–15, 134–35
   *New York Times* op-ed, 116–19, 122, 127
   and other Singlish writers, 129, 132, 133*t*, 137–38
   TED talk, 3–5
   See also *Spiaking Singlish* (Gwee)

Hainanese, 7, 10–11, 198–99. *See also* Chinese dialects
Hakka, 7, 10–11, 198–99. *See also* Chinese dialects
Hall, Stuart, 34
hashtags, 155–56, 157
heartlander ethos, 15, 31–32, 94
   *vs.* cosmopolitanism, 14–15, 33, 137, 179
   and resistance, 174–75
   and Singlish, 13, 22, 109, 112*t*, 113, 120, 121, 125, 171, 190
hegemony, 142, 145, 175–76, 180–81, 190, 211
   of English, 102, 112*t*, 174–75, 208
   of Mandarin, 148, 170
   in translation, 65, 75–76
Heinrich, Patrick, 53
Heller, Monica, 28
heteroglossia, 23, 59, 118–19, 139–40, 141–44, 166, 167, 210–11
   commoditized, 208
   in English writing, 106, 148, 149
   and grassroots multilingualism, 15, 22–23, 101, 145–46, 149, 165, 168–69, 172, 173–74 (*see also* SingPoWriMo [Singapore Poetry Writing Month])
   and translation, 153
   See also Anglophone literature
heterography, 108
Hindi, 7, 56
Hokkien, 7, 10–11, 12, 133*t*
   commodification of, 12–13, 193
   in heteroglossic writing, 144–45, 146–49, 152, 153–54, 166, 167–68, 172–73

   in Singlish, 105–6, 114, 131
   in state communications, 184, 187, 189, 189n.9
   on text-based memorabilia, 194, 195, 197–98, 199, 200–7
   See also Chinese dialects
Holden, Philip, 140n.1, 145, 149, 150, 150n.4, 154n.11
*Home and Away* (National Library Board), 78n.14, 79n.15, 84
humor:
   in multilingual commodities, 196, 197–98, 200, 204–5
   and Singlish, 4, 22, 125, 174
   in SingPoWriMo, 157–58, 171n.38, 175
   in *Spiaking Singlish*, 103, 104, 105, 106–7
   See also ludification; playfulness
hyperegalitarianism, 76, 81, 83–84, 99

indexical orders, 110–13, 112*t*
   and Singlish, 113–14, 120, 121, 137, 186–87
Indian languages, non-Tamil, 33, 56
institutional multilingualism, 5, 15, 16–17, 20–21, 26, 84, 100, 181, 211
   exclusions of, 59
   and Singlish, 185–86, 187, 190
   See also choreographies of multilingualism: institutional; language policy; neat multilingualism
institutional signage.
   See public signage
intelligibility, politics of, 149, 154–55, 171–72
Ip, Joshua, 94, 149, 150–51, 152, 153, 154–55, 167–68, 185, 192
   and SingPoWriMo, 92, 156n.13, 158n.16, 159–60, 161–62, 163

Japanese, 53, 54, 146, 149
Japanese occupation of Singapore, 146, 147, 148
Javanese, 7n.6, 56
Jaworski, Adam, 18, 26n.5
Johnstone, Barbara, 110, 111, 113, 114, 171n.37
*Journeys* (Thumboo et al.), 73, 81, 83

NLB (National Library Board), 78, 84, 87–88, 89–90, 91, 191–92. *See also* Read! Singapore
nontranslation, 65, 87–89, 90

original language (translation). *See* source language
Otsuji, Emi, 101–2, 114n.10, 168

parallel-text bilingualism, 28
parallel texts, 29, 48–49, 69–70, 76, 82, 86
paratextual analysis, 65–66, 76, 80, 88, 106–7, 198
Parra, Nicanor, 171
Patke, Rajeev Shridhar, 140n.1, 145, 149
PCK, 205, 206f. *See also* Phua Chu Kang
Pennycook, Alastair, 101–2, 114n.10, 168
People's Association (PA), 31–32
performativity, 17, 90, 103, 106, 116, 190
Phua Chu Kang, 13, 125, 129, 184–85, 205
Phuan, William, 92
Pittsburghese, 110–11, 112t, 113, 114, 127–28, 171n.37, 208
*place* (de Certeauean), 60, 141, 163
and literary anthologies, 99–100
*vs. space*, 18–21, 136, 177–79, 182, 191–92, 209
Platt, John, 145
playfulness, 103, 208, 211
of Singlish, 16, 118, 120, 121, 179
of SingPoWriMo, 156–57, 159–60, 167, 178–79
in *Spiaking Singlish*, 103, 105, 106, 107
*See also* ludification
poetry. *See* literary anthologies; SingPoWriMo (Singapore Poetry Writing Month)
Poetry Festival Singapore, 83
Poetry on Platforms, 90, 91, 91f
policy. *See* language policy
political correctness, 67–68, 72, 89
political incorrectness, 118–19, 132–34, 163, 208
Postcolonial English, 144
postmultilingualism, 209–12
prefiguration, 178–79, 209

public signage, 28, 60, 73, 179, 183
asymmetries on, 42, 53–54, 84–85
as institutional discourse, 16, 21, 24–25, 34, 69
nonlocal languages on, 55, 56
and the quadrilingual schema, 33, 59, 84, 100, 208
visual-spatial choreography of, 34, 58, 61, 66, 80
Punjabi, 7, 56

quadrilingualism. *See* language policy; neat multilingualism
quadrilingual schema, 21, 22–23, 25, 26–28
asymmetries within, 42–54
exclusions of, 56–57
as institutional choreography, 31, 33–34, 58–60
*See also* frames; sequence of languages
quadruple frames. *See* frames: quadrilingual
quadruple monolingualism, 142
in cultural literacy programs, 90, 96, 99
in literary anthologies, 83–85, 86, 87
on public signage, 27–28

racial harmony, 6, 7, 31–32, 81, 97. *See also* multicultural fantasy; multiculturalism
Raessens, Joost, 103
Ramachandran, Kamini, 94
Read! Fest, 78, 90
Read! Singapore, 78–81, 90, 92–94
anthologies, 78n.14, 80f, 84, 95–96
*Reflecting on the Merlion* (Thumboo, Yeo, et al.), 82
Reh, Mechthild, 28n.7
resemiotization, 91, 95, 97–98, 102, 106, 204–5
resistance, 20–21, 173, 174, 175–76, 180, 181, 183, 209, 211
commodification of, 205, 208–9
and heteroglossia, 149, 166–67, 171–72, 182
and language ideology, 4–5, 102, 114, 118, 126, 165, 168–69
and vernaculars, 16, 22, 107–8, 114, 117, 136